PRAI
LATTER-DAY RESPONSIBILITY

"How refreshing it is for voters in this year of Mitt Romney to have a voice that is both Mormon and libertarian. Here is that voice: Clear, compelling, full of faith, and understanding the need for limited government. Connor Boyack's *Latter-day Responsibility* should be on Governor Romney's desk, and the governor should read it for its extraordinary explanation of the shared values of Christianity, Mormonism, and personal freedom. This book will open your eyes to a well-spring of Western religious values that recognize the primacy of the individual over the state and insist that the government do the same."

—Judge Andrew P. Napolitano
Senior judicial analyst, Fox News Channel

"America's responsibility deficit is a more pressing challenge than anything we face in the economy, energy, education, or defense. Citizens must renew an individual ethic of doing the right thing by choice. People of faith, including my Mormon friends, understand this—but we need a sense of urgency and an action plan. Connor Boyack's wise, timely, and practical book provides exactly that."

—John Andrews
Former Colorado Senate president and author of
Responsibility Reborn: A Citizen's Guide to the Next American Century

"Many patriotic Americans demand a more limited government, but few seem to have figured out the path to reach that goal. Connor Boyack's important book explains in simple and compelling terms that limited government and liberty will be obtained through personal responsibility. The duty to take care of ourselves and those around us must be lived, encouraged, and popularized if we are to create a free society. *Latter-day Responsibility* helps pave the way for a restoration of this primary virtue."

—John Pestana
Cofounder, Omniture

"Connor Boyack makes a compelling case for a return to personal responsibility as the bedrock principle needed to maintain the best virtues of our society. In this highly readable and informative book, he explains why our desire for preserving freedom will not become a reality until we first emphasize the importance of personal responsibility. 'We will secure freedom for future generations,' Boyack writes, 'by first taking care of ourselves and those around us—a forgotten virtue that once permeated our culture. The battle for keeping our freedom alive and vibrant will not be won in the halls of Congress,' he claims, 'but in the hearts and homes of every individual.' Boyack's new book speaks to the heart of those who respect the role a spiritual perspective toward preserving freedom plays."

—Daniel L. Bolz
President, The Statue of Responsibility Foundation

Latter-day RESPONSIBILITY

Choosing Liberty
through
Personal Accountability

Connor Boyack
Author of *Latter-day Liberty*

CFI
An Imprint of Cedar Fort, Inc.
Springville, Utah

ISBN 13: 978-1-4621-1092-6

Published by CFI, an imprint of Cedar Fort, Inc.
2373 W. 700 S., Springville, UT 84663
Distributed by Cedar Fort, Inc., www.cedarfort.com

LIBRARY OF CONGRESS CATALOGING-IN-PUBLICATION DATA

Boyack, Connor, author.
 Latter-day responsibility : choosing liberty through personal accountability / Connor Boyack.
  pages cm
 Includes bibliographical references and index.
 ISBN 978-1-4621-1092-6 (alk. paper)
 1. Self-reliance--Political aspects--United States. 2. Self-reliance--Religious aspects--Church of Jesus Christ of Latter-day Saints. 3. Responsibility--Political aspects--United States. 4. Responsibility--Religious aspects--Church of Jesus Christ of Latter-day Saints. I. Title.

BJ1533.S27.B69 2012
241'.0493--dc23

                          2012032784

Cover design by Angela D. Olsen
Cover design © 2012 by Lyle Mortimer
Edited and typeset by Emily S. Chambers

Printed in the United States of America

10 9 8 7 6 5 4 3 2 1

Printed on acid-free paper

To Mom and Dad
Thanks for teaching me
to be responsible.

ALSO BY CONNOR BOYACK

Latter-day Liberty

CONTENTS

Preface ix

Introduction 1

Liberty 13

Self-Defense 21

Financial Freedom 57

Welfare and Charity 79

Preparedness and Self-Reliance 107

Education 135

Civic Duty 161

Food Production 185

Family 207

Faith and Morality 235

Conclusion 263

Americans Demand Increased
Governmental Protection from Selves 271

Personal Responsibility Is the Price of Liberty 274

Index 288

About the Author 294

Above this race of men stands an immense and tutelary power, which takes upon itself alone to secure their gratifications and to watch over their fate. That power is absolute, minute, regular, provident, and mild. It would be like the authority of a parent if, like that authority, its object was to prepare men for manhood; but it seeks, on the contrary, to keep them in perpetual childhood . . . . For their happiness such a government willingly labors, but it chooses to be the sole agent and the only arbiter of that happiness; it provides for their security, foresees and supplies their necessities, facilitates their pleasures, manages their principal concerns, directs their industry, regulates the descent of property, and subdivides their inheritances; what remains, but to spare them all the care of thinking and all the trouble of living?

Thus it every day renders the exercise of the free agency of man less useful and less frequent; it circumscribes the will within a narrower range, and gradually robs a man of all the uses of himself.[1]

—Alexis de Tocqueville

Liberty will not descend to a people, a people must raise themselves to liberty; it is a blessing that must be earned before it can be enjoyed.[2]

—Charles Caleb Colton

PREFACE

When I wrote *Latter-day Liberty* in 2011, it was meant to be a standalone volume. I consider what I wrote in that book to be extremely important not only for Latter-day Saints, but for every person, regardless of religion. Individual liberty is inexorably linked to agency, and these fundamental principles should guide not only our personal lives but also our interactions with others both directly and indirectly through government. It is my hope that what I perceive to be widespread ignorance on the subject will be increasingly corrected through the ideas presented in that book, as well as through the like-minded efforts by others working to advance the cause of liberty.

In the first few weeks after the book was published, many friends and supporters asked me if I was thinking of writing another. Given the time and energy required to write a book, I often replied that while I had a few ideas in mind, I probably would not attempt a second book for a few years. I have a young family, a busy career, and a significant time commitment to liberty-oriented activities and interests. The last thing I needed was to tackle another writing project so soon.

In what has become a long-standing cycle of course corrections in my life, I soon thereafter realized that my initial intentions would not last long. Just one month after the publication of *Latter-day Liberty*, the idea and structure of this book illuminated my mind with profound clarity while driving home one evening; I couldn't pull out my iPhone fast enough to make an audio recording of everything I was thinking. Once the brain dump was complete, I realized that I had the blueprint for what was the obvious and necessary companion to my first book. It made sense, and I felt foolish for not having previously realized that in *Latter-day Liberty*, I had presented only one half of a two-part equation.

This book does not reflect a change of position from the principles and policies contained in *Latter-day Liberty*. That book deals with a subject that merits its own focus and discussion in order to fully understand what liberty is and how it applies to government and politics. In a sense, it can and should stand alone to allow for a narrow study of the specific issues it presents. Amplifying that understanding, though, requires expanding the discussion to related concepts that influence the degree to which our liberty can be attained and enjoyed. This book serves, then, as a companion volume to address the other half of the equation, for with increased liberty comes the obligation to assume more responsibility.

Latter-day Responsibility provides additional and needed context to help readers understand what our responsibilities are as citizens, including working to restrain the government and defend individual liberty. Just as we would only enter into a fight if we had the proper armor and training, so too must we understand the content in this book before battling the state.

Notes

1. Alexis de Tocqueville, *Democracy in America*, vol. 2 (New York: The Century, 1898), 392.
2. Charles Caleb Colton, *Lacon: or, Many Things in Few Words*, vol. 2 (London: Longman, Rees, Orme, Brown, and Green, 1826), 123.

INTRODUCTION

If we wish to be free; if we mean to preserve inviolate those inestimable privileges for which we have been so long contending; if we mean not basely to abandon the noble struggle in which we have been so long engaged, and which we have pledged ourselves never to abandon until the glorious object of our contest shall be obtained, we must fight! I repeat it, sir, we must fight![1]

—Patrick Henry

Freedom is only part of the story and half of the truth. Freedom is but the negative aspect of the whole phenomenon whose positive aspect is responsibleness. In fact, freedom is in danger of degenerating into mere arbitrariness unless it is lived in terms of responsibleness.[2]

—Victor Frankl

Freedom is the best of things which can be found around the world if you can bear the burden.[3]

—Bishop Thomas Simonsson

As the saying goes, even a broken clock is right twice a day. So it was with a gentleman named George Bernard Shaw—an Irish playwright who cofounded the London School of Economics. Shaw was a staunch socialist and wrote many articles and brochures for the semi-secret Fabian Society[4]—a group dedicated to advancing socialism through politics and propaganda. Shaw's political clock, while usually incorrect, struck correctly when he wrote: "Liberty means

1

responsibility. That is why most men dread it."[5] For his many intellectual failings, Shaw's conclusion in the foregoing quote is accurate: liberty means responsibility.

It is not difficult to debate the various intellectual points of what liberty is and how it applies to government and politics. In doing so, it is easy to observe how the government is infringing on our rights and to point out problems needing correction. What is not so easy is understanding the related responsibilities, which is the corollary component of the equation, and how they apply to each of us. The following example illustrates this seeming paradox.

Thomas Paine was a master essayist during the seventeen hundreds known for his vitriolic and passionate pamphlets, in which he excoriated monarchy, oppression, and a government out of touch with its people. Paine wrote to convince the reader of the need to dismantle the reigns of unjust government. Frequently he wrote to point out violations of individual liberty at the hands of King George. John Adams was initially impressed with Paine's *Common Sense* and was flattered when some suspected he was the author of the originally anonymous document. But as biographer David McCullough notes, "the more [Adams] thought about it, the less he admired *Common Sense*." Writing to his wife Abigail in 1776, Adams commented that Paine was "a better hand in pulling down than building."[6] Adams's uneasiness with some of Paine's proposed ideas fueled a desire to propose his own. As McCullough notes:

> It was Paine's "feeble" understanding of constitutional government, his outline of a unicameral legislature to be established once independence was achieved, that disturbed Adams most. In response, he began setting down his own thoughts on government, resolved, as he later wrote, "to do all in my power to counteract the effect" on the popular mind of so foolish a plan.[7]

A decade later in a changed world, Adams reiterated his assessment of Paine's efforts in a letter to James Warren, a fellow patriot from Massachusetts: "It is much easier to pull down a government, in such a conjuncture of affairs as we have seen," he wrote, "than to build up at such season as present."[8] A few short years later on the issue of the French Revolution, Adams wrote in similar fashion to revolutionary Samuel Adams: "Everything will be pulled down. So much seems certain. But what will be built up? Are there any principles of political architecture? . . . Will the struggle in Europe be anything other than a change in impostors?"⁹

In today's world of rampant corruption, sky-high spending, and a pervasive erosion of the principles necessary for good government, it is tempting and—in fact—easy for each of us to be a modern Tom Paine. Many people expend significant amounts of time and energy tearing down offending politicians, pointing out violations of individual liberty, and attempting to throw off the heavy burdens of tyranny increasingly being imposed upon a once-free people. However, many of these well-intentioned individuals lack a principled, philosophical foundation upon which to build a solid substitute structure. They tear down without being ready to rebuild. They grasp in the dark for liberty without understanding how it applies to government and individuals and without being prepared to live it themselves. They claim to want liberty but do not want the corresponding responsibility.

This is not to say, of course, that all those who chafe against an encroaching government suffer from this intellectual dissonance. Indeed, many who realize the scope of the problem, and its darker implications, are often compelled to better understand true principles and engage themselves in a serious study of history and government. In this sense, their Paine-like criticisms are precursors to Adams-like study and actions.

Restraining government in order to secure individual liberty requires more than simply pulling down usurpations of power.¹⁰ As Shaw noted, liberty has a symbiotic relationship with responsibility; our opportunity and ability to defend individual liberty increase proportionally with our capacity and willingness to assume personal responsibility. Correspondingly, when we collectively disregard or delegate our responsibilities, we in turn lessen and ultimately risk losing our liberties. We should see personal responsibility as the price of liberty. We cannot properly claim the latter without also complying with the former.

For Latter-day Saints, this connection between liberty and responsibility should especially ring true. Lucifer's counterfeit plan to "redeem all mankind, that one soul shall not be lost" (Moses 4:1) would have necessarily nullified each individual's agency. With neither the power nor the opportunity to choose and reap the consequences of our choices, personal responsibility would become irrelevant. Satan's dictatorial desire opposed both liberty and responsibility, while God's plan of salvation elevates both as part of an "individual effort"[11] in which men are "punished for their *own* sins" (Article of Faith 12, emphasis added). God has given us our agency and the opportunity (and responsibility) "to choose liberty and eternal life, through the great Mediator of all men, or to choose captivity and death, according to the captivity and power of the devil" (2 Nephi 2:27). The relationship between responsibility and liberty, or agency, was further articulated by President David O. McKay:

> With free agency there comes responsibility. If a man is to be rewarded for righteousness and punished for evil, then common justice demands that he be given the power of independent action. A knowledge of good and evil is essential to a man's progress on earth.
>
> If he were coerced to do right at all times, or were helplessly enticed to commit sin, he would merit neither a blessing for the first nor a punishment for the second.
>
> Man's responsibility is correspondingly operative with his free agency. Actions in harmony with divine laws and the laws of nature will bring happiness, and those in opposition to divine truth, misery.[12]

In other words, the very purpose of our agency, or liberty, is to allow us to choose to do what is right—to do what God has commanded us to do. We are given our agency to see "if [we] will do all things whatsoever the Lord [our] God shall command [us]" (Abraham 3:25). This very agency provides us with the liberty to be either responsible or irresponsible. As Elder B. H. Roberts noted: "The agency of man would not be worth the name if it did not grant liberty to the wicked to fill the cup of their iniquity, as well as liberty to the virtuous to round out the measure of their righteousness."[13] If we are not free to choose wrongly and irresponsibly, then we are in fact not free at all.

To effectuate this mission of perpetuating free agency, we must refrain from two forms of wickedness: sins of commission and sins of omission. Most people recognize that it is wrong to commit adultery, to steal, or to unjustly use violence against another person. These are sins of commission and overtly interfere with the life, liberty, property, and therefore agency of other individuals. Some people, however, do not sufficiently understand the much more lengthy list of sins of omission, through which we surrender agency by neglecting responsibility. Not actively supporting good, honest, and wise men for positions of power and influence; not actively promoting morality in the public square; not learning skills and acquiring resources to be self-sufficient; not taking the steps necessary to provide for and protect those within our stewardship—these and many other responsibilities have been increasingly ignored in recent decades, yet they are part and parcel of promoting individual liberty. These responsibilities are generally recognized as being incumbent upon us, but they often go unfilled—a neglect of duty that has eternal consequences. As President John Taylor taught: "Besides the preaching of the Gospel, we have another mission, namely, the perpetuation of the free agency of man and the maintenance of liberty, freedom, and the rights of man."[14]

Simply abstaining from explicitly violating God's more well-known commands is not sufficient, neither for our individual salvation nor for the perpetuation of the individual liberty of mankind. Rather, we must proactively, willingly, and eagerly assume the personal responsibilities that are intertwined with individual liberty and, through persuasion (and never coercion), encourage others to act likewise. God has taught that "men should be anxiously engaged in a good cause, and do many things of their own free will, and bring to pass much righteousness . . . But he that doeth not anything until he is commanded . . . the same is damned" (D&C 58:27, 29). Fulfilling our personal responsibilities is how we "bring to pass much righteousness." It is an effort with eternal implications, and one that should not be treated as a mere checklist of burdensome items to muddle through.

The rise of the welfare state, the police state, and the nanny state[15] has occurred only because individuals have, in the aggregate, avoided the responsibility to take care of and to control themselves. As conservative columnist Walter Williams notes: "Our increased reliance on laws to regulate behavior is a measure of how uncivilized we've become."[16] It therefore follows that if we wish to dismantle the welfare, police, and nanny state, and to restore our lost liberties, we need to once again become civilized and responsible. We must relearn and assume the responsibilities that the government has taken over. Building up good government, as John Adams advocated, requires that we first build up ourselves.

Once more, individuals must recognize the importance of

responsibilities such as self-defense, self-reliance, charity, preparedness, financial freedom, education, food production, faith and morality, civic duty, and the family. Some of these can be supplemented or sometimes substituted with services by others through a division of labor. Nevertheless, we must recognize and personally act on the principle of personal responsibility. It is not our neighbor's duty, neither directly nor indirectly through government, to provide us with food, shelter, health care, or an education. The proverbial village should not shoulder the burden of raising our children for us. We should not consent to a government that competes with, and at times fully usurps, our natural responsibility to act in these and other areas of life.

John Adams, ever the builder, wrote to his wife, Abigail, in 1775:

> It should be your care, therefore, and mine, to elevate the minds of our children and exalt their courage; to accelerate and animate their industry and activity; to excite in them an habitual contempt of meanness, abhorrence of injustice and inhumanity, and an ambition to excel in every capacity, faculty, and virtue. If we suffer their minds to grovel and creep in infancy, they will grovel all their lives.[17]

Unfortunately, we have become a nation of dependents. A full 48.5 percent of Americans receive some form of financial assistance from the government.[18] Just as independence is secured by independents, so too do dependents foster dependence. Individuals today grovel at the feet of the state, begging to be cared for from cradle to grave. Even those who do not receive direct financial assistance from the government often strongly support government-run education, the "war on terror," the voluminous regulations imposed by the FDA/EPA/USDA, the use of taxation to finance social services both at home and abroad, and a host of other government interventions that encroach on individual liberties. Having outsourced or shirked the responsibility to care for itself, this body politic has proven it is neither able nor willing to reclaim its lost liberties. Americans have given up their liberty for economic, physical, and social safety, and as Benjamin Franklin warned,[19] we now have neither liberty nor safety.

Abigail Adams agreed with her husband, once remarking that "we have too many high-sounding words, and too few actions that correspond with them."[20] The actions that correspond with a sincere desire for individual liberty are those that demonstrate an individual's willingness to care for himself and those within his stewardship, along with a charitable outreach to others in need. It is not sufficient to simply talk about and work toward reducing the government's size and scope to the point at which we feel free—we must become free by living accordingly. When that point arrives, government will have no choice but to recede to its proper role and authority. We learn in the scriptures that "Satan shall have power over the hearts of the children of men, no more for a long time" (2 Nephi 30:18) specifically "because of the righteousness of [God's] people" (1 Nephi 22:26). Satan will not first be bound, providing people with the opportunity to become more righteous. His defeat will be secured because the people over whom he might otherwise exert control are already living righteously. The same pattern can and should apply to our relationship with the state: by becoming righteous and responsible, the state loses its power over us. President James E. Faust taught:

> The Lord said that it is important for the Church to "stand independent above all other creatures beneath the celestial world" (D&C 78:14). Members of the Church are also counseled to be independent. Independence means many things. It means being free of drugs that addict, habits that bind, and diseases that curse. It also means being free of personal debt and of the interest and carrying charges required by debt the world over.[21]

One might reasonably argue that the state is one such "creature" above which the Church is to stand independent. The Church's independence is predicated upon the independence of its members, and individual independence will only be secured as we each perform our personal responsibilities. Our eternally important mission to pursue "the perpetuation of the free agency of man and the maintenance of liberty," as President Taylor said, depends in large measure upon whether we are each acting as a wise steward in individually doing what agency and liberty requires.

Many are familiar with the prevailing, founding-era idea that, in George Washington's words, "religion and morality are the essential pillars of civil society."[22] In 1778, the Continental Congress passed a resolution declaring that "true religion and good morals are the only solid foundations of public liberty and happiness."[23] John Adams opined that "our Constitution was made only for a moral and religious people. It is wholly inadequate to the government of any other."[24] While these ideas are sound, some interpret them to mean that we do not deserve, and should not have, a government confined only to moral and legitimate powers until the people who comprise that government are righteous and peaceful. This argument suggests that because people refuse to take care of and control themselves, that a welfare, police, and nanny state becomes justified and necessary. While such individuals may claim to understand the importance of individual liberty, they disregard its application to the government today by pointing to the rampant irresponsibility of the people around them. Why do we deserve good government, they ask, when so many people are so bad?

The underlying question is whether liberty should be held hostage to responsibility. Should we as a people only be granted the privilege of enjoying our unimpeded individual liberty when we collectively have achieved some arbitrary societal standard of sufficient personal responsibility? Must we implicitly consent to a government that infringes on those rights until and unless we all are living our lives as we should? The answer is found in understanding the nature of the relationship between liberty and responsibility. The one implies the other, and each are codependent states. Liberty is not fully contingent upon responsibility, nor is the reverse true. Rather, each influences the other—as we become more responsible, we are able to enjoy more liberty. Conversely, as we become less responsible, we become less free.

Thus, while some would erroneously argue that individual liberty should not be fully enjoyed until each person is living responsibly (a standard that will never be reached in our fallen world), an increase of individual liberty would actually prompt higher levels of personal responsibility. Consider an example: if the Federal Emergency Management Agency were abolished, along with all of its state-based counterparts, individuals would realize that in the event of a disaster, they would not be able to rely upon a team of bureaucrats and government funding to arrange and pay for food, shelter, clothing, and to otherwise assist them in the weeks following the disaster. Accordingly, individuals would either acquire needed skills and supplies to prepare for a potential disaster, or they would suffer the consequences of their irresponsibility. Either way, they would have the individual liberty and use of their agency to do as they please, realizing that they will ultimately be held accountable for their choices. The same holds true in the reverse: by encouraging people to become more responsible—to prepare, to be charitable, to be financially independent, to have strong families and faithful lives—we reduce the influence and reach of the state and raise up an entire generation of independently minded people who do not need (and who therefore oppose) the government's overreach.

By confining the government to its moral size and scope, we likewise provide an opportunity for individuals to reclaim their responsibilities and become wise stewards. By removing the government's tentacles from so many aspects of our lives, we encourage people to learn to live independently as moral agents. Liberty is thus no longer held hostage by responsibility. Rather, both are augmented by reducing the reach of the state and persuading individuals to responsibly act rather than be acted upon.

If individual liberty is our desire, then personal responsibility is our duty. In discussing liberty, we concern ourselves primarily with what the government should not do. In discussing responsibility, we concern ourselves with what we as individuals should do. Lord Acton defined liberty as "the highest political end."[25] Responsibility, then, is the highest personal end. Without it, liberty cannot exist.

NOTES

1. Patrick Henry, Speech in Virginia Convention, Richmond, March 23, 1775.
2. Victor Frankl, *Man's Search for Meaning* (New York: Simon & Schuster, Inc., 1984), 155–56.
3. Bishop Thomas, "Freedom Ballad," accessed May 12, 2012, http://runeberg.org/vitaband/0128.html.
4. Shaw's contributions also included designing a stained-glass window, now on display at the London School of Economics, which features Shaw and fellow Fabian socialist Sidney Webb striking the Earth with hammers, as the caption describes at the top of the window, to "remould it nearer to the heart's desire." The Fabian crest, also included in the window's design, portrays a wolf in sheep's clothing—a symbolic reference to the group's avoidance of controversial and recognizable labels in aiming to instead advance its agenda incrementally and subtly through propaganda and legislation. At the bottom of the window, a group of people depicting the world's population is shown kneeling in adoration at a stack of books which promote socialism.
5. George Bernard Shaw, "Maxims for Revolutionists," *Man and Superman:*

A Comedy and a Philosophy (Westminster: Archibald Constable, 1903), 229.

6. Frank Shuffelton, ed., *The Letters of John and Abigail Adams* (New York: Penguin Group, 2004), 89.
7. David McCullough, *John Adams* (New York: Simon & Schuster, 2001), 97.
8. McCullough, *John Adams*, 373-4.
9. McCullough, *John Adams*, 418.
10. An example is found in Alma 60:36, in which Captain Moroni wrote: "I seek not for power, but to pull it down. I seek not for honor of the world, but for the glory of my God, and the freedom and welfare of my country." It might be argued that freedom relates to liberty, as welfare relates to responsibility. Thus, Moroni embodied both characteristics.
11. Dallin H. Oaks, "Repentance and Change," *Ensign*, November 2003, 40. The full quote reads: "The gospel plan is based on individual responsibility. Our article of faith states the eternal truth 'that men will be punished for their own sins, and not for Adam's transgression' (Article of Faith 1:2). This requirement of individual responsibility, which has many expressions in our doctrine, is in sharp contrast to Satan's plan to 'redeem all mankind, that one soul shall not be lost' (Moses 4:1). The plan of the Father and the Savior is based on individual choice and individual effort."
12. David O. McKay, In Conference Report, Apr. 1950, 33.
13. B. H. Roberts, *A New Witness For God* (Salt Lake City: George Q. Cannon & Sons., 1895), 48.
14. John Taylor, *Journal of Discourses*, vol. 23 (London, 1883), 63.
15. The "welfare state" is a term which references the collection of policies that provide for "free" resources for individuals allegedly in need, such as food stamps, unemployment insurance, health care, education, and so on. The police state is the collection of policies which turn the government into a militaristic institution that treats people as guilty until proven innocent, restricts or rejects the right to habeas corpus and due process, and which authorizes the strict regulation, invasion, and confiscation of personal property to allegedly suppress crime and punish those who have violated some statute. The nanny state is the collection of policies which aim to shape society and protect people from themselves, such as seat belt laws, business licensure, heavily taxing or completely prohibiting soda or cigarettes, and so on., each of which presumes that politicians and bureaucrats know better how to live our lives than we do.
16. Walter Williams, "Laws Are a Poor Substitute for Common Decency, Moral Values," *Deseret News*, Apr. 29, 2009, A15.
17. Shuffelton, Letters, 74.
18. "Nearly Half of U.S. Lives in Household Receiving Government Benefit," Wall Street Journal, October 5, 2011, accessed May 12, 2012,

http://blogs.wsj.com/economics/2011/10/05/nearly-half-of-households-receive-some-government-benefit/

19. Benjamin Franklin, *The Memoirs of Benjamin Franklin*, vol. 2 (Philadelphia: McCarty & Davis, 1834), 99. The quote reads: "Those who would give up essential liberty, to purchase a little temporary safety, deserve neither liberty nor safety."

20. Shuffelton, Letters, 28.

21. James E. Faust, "Responsibility for Welfare Rests with Me and My Family," *Ensign*, May 1986, 21.

22. Jared Sparks, ed., *The Life of George Washington*, vol. 2 (London: Henry Colburn, 1839), 315.

23. Continental Congress, *Journals of the Continental Congress, containing the proceedings from January 1, 1778*, to January 1, 1779 (Philadelphia, 1779), 590.

24. The Works of John Adams, vol. 9 (Boston: Little, Brown, 1854), 229.

25. Lord Acton, *The History of Freedom and Other Essays* (London: Macmillan, 1907), 22.

LIBERTY

I believe that a man is a moral, responsible, free agent.[1]

—Joseph Smith

To address the importance of responsibility as it relates to liberty, it is necessary to first understand liberty. While the subject is treated at length in *Latter-day Liberty*, a brief summary is presented here to ensure that the reader has the necessary context to continue through the material in this book.

Liberty is a commonly used word, especially during election seasons, but only a relative few have a foundational understanding of what it is and, more important, what it implies. Liberty is the right to peaceably act as one pleases, provided he does not violate anybody else's equal, unalienable rights. It is, as described by Thomas Jefferson, "unobstructed action according to our will, within limits drawn around us by the equal rights of others."[2] Elder Bruce R. McConkie similarly defined it as "the privilege to be free and to be unrestrained in all activity except that which interferes with the equally sacred rights of others."[3] President David O. McKay described it by teaching that "a man may act as his conscience dictates so long as he does not infringe upon the rights of others."[4] So long as you do not violate another person's rights, liberty demands that you be free to act as you peaceably please—whether that's ingesting a dangerous substance, owning a weapon, refusing to employ a certain type of people, or tearing out your front lawn and putting in a garden.

Liberty is an all-encompassing political philosophy that implies and requires economic freedom, political independence, and moral agency. It is an affirmation of each individual's unalienable right to life, liberty, and property—a position based on and supported by eternal principles and natural law. Liberty is a mindset and a comprehensive way of living wherein independent, self-reliant individuals affirm their ability to determine their own destiny, free from control by their peers either individually or collectively through government. In a way, liberty is rigid and stubborn. It often deals in absolutes, which runs contrary to how many people believe and behave. Just as a person cannot be partially alive, mostly alive, or almost totally alive, so too can a person not be partially, mostly, or almost totally free. We are either alive or dead. We either have liberty or we do not. If people are in bondage in one area of their lives, then they are not free. If they are dependent upon the government for anything, then they are not independent. If the state prohibits peaceful people from using their property how they please, then they do not have liberty. While freedom may be enjoyed in certain areas of our lives even while it is denied or discarded in other areas, a person who is not fully free cannot in fact say that he is free. Those who fight for liberty recognize its rigidity and work to remove the forceful arm of the state from all areas of their lives.

A political framework founded on liberty contemplates a society that functions through persuasion rather than through force. This is a key concept in the gospel of Jesus Christ, as we learn in the Doctrine and Covenants: "No power or influence can or ought to be maintained by virtue of the priesthood, only by persuasion, by long-suffering, by gentleness and meekness, and by love unfeigned; By kindness, and pure knowledge, which shall greatly enlarge the soul without hypocrisy, and without guile" (D&C 121:41–42). Liberty recognizes and respects the sovereignty and worth of each individual. It presumes that nobody (except God) knows how better to run a person's life than that person and therefore rejects policies that aim to control the actions of others without just cause. Those who champion this political philosophy see a great need for improving society, enforcing justice, encouraging charity, and promoting virtue. Unlike many, however, they know that the coercion by which the state operates cannot foster these important characteristics. Like the prominent journalist H. L. Mencken states, they "do not believe in even liberty enough to want to force it upon anyone."[5]

What does liberty have to do with responsibility? Consider, for example, a society in which each individual has unrestricted enjoyment to all his rightful liberties. This society has governments that in no way exceed their authority to only impose justice against those who violate another person's liberty by committing an act of aggression. In this scenario, there would still be poor people, criminals, natural and man-made disasters, and evil influences pervading society. The only feasible way such a society might exist is if the people who comprise it were independently and individually taking care of themselves, helping to take care of others, preparing for future emergencies, and promoting faith and family to spread the gospel of peace and persuasion. A society that enjoys unadulterated individual liberty cannot exist without the vast majority of individuals acting responsibly of their own accord. Responsibility is the prerequisite to liberty.

Considering the opposite scenario reinforces this point. A society of individuals who don't look after themselves—who refuse to learn new skills, work more than one job when necessary, prepare for the proverbial and inevitable rainy day, defend themselves and their property, get out of and avoid debt, promote sound political principles, and so on—is effectively asking for the state (or someone else) to take care of them. Rather than acting, they implicitly invite the consequence of being acted upon (see 2 Nephi 2:14). Into the vacuum created by inaction and irresponsibility, the state eagerly interjects itself. Thus, responsibility is an important trait that is inherently tied to individual liberty. More important, it is a core component of the agency God has given us.

THE AGENCY OF MAN

Agency is a fundamental doctrine and gift from God. It triggered an epic war in which a third part of God's children decided to follow Lucifer and as a result were denied the opportunity to experience mortality and progress toward becoming like their Heavenly Father. This agency led to their downfall yet enables us as individuals to be "free forever" (2 Nephi 2:26), if we utilize it correctly.

To better understand agency, consider the related word *agent*. An agent is an individual given responsibilities by the person he represents in a business transaction or other decision. Noah Webster defined agent in his 1828 dictionary as "one that exerts power, or has the power to act" and "one entrusted with the business of another."[6] While this word is used in modern scripture, the Bible identifies agents as *stewards*. The responsibility of a steward is his *stewardship*, just as the responsibility of an agent is his agency.

Both an agent and a steward are responsible to make decisions and take action and later be held accountable by the delegator of the agency or stewardship. Dozens of scriptures demonstrate this relationship. For example, God has said that "Every man shall be made *accountable* unto me, a *steward* over his own property" (D&C 42:32; emphasis added). We also learn that "it is required of the Lord, at the hand of every *steward*, to render an *account* of his *stewardship*, both in time and in eternity" (D&C 72:3; emphasis added). Further, we are told "as ye are *agents*, ye are on the Lord's *errand*; and whatsoever ye do according to the will of the Lord is the Lord's *business*" (D&C 64:29; emphasis added). Another scripture shows its importance: "For it is expedient that I, the Lord, should make every man *accountable*, as a *steward* over earthly blessings . . . I prepared all things, and have given unto the children of men to be *agents* unto themselves" (D&C 104:13, 17; emphasis added).

Thus, agency is simply one's stewardship—the duties assigned by God. We can only fully discharge that set of responsibilities when our agency is unimpeded. As Elder Bruce R. McConkie explained, agency's existence and effectiveness requires several components:

> Four great principles must be in force if there is to be agency: 1. Laws must exist, laws ordained by an Omnipotent power, laws which can be obeyed or disobeyed; 2. Opposites must exist—good and evil, virtue and vice, right and wrong—that is, there must be an opposition, one force pulling . . . the other; 3. A knowledge of good and evil must be had by those who are to enjoy the agency, that is, they must know the difference between the opposites; and 4. An unfettered power of choice must prevail.[7]

As stewards of the individuals and resources God places in our care, we have been given specific, associated responsibilities. If we do not act righteously of our own accord, guided by God's commandments, then we mismanage our stewardship and will suffer the consequences. As dictated by the law of the harvest, "whatsoever a man soweth, that shall he also reap" (Galatians 6:7). By sowing actions in fulfillment of our personal responsibilities, we reap increased liberty. If we fail to sow such actions, then we risk implicitly justifying our neighbors in trying to act upon us (supposedly with our best interests at heart) through the collective force of government. As Benjamin Franklin once observed, "Only a virtuous people are capable of freedom. As nations become corrupt and vicious, they have more need of masters."[8] If we as agents on the Lord's errand do not fulfill our responsibilities, we cannot feign surprise when others attempt to do it for us and seize our liberty in the process.

Agency, stewardship, consequences, responsibility, duty—these and other interrelated concepts all describe a relationship between God and his children. We are on earth to acquire a physical body, gain experience, and prove ourselves worthy to return to our Heavenly Father. That process occurs by using our agency to obey God's commandments and repenting of and learning from our mistakes and sins along the way. We obey God's commandments by carrying out the many responsibilities we are given, each associated with the stewardships we have. In our roles as parents, business owners, citizens, neighbors, caretakers, teachers, and so on, we have an associated list of duties we must perform if we are to be faithful and effective. If we use our agency to be irresponsible and fail to fulfill these duties, those needs will either go unfulfilled or will be met by another individual or institution. In a society where a large percentage of individuals shirk or evade their responsibilities, those in need begin to believe that the state should be their protector and savior, intervening to satisfy unfulfilled needs. One of the most effective ways to oppose the state's interventions, then, is to make them unnecessary by being wise stewards and using our agency to make good choices—in other words, by acting in accordance with our personal responsibilities and obeying God's commandments. We gain ground for individual liberty by simply becoming more responsible and encouraging others to do the same.

AGENCY MEANS LIBERTY

Just as was the case during the war in heaven, it is imperative that we fight here on earth to defend our agency against any who might wish to inhibit it or take it away. As President Hinckley taught, today's continuation of that protracted war is "between truth and error, between agency and compulsion," and requires "that we close ranks, that we march together as one."[9] It is arguably more important, however, that rather than simply defending agency, we promote its wise use. This entails, among other things, making good decisions, obeying God's commandments, and using our agency in a righteous and responsible manner. By acknowledging, accepting, and acting upon our personal responsibilities, and by encouraging others to do the same, we switch from playing defense to playing offense in the battle to preserve agency. We put Satan and his legions on the ropes, and we increase tactical advantages. We win battles and gain ground, rather than defensively trying to limit our casualties.

Responsibility is one of the three *R*s of agency, the other two being *right* and *results*. The right to choose is paramount and precedes the others, since having the unfettered ability to weigh and choose between different options is what allows agency to even be possible. This right comes directly from God, who made his children "agents unto themselves" (Moses 6:56) who are "free to choose" (2 Nephi 2:27) their course. The *responsibility* of choice requires taking accountability for one's decisions, suffering whatever the consequences of those choices are, whether for good or for bad. This leads to the *result* of choice, where the consequences of one's decision are brought to pass, whether immediately or in the future. The rights, responsibility, and results implicit in our agency are either a burden or a blessing, depending on how they are used. When we choose to fulfill our personal responsibilities—when we pay the price for the results we seek after—then we increase our ability to be free and independent. By choosing to abandon those responsibilities, the result will be much like what is occurring in the world around us: staggering debt, dependence upon the state, weak and broken families, and a general deviation from God's commandments.

By being responsible, we become wise stewards of the many things God has placed under our care. As wise stewards, we protect our agency and promote righteousness. In becoming righteous, we ensure that our individual liberty has a strong and sure foundation upon which to resist the encroachments of the state. It is a virtuous cycle. In short, only by "supporting and defending the principles of truth, right, and freedom"[10] can we truly preserve liberty. The cycle begins by choosing to be responsible.

NOTES

1. B. H. Roberts, ed., *History of the Church*, vol. 4 (Salt Lake City: Deseret Book, 1978), 78.

2. Joyce Appleby and Terence Ball, ed., *Jefferson: Political Writings* (New York: Cambridge University Press, 1999), 224.

3. Bruce R. McConkie, "Know Your Constitution," *Deseret News*, March 26, 1945.

4. David O. McKay, in Conference Report, October 1938.

5. Guy J. Forgue, ed., *Letters of H. L. Mencken* (New York: Knopf. 1961), 281.

6. "Agent," 1828 Webster's Dictionary, accessed May 2, 2012, http://1828-dictionary.com/d/search/word,agent.

7. Bruce R. McConkie, *Mormon Doctrine* (Salt Lake City: Deseret Book, 1979), 26.

8. Benjamin Franklin, *The Works of Benjamin Franklin*, vol. 6 (Philadelphia: Williams Duane, 1817), 199.

9. Gordon B. Hinckley, "An Unending Conflict, a Victory Assured," *Ensign*, Jun. 2007, 4–9.

10. L. Tom Perry, *Ensign*, Nov. 1987, 72. The full quote reads: "As Church members, we live under the banner of many different flags. How important it is that we understand our place and our position in the lands in which we live! We should be familiar with the history, heritage, and laws of the lands that govern us. In those countries that allow us the right to participate in the affairs of government, we should use our free agency and be actively engaged in supporting and defending the principles of truth, right, and freedom."

SELF-DEFENSE

The great object is, that every man be armed.[1]

—Patrick Henry

One loves to possess arms, though they hope never to have occasion for them.[2]

—Thomas Jefferson

QUESTIONS TO PONDER

1. If an intruder entered your home at night, intent on doing harm to your children, how would you respond?

2. Would you be prepared to defend yourself after a large disaster, when police could not quickly respond to your 911 call?

3. Should a person defend himself from an attacker or submit himself to harm?

4. Would America have been founded if the colonists did not own and know how to use firearms?

5. Are Americans free because they are armed, or are they armed because they are free?

The September 11, 2001, terrorist attacks on US soil created in their wake a pervasive sense of uncertainty and fear. In the days and weeks that followed, those feelings seemed to manifest themselves in a few common questions asked by many. Why were we attacked? Why do the terrorists hate us? Are we at war? Why didn't the government foresee and prevent this from happening? In response, the government quickly erected a massive police state. The first step was the rushed introduction of the USA Patriot Act through Congress six weeks later—a 240-plus page bill that was previously written, not available to the public prior to the vote, and barely available to the elected officials in Congress, *none of whom read it* before casting their vote.[3] This act expanded the federal government's ability to gather intelligence, engage in domestic surveillance and secret searches, and detain immigrants with little restraint—all in an alleged attempt to prevent a future attack like 9/11. On the same day it was introduced, October 23, the bill was brought to the floor of the House of Representatives for a vote. "No one has really had an opportunity to look at the bill to see what's in it," remarked one Representative.[4] It passed 357 to 66, was passed by the Senate on a 98 to 1 vote the very next day, and then was signed into law two days later by President George Bush.

Two weeks previous, President Bush had announced the establishment of the Office of Homeland Security to "develop and coordinate the implementation of a comprehensive national strategy to secure the United States from terrorist threats or attacks. The Office will coordinate the executive branch's efforts to detect, prepare for, prevent, protect against, respond to, and recover from terrorist attacks within the United States."[5] The office's efforts culminated in the creation of the Department of Homeland Security (DHS) one year later as a result of the Homeland Security Act of 2002. This law consolidated executive branch organizations related to "homeland security" into a single Cabinet department; twenty-two total agencies became part of this new apparatus.

A further attempt to prevent future terrorist attacks was the establishment of the Transportation Security Administration (TSA) on November 19, 2001, as a result of the Aviation and Transportation Security Act. Later folded into the DHS in 2003, this much-loathed agency[6] has become infamous for frisking, groping, and irradiating innocent individuals simply trying to visit a loved one or conduct business. Like the other institutionalized attempts to react to and prepare for future terrorist attacks, the TSA's efforts have created a colossal wake of collateral damage by violating the rights of peaceful people not suspected of having committed any crime—leading its own creator to call the entire agency he once spearheaded "a complete fiasco."[7] Toddlers being frisked,[8] elderly folks in wheelchairs with medical implants or devices being strip searched,[9] a nursing mother who emptied her bottles of breast milk to avoid a security hassle then being forced to actually demonstrate her breast pump to prove that the pump was really for that purpose,[10] a teacher having her frosted cupcake confiscated by TSA authorities because its gel-like frosting "counted as a [prohibited] gel-like substance,"[11] and thousands of stories like these all attest to a government boondoggle more interested in security theater[12] than in the actual security of each passenger.

These actions, and many more like them in the years following 9/11, could have been completely avoided—just as 9/11 could have been avoided. Understanding how requires a deep look into common questions like "Why do they hate us?" or "Why were we attacked?" We should have immediately considered the question of whether the attacks *could have been prevented*, and if so, how? One answer to this question could have been (and still is) the immediate termination of military interventions around the world. As the CIA has noted, the US government's foreign policy can be negatively impacted by the "blowback"[13] that occurs when the government's agents kill people around the world, leading the family, friends, and countrymen of those (often innocent[14]) people to become angry and seek revenge. Osama bin Laden himself stated that he and his cohorts were attacking America "because of their evil and injustice in the whole of the Islamic World, especially in Iraq and Palestine and their occupation of the Land of the Two Holy Sanctuaries [Saudi Arabia]."[15] While this is one answer, there is a much simpler one that is less known, and certainly much less controversial than complete military withdrawal.

To orchestrate the 9/11 attacks, terrorists commandeered planes using box-cutters as weapons. Why were pilots, charged with protecting their crew and plane, outmatched by a small piece of metal? The answer: just months before the attack, pilots were prohibited by a federal bureaucracy's regulation from possessing a gun on board their planes. Since 1961, regulations from the Federal Aviation Agency (now Federal Aviation Administration) exempted law enforcement officers and other authorized airline personnel, including pilots, from a general prohibition against possessing weapons aboard aircraft. On July 21, 2001, the

FAA bureaucracy banned pilots and other authorized personnel from being armed on board their planes—thus making the cockpit a "gun-free zone" in which men with box-cutters could dominate the unarmed victims and gain control of the plane.[16] Had that edict not been made by an unelected government employee, and had the pilots been armed, the tragic events of 9/11 may have been minimized if not altogether prevented.

Similar "gun-free zones" have been the setting of other catastrophic attacks. In 2006, Virginia Tech University lobbied their state legislature to prohibit concealed-permit holders from carrying a gun on campus. The bill which would have changed this policy in favor of permit holders was defeated at the committee level, prompting Virginia Tech's spokesman Larry Hincker to congratulate the legislature for denying students the use of firearms on campus. "I'm sure the university community is appreciative of the General Assembly's actions," Hincker said, "because this will help parents, students, faculty and visitors feel safe on our campus."[17] Whether they *felt* safe or not, the mass murder committed on that campus just one year later proves that they were in fact *not* safe. Over the course of two and a half hours, a cold-blooded gunman killed thirty-two defenseless people and injured twenty-five others. Had any of the victims or those who successfully escaped been carrying a gun and been willing to fight back, it is extremely likely that the shooter's rampage would have been substantially cut short; according to witnesses, the shooter often took his time and paused to reload.[18] Even the shooting at Fort Hood two years later, in which a disgruntled Army major killed twelve fellow soldiers and wounded thirty-one others can be blamed in part on the "gun-free zone" created by a rule requiring soldiers to not carry guns on base unless as part of a training exercise.[19] Soldiers who are highly trained and experienced in the use of their weapon, and with which they are constantly in contact while in potential combat zones, were disarmed and unable to minimize or prevent the assailant's aggression.

Fortunately, these draconian restrictions have not turned everyone's home into a "gun-free zone," though some states such as New York, New Mexico, Virginia, and a few others have limited or no laws that codify people's right to defend their person and property within their homes. An estimated one hundred-eighty million Americans[20] have a gun within the home, one of whom is Sarah McKinley of New York. In

September 2011, eighteen-year-old Sarah gave birth to a little boy. Three months later, on Christmas Day, her husband died of cancer. On New Year's Eve just one week later, Sarah was home alone with her infant son when two men, one armed with a knife in hand, attempted to forcibly enter her home. She called 911, retrieved a shotgun and handgun, and positioned herself defensively to use the guns if the would-be intruders were to successfully enter her home before police arrived. The men broke down the door, and as the first man entered the home, Sarah fired the shotgun and felled the intruder immediately. The other man fled and later turned himself in. Commenting later to reporters on her use of the gun to defend herself and her baby son, Sarah said: "I knew that I was going to have to choose [the intruders] or my son, and it wasn't going to be my son so I did what I had to do." [21] Sarah acted responsibly and successfully defended herself and her son.

Every thirteen seconds, an American uses a gun in self-defense according to a comprehensive 1994 study.[22] The study determined that in 15.7 percent of an estimated 2.5 million annual instances in which a gun was used in self-defense in America, the defender believed that someone "almost certainly" would have died had the gun not been used for protection. This suggests, if accurate, that a life is saved within the United States of America about once every 1.3 minutes. (In another 14.2 percent of cases, the defender believed that someone "probably" would have died had the gun not been used.) In over half of the gun defense incidents, the defender was being confronted by two or more attackers; three or more attackers were involved in over a quarter of incidents.

With millions of Americans finding themselves in circumstances where a gun is needed for defensive use, a need for the tools and training required to deter a threat is clearly needed. Of course, a gun is by no means the only weapon that can be successfully used to defend one's self and one's property. Six-year-old Rivers Hobbs was attacked by a mountain lion at Big Bend National Park in February 2012 as his family was walking to their room.[23] As the animal bit Rivers's face, his father pounced on it to break his son free. Mr. Hobbs quickly reached for a pocketknife he was carrying and stabbed the mountain lion in the chest, causing it to flee. Knives, baseball bats, pepper spray, a hammer, and even car keys—these and many other tools can be and often are successfully used in self-defense. Historically, however, guns have proven to be the most effective way at matching an assailant's threat while keeping the assailant at a safe distance. Yet despite so many examples of the responsible use of a firearm to literally save hundreds of thousands of lives, institutions and individuals continue to lobby for "gun control" laws, which violate the individual right to self-defense.

THE RIGHT OF SELF-DEFENSE

Most Americans know of the Second Amendment to the US Constitution, which reads: "A well-regulated militia being necessary to the security of a free state, the right of the people to keep and bear arms shall not be infringed." This right "to keep and bear arms" (put differently, to own and use guns) is important and foundational to the other constitutionally protected rights. As gun champion Charlton Heston once quipped, it "is the one right that allows 'rights' to exist at all."[24] It is not inaccurate to claim that there exists a right to own and defensively use a gun, but this right is incomplete. In truth, we possess a right to *self-defense*, not just a right to use a *gun* in self-defense. The right to defend ourselves against a would-be aggressor implies that any tool necessary can be employed to achieve that end, whether a gun, a knife, a baseball bat, or any other tool.

The right to self-defense is merely the extension of the right to own property. If a person has the right to his life and the property he owns, it then follows that he has the right to keep that property and protect it from the unjust and unauthorized aggression of others. Violence is justified in actual cases of aggression to defensively deter that threat, but no violence is justified in seeking revenge for an aggressive action that already occurred or in escalating the defensive response more than is necessary to terminate the threat. Further, violence is not justified in cases of indirect or perceived harm, such as a neighbor's unkempt property decreasing one's property values or an organized boycott against one's place of business. In short, the right to self-defense only relates to actual defense of life, liberty, and property, and nothing more.

This right is individual; we each inherently possess the moral authority to repel an aggressor. While that aggressor is often a common criminal, historically it has also been a tyrannical state sending its armed forces to disarm the populace, incarcerate innocent individuals, and kill

dissenters without due process. As the patriots from the founding generation demonstrated, and as was boldly proclaimed in the Declaration of
Independence, it is necessary at times "to throw off [despotic] government, and to provide new guards for [our] future security." Pitted against
a ruthless military machine in a quest to "secure the blessings of liberty,"
the seceding colonists had only one realistic recourse: their firearms.
Without guns, revolution would not have been possible. "Personal firearms were vitally important for the success of the American Revolution,"
notes one historian. "The brunt of the initial fighting during the war was
borne by state militias, composed of citizen-soldiers who carried their
own hunting rifles and personal weapons into combat."[25] The founders
exercised their right to self-defense, not only against individual aggressors, but also against other institutions, including government, which
committed acts of violence against them.[26]

While few people would object to the assertion of an individual
right to self-defense, many do not agree that a similar and subordinate
right to keep and bear arms exists. Such persons have argued that the
right to own weapons is a collective one only, allowing for military and
law enforcement officials to keep the peace through the use of arms.
To understand why this argument is wrong, and why the right to keep
and bear arms is an individual one, imagine that the government was
completely abolished. In such a scenario, does a person have the moral
authority to prevent his neighbor from obtaining and using a gun?
Would this person be justified in using violence against his peaceful
neighbor—imposing a fine upon him, incarcerating him in his basement, openly beating him, and so on—when that neighbor uses his
gun for recreation or self-defense? Clearly, peaceful individuals can in
no legitimate way be prevented by their peers in possessing and appropriately using a gun. When those neighbors collectively delegate some
of their powers to a government to execute on their behalf, they cannot
delegate a nonexistent power. Lacking the individual authority to prevent a person from having and using guns, government cannot therefore be delegated that power. As such, the right to keep and bear arms
(a subset of the right to self-defense) is one that predates and thus *super-
sedes* government. As articulated in a 1788 editorial by the *Pennsylvania
Gazette*, "the unlimited power of the sword is not in the hands of either
the federal or state governments, but where I trust in God it will ever
remain, in the hands of the people."[27]

The constitutional clause aiming to guarantee the right to keep and bear arms is commonly known, but it is not the first such appearance in the governing documents of early America. During the Revolutionary War, many colonies created declarations of rights, which explicitly recognized the individual right to bear arms. Virginia's declared "that a well regulated militia, composed of the body of the people, trained to arms, is the proper, natural, and safe defense of a free state."[28] Pennsylvania's stated "that the people have a right to bear arms for the defense of themselves and the state."[29] Vermont's asserted "that the people have a right to bear arms for the defense of themselves and the state."[30] The emphasis placed on the right to defend against both an individual aggressor and a tyrannical government was also indirectly supported by Massachusetts, which maintained that "the people have a right to keep and bear arms for the common defense."[31] By referencing the "common defense" alone, the argument that guns were only authorized for individual self-defense was preempted. However, some citizens of that state objected to the decision not to explicitly guarantee the right to individual self-defense. The man who drafted the language was John Adams, who did not intend to deny such a right, and who actually defended that right, noting that "arms in the hands of citizens [may] be used at individual discretion . . . in private self-defense."[32] The colonies' joint Declaration of Independence argued for the right to self-defense against both an individual and a government by affirming the unalienable right of individuals in "defending their lives and liberties . . . and protecting property . . ." The protection of one's life, liberty, and property extends to all enemies who might seek to do them harm—governments and their standing armies included. The developing worldview in early America, writes one expert on the subject, "entailed not only the right of individuals to keep and bear arms, but also the right to have and use arms in concern to defend their freedom against an oppressive government."[33]

Though the right exists in truth and allegedly is protected on paper, it is one that has been willingly rejected by many people. In his day, James Madison wrote that Americans, unlike those in Europe, had "the advantage of being armed," whereas in Europe "the governments are afraid to trust the people with arms."[34] Today, in contrast to two centuries ago, many Americans are afraid to trust *themselves* with arms, and their government shares in the skepticism. Sure, a majority of Americans are estimated to own a gun, but how many of those who bothered to procure a weapon have ammunition at the ready, have the training necessary to efficiently use it, and have the willingness to actually shoot another person were that to become necessary? Whether with guns or not, the right to self-defense implies a corresponding responsibility to exercise that right in order to protect it. If we do not defend ourselves, then the government will increasingly involve itself in the issue. Regulating gun ownership and use, restricting access to the necessary tools for self-defense, and criminalizing the right to carry the tools needed for such self-defense have become the byproducts of this intervention—an intervention brought about because too many individuals have shirked the responsibility to provide for their own protection.

THE RESPONSIBILITY OF SELF-DEFENSE

The leadership of The Church of Jesus Christ of Latter-day Saints authored and signed a document in 1995 titled "The Family: A Proclamation to the World." In that review of the importance of and responsibilities associated with the institution of the family, the following is included: "By divine design, fathers are to preside over their families in love and righteousness and are responsible to provide the necessities of life and protection for their families."[35] As this indicates, husbands and fathers have three primary roles in their stewardship,[36] which are generally prioritized and proactively worked on in the following order: provide, preside, and protect. Almost all men recognize the duty to work and provide for their family; most men do a good job at being the patriarch and being the leader of the family, and some take the issue of protection and defense seriously enough to assume the responsibility. In today's world of outsourcing and delegation, however, it seems that most prefer to appoint the duty of defense to the police department rather than concern themselves with weaponry and tactical training. Political fear-mongering, Hollywood hype, and a general misunderstanding of the history and practical use of guns has resulted in a massively successful campaign to create an atmosphere in which very few people know how or are ready to defend themselves.

To be sure, families face a variety of threats, including but not limited to violent attacks. Further, owning weapons increases the potential for an accident to occur with that tool, if stored or handled improperly. Like any responsibility, individuals must weigh the alternatives according to their circumstances to determine the best course of action for them. Any tool, whether it be a vehicle, chainsaw, computer, or gun, should be treated with care and used after instruction and training so as not to cause a mishap. But the infrequency of accidents that occur with such tools should not stand as a strong reason against their acquisition and use; fulfilling the responsibility to defend and protect yourself and others requires exploring what tools can assist in that duty.

Joseph Smith—himself known for organizing a strong defensive force when faced with personal threats—once commented on this subject as follows: "There is one principle which is eternal; it is the duty of all men to protect their lives and the lives of the household, whenever necessity requires, and no power has a right to forbid it, should the last extreme arrive, but I anticipate no such extreme, but caution is the parent of safety."[37] Also calling those who will not defend their families "cowards,"[38] the Prophet seemed to emphasize this basic responsibility of every man. A similar statement was unanimously approved for canonization in the "declaration of belief regarding governments" in section 134 of the Doctrine and Covenants:

> We believe that all men are justified in defending themselves, their friends, and property, and the government, from the unlawful assaults and encroachments of all persons in times of exigency, where immediate appeal cannot be made to the laws, and relief afforded. (D&C 134:11)

It is important to note the conditional in this verse: we are justified in defending ourselves, our family and friends, our property, and our nation "in times of exigency"—that is, when another (legitimate) recourse is not available given the time constraints. This caveat succinctly illustrates why every family should be armed and knowledgeable in defense. Many individuals presume that the police will defend them should something happen, likely not realizing that the average response time of a police officer nationwide is seven minutes.[39] This amount of time, of course, is an *eternity* when faced with an immediate threat. In fact, police rarely *prevent* crime at all—much of their job is to write crime reports after a crime has taken place and conduct an investigation to try and seek justice. By no means are they a proper and adequate substitute for personal defense since crimes can occur in mere seconds, and waiting around helplessly for police assistance will likely not work to your benefit.

For many, fear is the main deterrent in taking the necessary steps to become armed and skilled. First, there is fear of the threat itself. If faced with a physical threat, some would rather give up and die, throwing their life upon the mercy of the assailant. These seem to be the "cowards" the Prophet described—unwilling to do whatever is necessary to ensure the safety and security of themselves or their family.[40] The other fear is a fear of the weapon. This uneasiness stems largely from inexperience and ignorance. When necessary security and precautionary measures are implemented, a weapon inside the home is no more a threat than the matches in the garage or the swimming pool outside. Ignorance has never been a justifiable excuse for inaction; we cannot excuse our unwillingness to fulfill our personal responsibilities by claiming that we didn't know they existed. It is a husband's responsibility to seek the proper training, experience, and self-confidence that will help him better fulfill the duties he inherently has and responsibilities associated with his role as protector of his family. Women are not exempt from this; just as the police aren't able to continually guard everyone against potential aggressors, so too are husbands away at work or elsewhere on a regular basis. Many women are not married and must rely on themselves for protection. Thus, the individual right of self-defense is also an individual responsibility, and men and women alike need to equip themselves with the skills and tools necessary to successfully repel a would-be aggressor.

This responsibility isn't just a "good idea" and wise counsel—it carries the weight of being a commandment from God. So taught Brigham Young:

> We all believe that the Lord will fight our battles; but how? Will He do it while we are unconcerned and make no effort whatever for our own safety when an enemy is upon us? If we make no efforts to guard our towns, our houses, our cities, our wives and children, will the Lord guard them for us? He will not; but if we pursue the opposite course and strive to help Him to accomplish His designs, then will He fight our battles. We are baptized for the remission of sins; but it would be quite as reasonable to expect remission of sins without baptism, as to expect the Lord to fight

our battles without our taking every precaution to be prepared to defend ourselves. The Lord requires us to be quite as willing to fight our own battles as to have Him fight them for us. If we are not ready for an enemy when he comes upon us, we have not lived up to the requirements of Him who guides the ship of Zion, or who dictates the affairs of his kingdom.[41]

Brother Brigham's words are echoed in principle within the proclamation on the family, which affirms the responsibility we have to protect our loved ones. Additional instruction is found in the scriptures: Captain Moroni reminded his people of the Lord's counsel that "ye shall defend your families even unto bloodshed" (Alma 43:47); the same people were "taught to defend themselves against their enemies, even to the shedding of blood if it were necessary; yea, and they were also taught never to give an offense, yea, and never to raise the sword except it were against an enemy, except it were to preserve their lives" (Alma 48:14); under the Law of Moses, "If a thief be found breaking [in], and be smitten that he die, there shall no blood be shed for him" (Exodus 22:2); the apostle Paul's declaration that "if any provide not for his own, and specially for those of his own house, he hath denied the faith, and is worse than an infidel" (1 Timothy 5:8) applies as well, for protecting what you provide is as necessary as providing it in the first place; as previously noted, the Doctrine and Covenants states that "all men are justified in defending themselves, their friends, and property" when circumstances require it (D&C 134:11).

One who would prefer to abdicate his right of self-defense, shirk the corresponding responsibility, and submit himself to an attacker are certainly entitled to do so; it is, after all, his own life. This attitude, however, is cowardly and irresponsible—even more so when that individual is the guardian of other people. Oddly, almost everybody who can afford to do so goes to great lengths to obtain insurance for their lives and possessions, yet few take the proactive (and less costly) steps that would potentially make filing claims against such insurance unnecessary.

Those who value their lives—and the lives of those within their stewardship—have the responsibility to defend those lives should it ever come under attack. Fulfilling that responsibility requires an investment of time and money to become better equipped and trained. President Joseph F. Smith believed that "it is righteous and just for every people to defend their own lives and their own liberties, and their own homes, with the last drop of their blood."[42] While becoming armed is ultimately a personal decision that should absolutely not be undertaken carelessly, we must remember that this responsibility is justified of God and, as noted in the Proclamation, is part of his "divine design."

DISARMAMENT PRECEDES DEMOCIDE

History offers one devastating story after another of people who were unable or unwilling to defend themselves against aggressors. While assault and murder are as ancient as man, the modern trend of highly centralized government has produced a system of destruction and death that far surpasses the aggregate random acts of violence individuals may commit on their own. It is estimated that in the twentieth century alone, 262 million people were killed *by their own government*.[43] Known as "democide" (or the intentional killing of an unarmed person or people by their government), this statistic is hard to fathom yet tragically true.

For example: the USSR killed sixty-two million of its people; China killed forty-five million; Nazi Germany killed twenty-one million; Japan killed 6 million; Cambodia killed 2 million; the list continues to include many other countries whose repressive regimes physically pitted the state against the individual. Based on the population at the time—over eleven billion people lived during the twentieth century— this means that governments killed roughly 3.7 percent of the entire human race, or a number equal to over 80 percent of the population of the United States of America at the time. If all of these bodies were laid from head to toe, and assuming an average of five feet in length per body, they would span the entire circumference of the earth *ten times*. This number of government murders is *four times* more than the number of people who died in combat or as so-called "collateral damage" during all foreign and internal wars during the same century.[44]

While the dictatorships and authoritarian governments responsible for such reprehensible crimes were created and succeeded for various reasons, they all share the same vulnerability. One societal trend could have mitigated if not prevented these mass exterminations of human life: widespread civilian gun ownership. No well-armed society has been susceptible to such a degree of tyranny, nor is it difficult to understand why this trend exists. Yet even among countries that enjoy a rich pro-gun culture (such as the United States of America), an overwhelming amount of propaganda is consistently promoted in the public square and adopted by government to hamper the right to self-defense.[45] Given that democide is a condition in which the government kills its *unarmed* citizens, it may be correctly argued that gun prohibition is far more deadly than gun ownership. Put differently, the estimated 262 million deaths by government in the twentieth century could be blamed on "gun control"—government policies which violate the right to self-defense by prohibiting civilians from owning and using guns. As the saying goes, "When guns are outlawed, only criminals (and the government!) will have them." The world is witness to what results such policies produce.

Disarmament of the civilian population is a key step in the rise of all dictatorships. Whether freely elected like Adolf Hitler and Hugo Chavez, or instituted after a violent revolution such as Mao Tse-Tung and Fidel Castro, dictators cement their newfound control by confiscating and prohibiting guns amongst the general population, thereby facilitating the extermination of any opposition. Just as 9/11 could have been partially or fully prevented had the pilots been armed, so too could these oppressors have been checked in their coercion by an armed populace.

Nazi Germany provides an instructive lesson. During the Weimar Republic, licensing and registration of guns became an exhaustive, mandated effort.[46] Passed under the guise of public safety, these detailed registration records gave Hitler the ability to begin a complete disarmament; knowing precisely who owned how many guns, he was able to selectively target the Jews and others deemed untrustworthy of being armed. As historian Stephen P. Halbrook notes:

> The existence of firearms regulations providing for records on all individuals lawfully possessing firearms, coupled with searches and seizures of firearms from the houses of potential dissidents, guaranteed that firearms would be possessed only by supporters of Nazism. These firearms policies made it far easier to exterminate any opposition, Jews, and unpopular groups.[47]

What was intended for the public good became used for public evil. Though the narrative today is that the Jews were collectively slaughtered—and most in fact were—there were pockets of resistance where emboldened individuals gathered whatever weapons they could find in order to mount a defense. One well-known story is that of the Warsaw Ghetto Uprising, in which up to one thousand Jews who knew they had almost no chance of survival decided, rather than being sent to die in a gas chamber, that they would die fighting their enemies. As one person wrote in his journal of the event: "We took stock of our position and saw that this was a struggle between a fly and an elephant. But our national dignity dictated to us that the Jews must offer resistance and not allow themselves to be led wantonly to slaughter."[48] Warsaw was the first of many other civilian uprisings against the Nazis throughout Europe. For these Jews and almost all others hoping to repel their would-be murderers, guns were scarce. As two thousand troops marched into the ghetto in 1943 to exterminate the remaining Jews, they were surprised to encounter resistance. Equipped only with a few guns, grenades, and limited ammunition they had acquired from soldiers who had previously attempted to raid the ghetto, the Jewish Combat Organization was able to hold off the Nazis for almost a month, killing three hundred of its highly trained and fully equipped soldiers in the process. Some of the Jews escaped, others committed suicide, but not one of them was captured and sent to the gas chambers. Guns—even when in extremely limited supply—and the bravery to use them created opportunity for resistance and defense of life, liberty, and property.

As Holocaust historian Abram L. Sachar writes, "the difference between resistance and submission depended very largely upon who was in possession of the arms that back up the will to do or die."[49]

Guns also made the difference for the Bielski brothers. These Jewish siblings assisted in saving and protecting the elderly, women, and children who otherwise would have been rounded up and summarily killed; nobody who fled to their group in the forest was turned away. Growing to over twelve hundred people, they enjoyed a 95 percent survival rate—the highest among the Nazi's victims.[50] In less than one year, roughly one hundred fifty of their group who had engaged in active resistance carried out thirty-eight combat missions, destroyed two locomotives, twenty-three train cars, thirty-two telegraph poles, four bridges, and killed three hundred-eighty-one enemy fighters.[51] This was made possible by their ability to repair broken guns and assemble new ones from spare parts. Sachar notes: "The indispensable need, of course, was arms. As soon as some Jews, even in the camps themselves, obtained possession of a weapon, however pathetically inadequate—a rifle, an ax, a sewer cover, a homemade bomb—they used it and often took Nazis with them to death."[52]

These stories and hundreds more like them demonstrate a trend found among disarmed societies. Guns (and other weapons) are important and necessary, both for our individual self-defense against would-be aggressors and for the preservation of liberty against the encroachments of an oppressive government. In 1967, the International Society for the Prevention of Crime held a congress in Paris to discuss the prevention of genocide. This body concluded that "defensive measures are the most effective means for the prevention of genocide. Not all aggression is criminal. A defense reaction is for the human race what the wind is for navigation—the result depends on the direction. The most moral violence is that used in legitimate self-defense, the most sacred judicial institution."[53] The illegitimate, anti-liberty action of confiscating guns from peaceful individuals by the state that governs them renders those individuals unable to resist the democidal destruction that is soon to follow.

People recognize that armed and trained soldiers are an important asset to protecting a group of people from external threats, such as an invasion from another country. But what happens when those soldiers are commanded by their superiors to turn on you? The framers of the Constitution knew from experience the importance of firearms both as a personal tool (for protection, hunting, and so on) and as a method of actively resisting unjust government. Noah Webster, the founding-era statesman and prolific author, voiced their common views as follows:

> Before a standing army can rule, the people must be disarmed; as they are in almost every kingdom in Europe. The supreme power in America cannot enforce unjust laws by the sword; because the whole body of the people are armed, and constitute a force superior to any band of regular troops that can be, on any pretense, raised in the United States. A military force, at the command of Congress, can execute no laws, but such as the people perceive to be just and constitutional; for they will possess the power, and jealousy will instantly inspire the inclination, to resist the execution of a law which appears to them unjust and oppressive.[54]

It is important that we recognize this historical trend toward tyranny. Many Americans think that it couldn't happen in their country, but so did many of those who are now unknown to history, other than being a simple statistic—one of hundreds of millions of unarmed individuals put to death by an oppressive government. Tyranny is not limited by geography; the same trend can happen in America. Dr. Miguel Faria, a Cuban doctor who escaped his native country during Castro's takeover, has written about the connection of gun registration, confiscation, and authoritarianism. After noting the connection between disarmament and democide, he observed the failure of many Americans to consider such a trend in their own country:

> When presented with these deadly chronicles [of democide] and the perilous historic sequence, Americans often opine that it cannot happen here. As to the dangers of licensing of gun owners and registration of firearms, they frequently retort, "If you don't have anything to hide, then you don't have anything to fear!" Followed by, "I see nothing wrong with gun registration because we have to do something; there are just too many guns out there that fall into the wrong hands." These naïve attitudes ignore the penchant of governments to accrue power at the expense of the liberties of individuals.[55]

Those observing this trend and wishing to prevent its future occurrence must identify early and seemingly innocuous actions (such as mandatory registration) that may lead to later, deathly consequences. Americans cannot claim that confiscation will not happen here—it has already happened here. The revolution of 1776 was fomented in large measure by the ruling government's attempts to disarm its citizens. Using arbitrary searches and seizures, false promises of safekeeping, entrapment, and a ban on the export of arms and ammunition from England to the colonies, King George's empire had clamped down on the colonists' right to keep and bear arms. Samuel Adams wrote that the British "told us we shall have no more guns, no powder to use, and kill our wolves and other game . . ."[56] Indeed, in a confidential order written on October 19, 1774, King George forbade the exportation of arms and gun powder to the colonies and mandated that the various governors prevent importation of such items into their jurisdictions.[57] In defiance of such actions, Patrick Henry's famous "liberty or death" speech directly confronted the importance of an armed people:

They tell us, sir, that we are weak—unable to cope with so formidable an adversary. But when shall we be stronger? Will it be the next week or the next year? *Will it be when we are totally disarmed*, and when a British guard shall be stationed in every house? Shall we gather strength by irresolution and inaction? Shall we acquire the means of effectual resistance, by lying supinely on our backs, and hugging the delusive phantom of hope, until our enemies shall have bound us hand and foot? Sir, we are not weak, if we make a proper use of those means which the God of nature hath placed in our power. *Three million people, armed* in the holy cause of liberty . . . are invincible by any force which our enemy can send against us.[58]

Less than one month later, in April 1775, the governor of Massachusetts dispatched around seven hundred soldiers to seize the arms and munitions being stored by the colonial militia in Concord. On the way to their destination, the soldiers were confronted by the minutemen—select members of the militia serving as a highly mobile, responsive force—who had gathered to block the way. Major John Pitcairn and his fellow officers demanded that the men throw down their weapons and disperse. The minutemen stood their ground, willing neither to disperse nor surrender their weapons. That defiance resulted in the confrontation that today is known as "the shot heard 'round the world," when an unknown person fired the first shot which led the British Army regulars to open fire and charge with bayonets, despite not having been given that order. As revolution broke out in the months ahead, disarmament policies were still promoted as a means to curtail the opposition's success in resisting. In 1777, the Under Secretary of State in the British Colonial Office drafted a proposal advocating disarming all Americans and relying only on a standing army:

The Militia Laws should be repealed and none suffered to be re-enacted, & the Arms of all the People should be taken away, & every piece of Ordnance removed into the King's Stores, nor should any Foundry or manufactory of Arms, Gunpowder, or Warlike Stores, be ever suffered in America, nor should any Gunpowder, Lead, Arms or Ordnance be imported into it without License; they will have but little need of such things for the future, as the King's Troops, Ships & Forts will be sufficient to protect them from any danger.

Standing armies were scary institutions to most of the founders, and rightly so. They knew from experience how often these soldiers, who were organized in the name of defending the country against external threats, had instead become used to violate the life, liberty, and property of the very people they were employed to protect. In the debate surrounding what became the Second Amendment to the US Constitution, Representative Elbridge Gerry of Massachusetts emphasized the importance of the militia—armed and trained civilians—over standing armies. "What, sir, is the use of a militia?" he asked. "It is to prevent the establishment of a standing army[,] the ban[e] of liberty . . . . Whenever Governments mean to invade the rights and liberties of the people, they always attempt to destroy the militia, in order to raise an army upon their ruins."[59] As President, James Madison spoke to Congress on the importance of the militia: "An efficient militia is authorized and contemplated by the constitution, and *required by the spirit and safety of free government*."[60] Being an association of armed and trained citizens, the militia makes it possible to repel democidal governments and their standing armies; an unarmed public unable and unwilling to defend itself enjoys no such liberty.

Whether loosely organized as a militia or operating independently as sovereign individuals, the people's right to self-defense is rightly perceived as a threat by would-be dictators. Adolf Hitler, himself a dictator who had consolidated power by disarming his enemies, noted: "The most foolish mistake we could possibly make would be to allow the subject races to possess arms. History shows that all conquerors who have allowed their subject races to carry arms have prepared their own downfall by so doing."[61] While we may be led to believe that we live in one of the freest nations and still enjoy a healthy amount of individual liberty, the historical trend toward tyranny should suggest the wisdom of proactively fulfilling the personal responsibility to defend one's life, liberty, and property. Joseph Story, an early American lawyer who served on the Supreme Court, wrote that the right to keep and bear arms is liberty's best defense since "it offers a strong moral check against the usurpation and arbitrary power of rulers; and will generally, even if these are successful in the first instance, enable the people to resist and triumph over them."[62] While we should hope that another armed revolution will never be necessary, we must ask ourselves whether armed resistance would even be possible. If we continually submit to gun registration, regulation, confiscation, and related steps leading toward a future dis-armament, we will be forsaking our rich American heritage regarding the right to keep and bear arms, and instead we will be casting our lot with the 262 million dead by democide. The Constitution states that a well-regulated militia—armed and trained citizens ready and willing to use their weapons in self-defense—is "necessary to the security of a free State." If we don't fulfill this essential responsibility, we cannot ade-quately defend liberty; a state will exist, but it will not be a "free" one.

SHIRKING THE RESPONSIBILITY

The "gun control" lobby—a coalition of anti-gun political groups such as the Brady Campaign to Prevent Gun Violence and sympathetic politicians—promotes its restrictive policies on the basis of an inter-pretation of the Second Amendment which argues that the militia is today's National Guard, suggesting that trained professionals are those for whom this right is guaranteed. This was an opinion held by the Supreme Court in 1965, which concluded that "the National Guard is the modern Militia reserved to the States by Art. I. 8, cl. 15, 16, of the Constitution. . . . The passage of the National Defense Act of 1916 materially altered the status of the militias by constituting them as the National Guard."[63] Thus, according to this view, the right to keep and bear arms serves as a military or law enforcement function only, and the government-sanctioned entities organized to perform those duties are therefore constitutionally guaranteed the right to equip themselves as necessary for the common defense. While citizen militias were impor-tant and necessary in the early days of the nation, proponents of this argument claim that the creation of National Guard units "modern-ized" this anachronistic idea of each person wielding and using their own gun.

This misguided interpretation of the Second Amendment—a con-stitutional clause that explicitly states that keeping and bearing arms is a "right of the people," as individuals—is merely a manifestation of a more fundamental belief. The central argument underlying all "gun control" legislation is that individuals don't need firearms because the police or military are there to protect us all from crime. Further, these individuals argue that guns in the wrong hands unnecessarily kill people, and by limiting or denying individuals the ability to own and use firearms, the related death count would substantially decrease.

This belief is completely false for two reasons. First, the police simply cannot protect everybody from crime, nor do they. This flies in the face of what the "gun control" lobby claims, as exemplified by one of its most famous advocates, James Brady—the former assistant to President Ronald Reagan who was nearly killed during an assassination attempt on the president's life. When asked whether handgun ownership is legitimate, Brady replied: "For target shooting, that's okay. Get a license and go to the range. For defense of the home, that's why we have police departments."[64] One story (of thousands more like it) shows the danger and factual bankruptcy of this claim. Leasa Ivory of Florida contacted her husband by telephone one day in 1998 to inform him that he was not the father of her six-month-old son.[65] Enraged, the husband drove to their apartment and attempted to enter. Ivory called 911 hoping for help, as her husband had a history of abuse. "He's trying to get in. Hurry up, hurry up," she yelled to the 911 operator. "He's taking the door off the hinges and coming in!" The call concluded with the sound of Ivory's phone crashing to the floor and her subsequent screams. When police arrived just two minutes later—an impressive feat given the average response time for most 911 calls—they found Ivory stabbed in the back three times with a six-inch fishing knife, lying in a pool of her own blood. Though the police officers responded in a timely fashion, they were unable to save Ivory's life. Brady's contention that police departments exist to defend us in our homes is completely misguided and demonstrably false. This rebuttal is backed up by more than just anecdotal evidence such as this story—the data itself disproves Brady's claim.

In 2010 alone, 1,246,248 violent crimes were reported in the United States.[66] Of that number, 14,748 people were murdered, 84,767 were raped, and 367,832 were robbed—all within a single year. This turns out to be one violent crime committed every 25.3 seconds—a murder every 35.6 minutes, a rape every 6 minutes, and a robbery every 1.4 minutes. *All of these crimes were not prevented by police.* In cases where victims have advance warning of the attack and are able to call 911 for help, rarely do police arrive in time to be of any real assistance. A 2004 report by the *Washington Times* found that the average time for police officers to respond to a high-priority 911 emergency call was *over eight minutes* in several major cities around the country.[67] Detroit's average is twenty-four minutes,[68] Atlanta's is eleven minutes,[69] and Oakland's is fifteen minutes.[70] The familiar saying "When seconds count, the police are only minutes away" may sound humorous, but it represents a matter of life and death played out many times each day across the country. The primary activity of police officers is not the deterrence of a future crime, but the investigation and pursuit of justice once a crime has already been committed. For victims, this is often too little, too late.

The second reason that the police protection argument is false is that the government has no legal obligation to protect people from crime. A well-known example graphically illustrates a common policy across the nation. On March 16, 1975, two men broke into a three-story home in Washington, DC. A woman on the second floor was sexually attacked, and her housemates on the floor above her heard her screams. The housemates called 911 and police were dispatched on a low-priority assignment to check out the incident. After knocking on the door and receiving no answer, the police left the scene. The frantic housemates, responding to the woman's continued screams, called 911 a second time. The dispatcher promised the women that help would come, but no officers were even sent. The attackers discovered the other women, and all three women were kidnapped, raped, and beaten over the next fourteen hours. When they later sued the city and its police department for failing to protect them and for not even responding to their second call, the court dismissed the case, stating that the police have no duty to help individuals and only exist to provide services to the "public at large." There exists a "fundamental principle," argued the court, "that a government and its agents are under no general duty to provide public services, such as police protection, to any particular individual citizen."[71] "Accordingly," they continued, "courts have without exception concluded that when a municipality or other governmental entity undertakes to furnish police services, it assumes a duty only to the public at large and not to individual members of the community." This is not just the opinion of a few judges, but a pervasive policy regarding police services throughout the nation.

Many states have explicitly codified this refusal to defend individuals into their law. California law states that "Neither a public entity nor a public employee [may be sued] for failure to . . . provide sufficient police protection service . . . [or] for injury caused by the failure to make an arrest."[72] Illinois law says the same thing, adding that police officers are not liable for "failure to prevent the commission of crimes, failure to detect or solve crimes, and failure to identify or apprehend criminals."[73] Delaware offers immunity to all levels of government and their employees provided that they are performing their duties in good faith, are exercising discretionary powers, and are not acting with gross negligence.[74] The Court of Appeals in Kentucky commented on the law of its state, which is common amongst a majority of the other states: "The general rule of thumb, in the absence of some 'special relationship,' is that a municipality or a law enforcement agency or official does not owe individual citizens a duty to protect them from crime."[75] Put more bluntly by a California appellate court, "Police officers have no affirmative statutory duty to do anything."[76]

In other words, we're on our own.

Most people believe that the core function of government is to defend and protect individuals from those who would do them harm. After all, this is an innate right we each have and therefore can legitimately delegate to the government. Some people, however, incorrectly understand the principle of delegation and feel that since police officers exist and are paid to protect us, that we don't need to worry about protecting ourselves. They then completely set aside the responsibility of self-defense—an action that is especially problematic in light of the information in this chapter. As they refuse to defend themselves, and will not be defended by the police whose job they think it is, they unnecessarily expose themselves to the actions of an aggressor.

The gun control movement perpetuates this promotion of a paradox wherein individuals are denied the ability to adequately defend themselves because that's what police are for, yet police are freed of any liability for failing to protect them. One expert on the subject notes the same trend, which he dubs a "fatal irony": "while the government owes no duty to protect citizens, the government is also taking away the citizens' ability to protect themselves."[77] While many law enforcement officials support the right of individuals to keep and bear arms, plenty do not. Former Chicago Mayor Richard Daley famously declared, "If it was up to me, no one except law enforcement officers would own a handgun."[78] This line of thinking was proven absurd in a case from 1959 when a New York man, Burt Pugach, threatened his lover, Linda Riss, for wanting to leave him after she found out that he was married and had a child. Riss reported the threat to the police, who did nothing. Worried about her lack of police protection, she applied for a gun permit but was denied. On the night of a party celebrating her engagement to another man, Riss received a phone call warning her that it was her "last chance." She frantically called the police, begging once more for protection, but they still refused to assist her. The next day, a thug hired by Pugach threw acid in her face, blinding and permanently disfiguring her.

Unsurprisingly, given the policies and precedent listed here, Riss's lawsuit against the City of New York was unsuccessful. An appeal to the state's Supreme Court resulted in the previous ruling's affirmation, meaning that judges all the way up the chain in New York agreed that the police held no responsibility for failing to respond to Riss's repeated requests for protection. The lone dissenting judge on the New York Supreme Court noted the paradox in this case:

> What makes the city's position particularly difficult to understand is that, in conformity to the dictates of the law, Linda did not carry any weapon for self-defense. *Thus, by a rather bitter irony she was required to rely for protection on the City of New York which now denies all responsibility to her.*
>
> It is not a distortion to summarize the essence of the city's case here in the following language: "Because we owe a duty to everybody, we owe it to nobody." Were it not for the fact that this position has been hallowed by much ancient and revered precedent, we would surely dismiss it as preposterous.[79]

Police claim a responsibility to protect the "public at large" but not the individuals who comprise the public. Those who believe that they need neither the tools nor training to defend themselves assume a significant risk that need not—and should not—exist. The right to self-defense, and the corresponding responsibility to defend ourselves, does not become unnecessary merely because the government provides police services. In cases where the police are willing to respond, they will almost assuredly be too late to defend us from an aggressor. In cases where the police are not willing to respond, we are left to our own devices.

The simple truth is that this right and responsibility cannot be completely delegated to another group, such as the police, military, or even private security. Our own protection requires that we take the steps necessary to protect ourselves. Though it may be tempting to believe that trained police officers will be our primary line of defense, both history and legal precedent clearly explode this myth. We are effectively on our own, so we should prepare and act like it.

The Media Bias

Since law enforcement officers are often unable (and sometimes unwilling) to defend us from aggressors, one might assume that there would be a public recognition of the importance of defending ourselves by obtaining the necessary resources and training to do so. Along with that assumption, one would conclude that the media would highlight stories of successful self-defense to demonstrate the importance of fulfilling this basic and essential responsibility. As it (perhaps unsurprisingly) turns out, the opposite is true.

Major news agencies can and do shape public opinion both by what they selectively choose to report, and by what they decide to exclude. The media, for example, overwhelmingly and almost universally excludes stories about successful self-defense using guns. During 2001, the *New York Times* printed 104 news articles related to crimes when guns were used, for a total of 50,745 words. They printed only one story where a gun was defensively used, for a total of 163 words.[80] *USA Today* devoted 5,660 words to gun-related crimes and zero words for the defensive use of guns.[81] The *Washington Post* spent 46,884 words describing gun-related crimes that year while offering up only 953 words reporting on their use in self-defense.[82] Further, the stories that actually do mention self-defense using a gun are almost always local, while the gun-related crime stories often are given national and international attention. There is clearly a media bias as it relates to the omission of information describing the successful and responsible use of firearms to defend life, liberty, and property.

Even when the media report on a gun-related issue, they often omit information that demonstrates the appropriate use of firearms in self-defense. For example: on January 16, 2002, a former student at the Appalachian School of Law in Virginia returned to campus and used a gun to kill three people and wound three others. The event made international headlines with most commentators clamoring for more "gun control." What was omitted from the overwhelming majority of reports was the fact that the attacker was stopped by two students who had guns in their cars, retrieved them, and pointed them at the assailant to demand he stop. Out of two hundred eight news stories in the week after the event, just *four* mentioned that the students who stopped the attack did so using guns.[83] Most simply stated, as did the *Washington Post*, that the students "pounced on the gunman and held him until help arrived." *Newsday* said that the attacker was simply "restrained by students." Seventy-two news stories described how the attack was stopped without so much as mentioning that the student heroes were armed with guns.[84]

Millions of people consuming this "news" therefore conclude, even if only subconsciously, that instances of a successful defense using guns must be rare if not nonexistent. This helps perpetuate the fallacious and detrimental belief that the police should and do exist to protect us. Those who hold this belief, molded by what they've been told and by what they haven't been told, do not recognize their right to—and responsibility of—self-defense. If a person is not aware of the responsibility (or if they are aware of it but simply have not made it a priority), then they will not act upon it. As with all other responsibilities, education precedes action.

Guns are used far more often in self-defense than they are in a crime, yet as previously shown, the media overwhelmingly reports their wrongful use. Further, by downplaying the benefits and successful use of firearms, the media encourages ignorance as to the best form of defense, effectively endangering the lives of their customers. Fortunately, positive stories of the responsible and successful use of guns still circulate through the Internet and other media sources, and sometimes in the mainstream media. Ultimately, providing the necessary balance against the media's anti-gun campaign is left up to us by educating and encouraging those within our sphere of influence to recognize and act upon the right and responsibility of self-defense.

A NATION OF FREEMEN

During the Massachusetts ratifying convention for the US Constitution, delegate William Symmes warned (some might say prophesied) that the proposed federal government at some point "shall be too firmly fixed in the saddle to be overthrown by anything but a general insurrection."[85] As the discussion later turned to standing armies and the likelihood of their assisting that government to become so "firmly fixed," delegate Theodore Sedwick rhetorically asked that if such a threat were to exist, "whether they [the standing army] could subdue a nation of freemen, who know how to prize liberty, and who have arms in their hands?"[86] In pondering such a question, consider two alternatives to Sedwick's perception of what a future America would look like: A nation of men who are well armed but who do not know how to prize liberty might be one where everybody's firearms gathered dust, were considered unnecessary or only for recreational use. Alternatively, it might encourage rampant crime and wrongful use of those weapons in a society of individuals who do not value their liberty nor the liberty of those around them. On the other hand, a nation of unarmed men who prize liberty is one in which that liberty will not long exist, for they lack the ability to effectively secure and defend it against dictators and despots.

The founding generation of America was one in which individuals were well armed *and* prized liberty. The revolution against their oppressors would not have been won without armed, supplied, and skilled shooters. What would they say of our generation? Are we armed? Are we disciplined? Do we prize liberty?

Self-defense is both a right and a responsibility—one that Joseph Smith called "eternal."[87] It cannot be fully delegated to another individual or institution. While we may employ others to assist us in aspects of our own protection, we cannot exempt ourselves from this responsibility. Though we may petition God for protection or assistance in repelling a threat, as Brigham Young taught, divine aid will come as we "tak[e] every precaution to be prepared to defend ourselves." For our own sake, and for that of each person within our stewardship, it is imperative that we become responsibly armed in order to protect and defend our lives, our liberty, and our property.

SUGGESTIONS

The following suggestions are offered on how to better fulfill the responsibility of self-defense:

1. CHOOSE YOUR WEAPON.

If you are interested in acquiring a gun, visit your local shooting range and talk to the store clerk. These experienced salesmen can help you determine what your best options are given your personal circumstances. Where possible, rent the gun you're interested in and practice using it at a shooting range to ensure that you are comfortable with and able to use it. If you are nervous around guns or for other reasons (including restrictive laws) choose to obtain a less lethal weapon. Do some research to determine what option is best for you—whether a pocketknife, taser, pepper spray, or other device. Be sure to also get holsters, ammunition, or other accessories your weapon may need to be as effective and versatile as possible. Be sure not to discount close combat skills such as martial arts; if you are unarmed or disarmed by your attacker and are being restrained, it would be helpful to have the strength and skills necessary to fight back and escape.

Acquiring firearms and other self-defense tools should be done only after first reviewing the related laws which govern their purchase, ownership, storage, and use.

2. GET EDUCATED.

Just as a responsible driver first learns the mechanics of driving through an educational course and then receives training from an experienced driver, so too should individuals receive both educational and hands-on instruction to become disciplined in the use of their defensive weapon of choice. Gun owners should seriously consider a training course such as those offered by Front Sight Firearms Training Institute in Nevada (or many comparable companies around the country) in order to become both mentally educated and physically trained with their preferred weapon. Many of these companies also offer courses on hand-to-hand combat, knife training, and related defensive skills that are not gun-specific. Ask the salesmen at your local shooting range for recommendations on where you might receive training.

3. TRAIN WITH YOUR WEAPON.

In his first annual address to Congress, President George Washington stated that "a free people ought not only to be armed, but disciplined."[88] Simply purchasing a gun is not sufficient and can in certain circumstances be more dangerous than not owning one at all, such as if the untrained owner does not responsibly secure the gun, and a child later finds it and accidentally takes his own life.[89] When seconds count, police are only minutes away, and in those mere seconds where an attacker may injure or kill you, being able to successfully defend yourself requires being able to quickly retrieve and properly use your weapon of choice. Routine practice with that weapon is an important preparation for ever having to use it. If the time comes to use a weapon defensively, an individual will almost always not rise to a level of heroic greatness, but rather fall to whatever practice and experience he has had. Converting the actions of self-defense into muscle memory through training and frequent practice will increase your chance of success should the need for self-defense ever arise.

4. BE SECURE AND ALERT.

Being able to successfully defend yourself also requires taking defensive measures to help ensure that such a situation never presents itself in the first place. Secure your home with adequate locks, keeping in mind windows and other points of entry into your home such as a side or back door. Learn to observe the environment you're in each day, constantly evaluating it and watching out for any form of danger or concern. Learn the "Cooper Color Codes" (you can find them online) to develop a state of awareness necessary to quickly and successfully react to a threat.

NOTES

1. Jonathan Elliot, ed. *The Debates in the Several State Conventions, on the Adoption of the Federal Constitution*, vol. 3 (Washington DC: Jonathan Elliot, 1836), 386.
2. John P. Foley, ed., *The Jefferson Cyclopedia: A Comprehensive Collection of the Views of Thomas Jefferson* (New York: Funk & Wagnalls, 1900), 247.
3. "Congress Had No Time to Read the USA PATRIOT Act," Sunlight Foundation, accessed May 2, 2012, http://sunlightfoundation.com/blog/2009/03/02/congress-had-no-time-to-read-the-usa-patriot-act/.

4. Rep. Bobby Scott (D-Virginia), C-SPAN, October 23, 2001, accessed May 2, 2012, http://www.c-spanvideo.org/appearance/596268063.

5. "President Establishes Office of Homeland Security," Summary of the President's Executive Order, October 8, 2001, accessed May 2, 2012, http://www.dhs.gov/xnews/releases/press_release_0010.shtm.

6. "TSA At The 'Tipping Point': Passenger Anger at Airport Pat-Downs Threatens to Boil Over," *Associated Press*, November 21, 2012, accessed May 12, 2012, http://www.huffingtonpost.com/2010/11/21/tsa-pat-downs-passenger-anger_n_786493.html.

7. "TSA Creator Says Dismantle, Privatize the Agency," Human Events, September 12, 2011, accessed May 12, 2012, http://www.humanevents.com/article.php?id=46114.

8. "Wheelchair Bound Toddler Searched for Explosives by TSA, Causes Outrage," the *Christian Post*, March 19, 2012, accessed May 12, 2012, http://www.christianpost.com/news/wheelchair-bound-toddler-searched-for-explosives-by-tsa-causes-outrage-video-71707/.

9. "TSA apologizes for searching elderly women," Reuters, January 19, 2012, accessed May 12, 2012, http://www.reuters.com/article/2012/01/19/us-usa-stripsearch-apology-idUSTRE80I29T20120119.

10. "Mom with Breast Pump 'Humiliated' by TSA," *ABC News*, March 2, 2012, accessed May 12, 2012, http://abcnews.go.com/Travel/hawaiian-mom-breast-pump-humiliated-tsa/story?id=15835844

11. "'Security Theater'? TSA Confiscates Woman's Frosted Cupcake," ABC News, December 24, 2011, accessed May 12, 2012, http://abcnews.go.com/blogs/headlines/2011/12/security-theater-tsa-confiscates-womans-frosted-cupcake/.

12. "Smoke Screening," *Vanity Fair*, December 20, 2011, accessed May 12, 2012, http://www.vanityfair.com/culture/features/2011/12/tsa-insanity-201112

13. "Blowback" is a CIA term first used in a March 1954 report on the 1953 operation to overthrow the government of Mohammed Mossadegh, the democratically elected leader of Iran. It is a metaphor for the unintended consequences of covert operations against foreign nations and governments, noting that our government's foreign interventions are likely to provoke a retaliatory response. The attacks of September 11, 2001, on the World Trade Center and the Pentagon were instances of blowback from American clandestine operations in the Middle East for the past many years.

14. "Civilians have borne the brunt of modern warfare, with ten civilians dying for every soldier in wars fought since the mid-twentieth century, compared with 9 soldiers killed for every civilian in World War I, according to a 2001 study by the International Committee of the Red

Cross." See "A Grim Portrait of Civilian Deaths in Iraq," *New York Times*, October 22, 2012, accessed May 12, 2012, http://www.nytimes .com/2010/10/23/world/middleeast/23casualties.html.

15. IntelCenter, *Words of Osama bin Laden*, vol. 1, (Alexandria, VA: Tempest Publishing, 2008), 14.

16. "Background Information on Arming Pilots," United States General Accounting Office report, June 28, 2002, accessed May 2, 2012, http:// www.gao.gov/assets/100/91330.pdf.

17. "Gun bill gets shot down by panel," the *Roanoke Times*, January 31, 2006, accessed May 12, 2012, http://www.roanoke.com/news/roanoke/ wb/wb/xp-50658.

18. "Drumbeat of Shots, Broken by Pauses to Reload," *New York Times*, April 17, 2007, accessed May 12, 2012, http://www.nytimes .com/2007/04/17/us/17scene.html.

19. "Motive a mystery after 12 die in Fort Hood rampage," *Associated Press*, November 5, 2009, accessed May 12, 2012, http://www.chron. com/news/article/Motive-a-mystery-after-12-die-in-Fort-Hood- rampage-1611054.php.

20. "How Many Americans Own Guns Revisited," *Extrano's Alley*, accessed May 12, 2012, http://extranosalley.com/?p=16213.

21. "Teen mom shoots intruder while on phone with 911," *ABC7 Eyewitness News*, January 4, 2012, accessed May 2, 2012, http://abclocal.go.com/ wabc/firstatfour/story?section=firstatfour&id=8490359.

22. Gary Kleck and Marc Gertz, "Armed Resistance to Crime: The Prevalence and Nature of Self-Defense with a Gun," *Journal of Criminal Law and Criminology*, Northwestern University School of Law, vol. 86, no. 1, 1995.

23. "Texas boy, 6, attacked by mountain lion at Big Bend National Park," Fox News, February 8, 2012, accessed May 12, 2012, http://www. foxnews.com/us/2012/02/08/texas-boy-6-reportedly-snatched-by- mountain-lion-at-big-bend-national-park/

24. Jeffrey L. Rodengen, *NRA: An American Legend* (Fort Lauderdale: Write Stuff Enterprises, Inc., 2002), 258.

25. Gregg Lee Carter, ed., *Guns in American Society: An Encyclopedia of History, Politics, Culture and the Law*, vol. 2 (Santa Barbara: ABC-CLIO, Inc., 2002), 17.

26. As noted in the Declaration of Independence: "Prudence, indeed, will dictate that Governments long established should not be changed for light and transient causes; and accordingly all experience hath shewn that mankind are more disposed to suffer, while evils are sufferable than to right themselves by abolishing the forms to which they are accustomed." Accordingly, the use of defensive force against the aggression of the state is almost always inadvisable, even when justified. There are, quite simply,

much safer ways to check the state's aggression than to open fire against its agents. This author does not in any way suggest nor advocate the use of force against the government, even when it violates your rights. You may have a gun, but they have thousands more . . .

27. *Pennsylvania Gazette*, Feb. 20, 1798, as quoted in Stephen P. Halbrook, *That Every Man Be Armed* (Oakland: The Independent Institute, 1984), 69.

28. Ibid., 64.

29. Ibid.

30. Ibid.

31. Ibid.

32. Ibid., 65.

33. Ibid., 57.

34. John C. Hamilton, ed., *The Federalist: A Commentary on the Constitution of the United States* (Philadelphia: J. B. Lippincott, 1864), 371.

35. "The Family: A Proclamation to the World," *Ensign*, Nov. 1995.

36. The proclamation notes that while this responsibility primarily falls to the men, women are "obligated to help," indicating that these and other responsibilities are shared amongst the couple. Unmarried individuals are not exempt; the proclamation also notes that "Disability, death, or other circumstances may necessitate individual adaptation."

37. B. H. Roberts, ed., *History of the Church*, vol. 6 (Salt Lake City: Deseret Book, 1978), 605.

38. Andrew F. Ehat, Lyndon W. Cook, eds., *The Words of Joseph Smith* (Orem, UT: Grandin Book, 1991), 166.

39. "A 'Faster, Stronger, Smarter' Police Force," *The Daily*, January 9, 2008, accessed May 12, 2012, http://dailyuw.com/news/2008/jan/09/a-faster-stronger-smarter-police-force-seattle-pd/.

40. Some believe that the Anti-Nephi-Lehies (see Alma 24) offer a better way, since they voluntarily laid down their lives rather than taking up their weapons. However, this was a group of people who were once extremely wicked and had murdered many innocent people. Their refusal to take up arms was not a general action to be replicated by all (indeed, the Nephites were obligated through a treaty to offer them defense services [Alma 27:22–24], and their children engaged in military activities [Alma 53:16–19]), but a personal demonstration of repentance in light of their specific sins. To claim this as behavior worthy of being implemented by all Latter-day Saints is to contradict commandments given directly by God.

41. G. D. Watt, E. L. Sloan, D. W. Evans, eds., *Journal of Discourses*, vol. 11 (Liverpool: Brigham Young, 1867), 131.

42. Joseph F. Smith, *Gospel Doctrine* (Salt Lake City: Deseret Book, 1938), 418–19.

43. See R. J. Rummel, *Death by Government* (New Brunswick: Transaction Publishers, 1994).

44. See Matthew White, "Historical Atlas of the Twentieth Century," accessed May 12, 2012, http://users.erols.com/mwhite28/warstat8.htm. Roughly 64 million people were killed in or because of combat in international and domestic wars.

45. See John R. Lott, Jr., *The Bias Against Guns* (Washington, DC: Regnery Publishing, 2003).

46. See Stephen P. Halbrook, "Nazi Firearms Law and the Disarming of the German Jews," 17 *Arizona Journal of International and Comparative Law*, no. 3, 2000, 483–535.

47. Ibid., 534.

48. Yuri Suhl, *They Fought Back: The Story of the Jewish Resistance in Nazi Europe* (New York: Schoken Books, 1967), 6.

49. Abram L. Sachar, *The Redemption of the Unwanted: From the Liberation of the Death Camps to the Founding of Israel* (New York: St. Martin's Press, 1983), 60.

50. Nechama Tec, *Resilience and Courage: Women, Men, and the Holocaust* (New Haven: Yale University Press, 2003), 354.

51. Peter Duffy, *The Bielski Brothers* (New York: HarperCollins, 2002), 282.

52. Sachar, *Redemption*, 47–48.

53. V.V. Stanciu, "Reflections on the Congress for the Prevention of Genocide," in *Yad Vashem Studies on the European Jewish Catastrophe and Resistance*, vol. 7 (Jerusalem: Yad Vashem, 1968), 187.

54. David Wootton, ed. *The Essential Federalist and Anti-Federalist Papers* (Indianapolis: Hackett Publishing, 2003), 132.

55. Miguel A. Faria Jr., "National Gun Registration: The Road to Tyranny," *The Freeman*, vol. 51, no. 3, Mar. 2001.

56. William Vincent Wells, ed., *The Life and Public Services of Samuel Adams*, vol. 2 (Boston: Little, 1865), 283.

57. Public Papers of George Clinton, *First Governor of New York*, vol. 1 (New York: Wynkoop Hallenbeck Crawford, 1899), 89.

58. Hezekiah Niles, ed. *Principles and Acts of the Revolution in America* (Baltimore: William Ogden Niles, 1822), 310, emphasis added.

59. George Athan Billias, Elbridge Gerry: *Founding Father and Republican Statesman* (Columbus: McGraw-Hill, 1976), 232.

60. *The Addresses and Messages of the Presidents of the United States From 1789 to 1839* (New York: McLean and Taylor, 1839), 192; emphasis added.

61. Gerhard L. Weinberg, ed., *Hitler's Table Talk, 1941–1944* (New York: Enigma Books, 2007), 321.

62. Joseph Story, *Commentaries on the Constitution of the United States* (Boston: Hilliard, Gray, 1833), 607.

63. *Maryland v. United States*, 381 US 41, 46 (1965).

64. Gregg Lee Carter, ed., *Guns in American Society* (Santa Barbara: ABC-CLIO, Inc., 2002), 263.

65. "Woman killed after 911 call in which she begged police to 'hurry'," Associated Press, Apr. 21, 1998.

66. "Crime in the United States, 2010," Federal Bureau of Investigation, accessed May 2, 2012, http://www.fbi.gov/about-us/cjis/ucr/crime-in-the-u.s/2010/crime-in-the-u.s.-2010/violent-crime/violent-crime

67. "Police response to 911s slowing," the *Washington Times*, May 10, 2004, accessed May 2, 2012, http://www.washingtontimes.com/news/2004/may/10/20040510-122711-8996r/.

68. "In Detroit, Improved 911 Response Times," *Time*, April 19, 2010, accessed May 2, 2012, http://detroit.blogs.time.com/2010/04/19/in-detroit-improved-911-response-times/.

69. "Atlanta police lag in emergency response time," Atlanta-Journal Constitution, March 22, 2009, accessed May 2, 2011, http://www.ajc.com/services/content/metro/atlanta/stories/2009/03/22/atlanta_police_response.html?cxtype=rss&cxsvc=7&cxcat=13.

70. "Oakland police seek to cut response time," *San Francisco Chronicle*, May 8, 2010, accessed May 2, 2012, http://articles.sfgate.com/2010-05-08/news/20889768_1_dispatchers-domestic-violence-officers

71. *Warren v. District of Columbia*, 444 A.2d 1 (DC Ct. of Ap., 1981).

72. California Government Code, Sections 845, 846.

73. 745 Illinois Compiled Statutes 10/4–102.

74. Delaware Code Annotated 10 § 4001

75. *Ashby v. City of Louisville*, 841 S.W.2d 184, 189 (Ky. App. 1992).

76. *Souza v. City of Antioch*, 62 California Reporter, 2d 909, 916 (Cal. App. 1997).

77. Richard W. Stevens, *Dial 911 and Die* (Hartford: Mazel Freedom Press, Inc., 1999), 6.

78. "The Words of Mayor Richard Daley," *Chicago Tribune*, Apr. 29, 2011, accessed May 2, 2012, http://articles.chicagotribune.com/2011-04-29/news/chi-daley-quotes-20110429_1_flight-attendants-flight-delays-chicago-river

79. *Riss v. New York* 240 N.E.2d 860 (N.Y. 1968); emphasis added.

80. Lott, *The Bias Against Guns*, 40.

81. Ibid.

82. Ibid.

83. Ibid., 25.

84. Ibid.

85. Elliot, *Debates*, 74.

86. Ibid., 97.

87. Roberts, *History*, 605.

88. Jared Sparks, ed., *The Writings of George Washington*, vol. 12 (Boston: American Stationers' Company, 1837) 8.

89. Tragic though they may be, accidental gun deaths each year account for only a very small percentage of accidental deaths. According to the National Safety Council's Injury Facts, firearm fatalities account for only 1 percent of accidental fatalities in the home. As gun ownership has more than doubled over the past three decades, the total number of accidental firearm fatalities has been reduced by over 70 percent.

FINANCIAL FREEDOM

I am convinced that it is not the amount of money an individual earns that brings peace of mind as much as it is having control of his money. Money can be an obedient servant but a harsh taskmaster.[1]

—N. Eldon Tanner

But, ah! Think what you do when you run into debt. You give to another power over your liberty.[2]

—Benjamin Franklin

What a wonderful feeling it is to be free of debt, to have a little money against a day of emergency put away where it can be retrieved when necessary.[3]

—Gordon B. Hinckley

QUESTIONS TO PONDER

1. How does a person feel who is mired in debt? Is he free? Does he enjoy the full use of his God-given agency?

2. What would you do with a million dollars?

3. Can the cause of liberty succeed without people able to help fund it?

4. If you currently have any debt, how can you more quickly pay it off?

*M*any of the men who signed the Declaration of Independence were men of distinction and wealth. Most of them had inherited land and money. When his uncle died, for example, John Hancock inherited a substantial amount of money. George Wythe had been given a large family farm and married into a wealthy family as well. At age twenty-one, Thomas Jefferson inherited five thousand acres of land. Others had "rags to riches" stories and had personally built their wealth. John Adams, for example, was born into a family of average financial means but went on to build his own highly successful legal practice in Boston. Robert Morris became wealthy through his business acumen and as a result was able to help finance the Revolution. Only one or two of the signers might have been considered poor.

During the debate on the Declaration, the soon-to-be signers were quite aware of the risks involved and reminded one another of them—they were, after all, considering committing treason. As such, the risk to their financial holdings was significant if they were defeated or caught. Affixing their signatures to the final document was a point of no return; either they were going to gain their independence from England and "provide new guards for their future security," as the Declaration said, or they were going to lose the war to the world's most powerful military, forfeit all of their possessions, ruin their families, and be hanged, drawn, and quartered.[4] Their resolve was recorded in the document as follows: "for the support of this declaration, with a firm reliance on the protection of divine providence, we mutually pledge to each other our lives, our fortunes, and our sacred honor." The commitment to independence was a moral, spiritual, political, and inescapably financial one.

Imagine if the eminent men participating in that process were poor and barely able to provide for their families after a full day's toil in the fields. If the individuals who comprised the founding generation were necessarily preoccupied with meeting their families' basic needs, they would not have had the free time, energy, and resources needed to be engaged in the revolutionary events that changed the course of history. Because of their economic situations, they were afforded the opportunity to pursue other interests. Had these specific men not had the financial wherewithal to be away from their homes for so long a period, who might have been sent in their place? Would other wealthy men have been as courageous and principled? If principled men with sufficient financial means were not willing and able to serve when needed, would the circumstances have been left up to other wealthy but *un*principled men?

Pondering these questions, one might conclude that the war for America's independence was predicated in part upon the financial independence of the founding statesmen. Defending individual liberty and promoting personal responsibility can be a part-time activity added on to work, family, church, and other demands on one's time, but in certain circumstances it may require much more time and energy than a person can afford who is spending most of his waking hours in pursuit of the next paycheck. Being financially free allows individuals to more easily fulfill their other personal responsibilities and thus enables them to better defend their individual liberty. In short, political independence is influenced by financial independence.

DEBT IS BONDAGE

If financial freedom leads to independence and allows somebody to more easily and effectively defend his liberty, then it is possible that the opposite state of being might lead to dependence and a decrease in liberty. That opposite is debt, a financial circumstance common to nearly every adult. Used prudently, it can be a tool to leverage loaned resources to pursue a more successful business initiative, own a home, or finance an advanced education. When abused, it leads to the alarming trend that has now become reality: in the United States alone, consumer debt (borrowed money for purchasing goods that are consumable, which excludes things like mortgages and education) is at $2.4 *trillion*.[5] This equates to almost $8,000 for every individual, with roughly $5,000 of that debt charged on credit cards. More than two million households in America each have more than $20,000 in credit card debt. Astoundingly, over 40 percent of families spend more than they earn.[6] Individuals are deep in debt, and thus mired in financial bondage.

"Debt is a form of bondage," taught Elder Joseph B. Wirthlin. "It is a financial termite. When we make purchases on credit, they give us only an illusion of prosperity. We think we own things, but the reality is, *our things own us*."[7] President J. Reuben Clark taught likewise: "Once in debt, interest is your companion every minute of the day and night; you cannot shun it or slip away from it; you cannot dismiss it; it yields neither to entreaties, demands, or orders; and whenever you get in its way or cross its course or fail to meet its demands, it crushes you."[8] God himself equated debt with bondage when instructing Martin Harris to "release thyself from bondage" by "pay[ing] the debt thou has contracted" (D&C 19:35). Calling debt an "oppressive burden," President Thomas S. Monson observed that "too many in the Church have failed to avoid unnecessary debt."[9] The accumulation of debt—especially the unnecessary type, such as for consumer goods—makes the debtor dependent upon another person and accountable to him for repayment with interest. This debt prevents the individual from being a righteous steward over the resources he has been given; for charity, savings, and personal needs must be deferred at times in order to repay a loan. Rather than freely acting, the debtor puts himself in a situation where he necessarily becomes "acted upon" (see 2 Nephi 2:14) by his creditor. This is a situation we are strenuously taught to avoid. "We should avoid bondage," taught President Ezra Taft Benson, "by getting out of debt as soon as we can, pay as we go, and live within our incomes."[10] As President Gordon B. Hinckley said, "One has neither independence nor freedom from bondage when he is obligated to others."[11]

Independence is important as individuals and also as a Church. In a revelation that commanded Joseph Smith and the Saints to establish the first bishop's storehouse to help provide for the poor, the Lord stated that a goal of the newly established church was so that it "may stand independent above all other creatures beneath the celestial world" (D&C 78:14). While this independence has many factors, the most important of which are spiritual and moral, the financial component cannot be ignored. In the late eighteen hundreds, heavy debt burdened the Church. The federal government had seized virtually all of the Church's properties in the 1880s, and a lackluster commitment to paying tithing by members made it difficult to pay off the bonds it had issued. In May 1899, President Lorenzo Snow suddenly paused during a talk he was giving at a conference in St. George, Utah, and after a moment of revelation, began to speak on the subject of tithing. "The word of the Lord is: The time has now come for every Latter-day Saint . . . to do the will of the Lord and to pay his tithing in full," he said. "That is the word of the Lord to you, and it will be the word of the Lord to every settlement throughout the land of Zion."[12] In the year following the revelation, the Saints sent in twice as much money in tithing than they had during the previous two years. Within eight years, the Church was able to pay off all of its debts and since that time has been completely debt-free. "Today the Church of Jesus Christ of Latter-day Saints owes not a dollar that it cannot pay at once," announced President Joseph F. Smith in 1907. "At last we are in a position that we can pay as we go. We do not have to borrow any more, and we won't have to if the Latter-day Saints continue to live their religion and observe this law of tithing."[13]

This positive and praiseworthy development might lead one to conclude that the Church now "stand[s] independent" financially. But as Elder J. Thomas Fyans stated, this is not quite so:

> The Church can be no more independent than the collective independence of its individual members. We fear that some may misunderstand the intent of the resources of the welfare program of the Church and fall into a false sense of security that will lead to reduced efforts toward self-sufficiency. . . . For the Church, as an organization, to be independent, it would basically have to duplicate the economy of the individual members. This is neither practical, possible, nor prudent. We have all been taught that dependence on the government is not good. Neither is dependence on the Church—that principle runs as deep as free agency itself.[14]

While the institutional Church has long been debt-free, its members have not followed its example of financial management.[15] For individuals to become debt-free and independent, the Church's example offers two important principles. President Hinckley noted them as follows:

> In the financial operations of the Church, we have observed two basic and fixed principles: One, the Church will live within its means. It will not spend more than it receives. Two, a fixed percentage of the income will be set aside to build reserves against what might be called a possible "rainy day."[16]

Following these basic steps can remove the shackles of financial bondage brought about as a result of unnecessary or unwise debt. Entertainment, leisure, costly food, clothing, Internet, mobile devices, vacation—all of these and many more secondary financial considerations can and should be delayed when they cannot be afforded and when an individual has existing financial obligations that must come first. Second, money should routinely be set aside as savings for a future time of need, such that needed expenditures will not require going into debt during a time of financial hardship. While they are basic, these elementary steps will steer one's financial ship in the right direction: out of debt and toward freedom.

These ideals have not yet been achieved, as is evidenced by the staggering debt which individuals (and Latter-day Saints specifically) shoulder as a result of their poor financial management. This situation stands as an unfortunate, partial fulfillment of a prophecy by President Heber C. Kimball in 1868. Speaking of a future time when Gentiles would "gather by the thousands" to Utah, he said: "A spirit of speculation and extravagance will take possession of the Saints, and the results will be financial bondage."[17] Each person will have to determine the extent to which this prophetic observation has been fulfilled, considering home values[18] and the real estate bubble bursting, the proliferation of multilevel marketing schemes,[19] the prevalence of "affinity fraud" investment scams with leaders and members of the Church fraudulently pilfering one another's money,[20] the disproportionately popular cosmetic surgery industry relative to other states,[21] and a host of other socioeconomic factors. It's not difficult to argue that President Kimball's words have found their fulfillment.

Because the Saints are not financially free, they are therefore in bondage. God's opinion on the matter is clear: "it is not right that any man should be in bondage one to another" (D&C 101:79). Being indebted to a creditor places a person in a state of voluntary financial bondage, whether the money is used for acceptable things such as an affordable mortgage or advanced education[22] or other things such as a nicer car, recreational expenditures, or unnecessary consumer goods. Either way, the individual cannot fully become politically independent while financially dependent upon a creditor. This bondage impedes our agency and thus our liberty, as noted by Elder Robert Hales:

> When we go into debt, we give away some of our precious, priceless agency and place ourselves in self-imposed servitude. We obligate our time, energy, and means to repay what we have borrowed—resources that could have been used to help ourselves, our families, and others. . . .
>
> To pay our debts now and to avoid future debt require us to exercise faith in the Savior—not just to do better but to be better. It takes great faith to utter those simple words, "We can't afford it." It takes faith to trust that life will be better as we sacrifice our wants in order to meet our own and others' needs.[23]

Our agency was the central issue in the war in heaven, which continues today. We cannot afford to jeopardize this divine gift by willingly placing ourselves in unnecessary bondage, especially for things of no lasting or significant value. Being unable to *act* to gain ground in the battle for liberty turns a would-be independent individual into a dependent who becomes *acted upon* by the demands of his creditors. Lacking the freedom to do as he pleases with his resources, he is therefore in bondage.

Keeping Up with the Joneses

Recognizing bondage is a relatively easy thing to do. Though a person in debt carries no shackles around his wrists and ankles, the outward signs of this form of bondage become increasingly evident as the bondage deepens. A person in this position often must work multiple jobs, has increased stress, has marital or family conflict, has problems sleeping, has anxiety, has depression, and even has heart attacks.[24] Recognizing the steps that lead to bondage is not nearly as easy. When a drunk driver crashes his car into a telephone pole, the tragic event is easily understood: the individual consumed alcohol and then got behind the wheel of a car. Understanding the influencing factors involved in the accident becomes more difficult. Why was the man drinking alone, and why did he not have a designated driver? What life circumstances led him to consume as much alcohol as he did? Why was he not at home with his family? While the smaller decisions and factors that led up to the accident did not *cause* the accident, they nevertheless led the individual down the path that culminated in the decision to drink and drive and therefore crash his car and risk his life.

The same holds true with financial bondage. Simply seeing numbers on a paper does not tell the whole story, nor does it address the underlying problems that led to the various decisions to take out loans or to charge things to credit that perhaps were not needed. Just as a good doctor will treat the symptoms of a disease but then also work to diagnose and remedy its underlying cause, so too should those who suffer from the bondage of debt scrutinize the various influencing factors that have led them to that circumstance. Doing so will help them to both eliminate their existing debt and stay out of debt in the future.

There are many reasons why people voluntarily place themselves in bondage, and thus surrender a degree of their liberty. One stands out from the rest and was pointed out by President Ezra Taft Benson as follows:

> Another reason for the increase in debt, I believe, is deeper—and causes greater concern. This is the rise of materialism as contrasted with spiritual values. Many a family, in order to make a "proper showing," will commit itself for a larger and more expensive house than is needed, in an expensive neighborhood. Again almost everyone would, it seems, like to keep up with the Joneses. With the increasing standard of living, that temptation increases with each new gadget that comes on the market. The subtle and carefully planned techniques of modern advertising are aimed at the weakest points of consumer resistance. And there is a growing feeling, unfortunately, that material things should be had now, without waiting, without saving, without self-denial. How many people stop to think when they buy on a thirty-six-months-to-pay basis that they place their future earnings for three years ahead in the hands of moneylenders.[25]

This "keeping up with the Joneses" mentality is little more than coveting what one's neighbor has, and desiring it for one's self. It is a jealous drive for increased consumerism, aligning one's financial priorities with peer pressure rather than God's requirements of the stewardship that individual has been given. It stands in stark contrast to the commandment "Thou shalt not covet" (Exodus 20:17). In modern times, the Lord expressed his displeasure at seeing that the Saints "seek not earnestly the riches of eternity, but their eyes are full of greediness" (D&C 68:31). Commenting on this trend, President Hinckley said:

> There have been many changes in this world since that time [when the "Thou shalt not covet" commandment was given to Moses], but human nature has not changed. I have observed that there are many in our present generation who with careful design set out on a course to get rich while still young, to drive fancy automobiles, to wear the best of clothing, to have an apartment in the city and a house in the country—all of these, and more. This is the total end for which they live, and for some the means by which they get there is unimportant in terms of ethics and morality. They covet that which others have, and selfishness and even greed are all a part of their process of acquisitiveness.

As is noted, there are many who intentionally "set out on a course" of materialism. For others, they are tempted and financially enslaved by the "subtle and carefully planned techniques of modern advertising," as President Benson observed—acted upon by others "at the weakest points of consumer resistance." The covetous mentality is thus fostered and propagated by an industry dedicated to determining how best to get people to spend their money, or money they don't even have, to buy the latest and greatest commodity. An estimated $497 billion was spent globally on advertising in 2011, up $21 billion from the year before.[26] That number is expected to increase to $600 billion by 2015—a figure larger than the GDP[27] of Sweden, Saudi Arabia, or Taiwan. Massive amounts of money are being spent to sell us stuff—often stuff we do not need. The distortion of reality the advertising industry produces in order to accomplish this goal is not a secondary side effect, but in many cases a primary and conscious component. As one advertising executive observed: "Advertising doesn't mirror how people are acting but how they are dreaming."[28] In other words, what objects might otherwise be a dreamt of and delayed gratification (such as a nicer car, a swimming pool in the backyard, or remodeling the kitchen) becomes, through those "subtle and carefully planned techniques of modern advertising," an object of immediate gratification. Through the propaganda generated by those who wish to sell their product, material dreams are made reality far sooner than they normally would have been, at the expense of more worthy goals such as independence and financial security. The once-common pioneer spirit of "use it up, wear it out, make it do, or do without" has been exchanged for a lifestyle of upgrades and enhancements that pushes a person to constantly desire the latest and greatest model of what he already owns. Financial bondage thus takes hold, and that person's liberty is diminished.

With the responsibility of pursuing financial freedom or any of the other responsibilities listed in this book, specific and proactive steps are needed in order to obtain and defend the independence and liberty that follow. In the consumer world, the threat of financial bondage is carried out through attacks "aimed at the weakest points of consumer resistance," as President Benson said. A large army of advertisers continually research and refine their methods to determine the most compelling and persuasive methods of enticing a person to purchase its product. "Effective advertising," notes one book on the subject, "is, almost always, persuasive advertising; and advertising that does not seek to persuade . . . is really missing an opportunity."[29] While true, it's important to note that persuasion is a two-edged sword. Persuasion is perfectly justified when used in respect of the other person's agency, seeking to inform, edify, and assist him. Encouraging somebody to read a good book, become baptized, or render service to another are forms of positive persuasion. Alternatively, persuasion is dangerous and potentially destructive to one's agency when used to encourage an action that is unnecessary or harmful to the individual—especially when pursued by preying on the person's ignorance, weakness, or other character deficiency. Enticing an unsuspecting person to participate in an investment scam, convincing the smart kid in class to share his test questions, or applying peer pressure to get somebody to do drugs are all examples of this. The former type of persuasion helps an individual become more independent and able to act upon their individual liberty. The latter type brings bondage and is thus harmful to the person's liberty.

Captain Moroni understood the danger of unprotected weak points in his day. Facing a military threat in the form of Amalickiah, a Nephite dissenter who had gained control of the Lamanite armies and sought to extinguish his former countrymen, Moroni prepared his people defensively for the onslaught that would soon come. While his opponent had been "obtaining power by fraud and deceit" (Alma 48:7), Moroni was "throwing up banks of earth round about to enclose his armies, and also building walls of stone to encircle them about" (Alma 48:8). Further, and most important, "in their weakest fortifications he did place the greater number of men" (Alma 48:9). This strategy proved successful, for when the Lamanites later attacked, "to their astonishment, the city of Noah, which had hitherto been a weak place, had now, by the means of Moroni, become strong" (Alma 49:14). The application of this principle is important for those seeking financial freedom. A person who is currently in the bondage of debt, or who finds difficulty in maintaining an appropriate budget, or who feels his priorities are not aligned with what God requires of the stewardship he has been given, must assess where his weak points are and take appropriate steps to strengthen them. The desire to "keep up with the Joneses" or any other distraction that would undermine one's path toward financial freedom is a threat to individual liberty by leading a person to become dependent, both upon one's neighbors for determining financial priorities and their popularity, and upon creditors for financing those unnecessary pursuits.

INDEPENDENTS AND INDEPENDENCE

Financial freedom is a fundamental component of one's enjoyment and use of individual liberty. Because bondage is the antithesis of liberty, we cannot simultaneously be independent while also being dependent on others. In other words, our independence requires that we be *independents*—individuals who are financially free and not in bondage to any other person. Put differently, a person can better defend his liberty as he becomes financially free. The alternative is a system of perpetual debt and worsening credit, with corresponding government bailouts, bankruptcies, and misplaced financial priorities.

The relationship between financial freedom and individual liberty manifests itself in two different ways, the first of which is in regard to a person's own life. An individual who wishes to enjoy and exercise his natural rights to their fullest degree cannot do so while having voluntarily placed himself in financial bondage as a result of acquiring debt. Consider a recent college graduate who has tens of thousands of dollars in student loans, a car loan, credit card debt, and a lengthy list of expenditures that exceed his income. Is this individual free? Is he independent? Is he able to use his resources as he pleases for his own benefit? In struggling to make the minimum payments for the debt he has acquired, this person neither feels free nor *is* free. His financial condition is tightly regulated, his income is quickly diverted to impatient creditors, his life becomes stressful as he uncomfortably eliminates one unnecessary expense after another so as to cut costs, and he feels inadequate in not being able to make more money and get out of debt. This situation represents millions of individuals who manage differing amounts of debt in their lives and prioritize payments as needed to comply with a previous commitment to secure a loan or prematurely purchase an item for which they did not have the money to pay. While those with debt are not fully in bondage, unable to say or act as they please, they are fettered by a financial bondage that curtails their freedom and limits the degree to which they can enjoy their individual liberty.

The second way in which the relationship between liberty and financial freedom manifests itself is in regards to publicly promoting the cause of liberty—reaching outside one's own stewardship to persuade and educate others. Those individuals who have the freedom and flexibility to include activities in their schedule that don't provide an income (and that often cost money, sometimes a *lot* of money) are better positioned to become active, productive champions of liberty. A person who works at a nine-to-five job, and who has to accommodate other necessary demands on nights and weekends (such as family, church, community service, and so on), is less likely to be able to dedicate a significant amount of time, energy, and resources to political activity. Recall the key players in the founding generation who through their industry or inheritance were able to dedicate significant quantities of time and energy to creating a new nation. Can those who are financially limited, whether through incorrect choices or employment constraints, have such an impact?

Clearly, our attention and priority must be devoted first to ourselves and our families. To the extent that a person's situation, through no fault of his own, requires a strenuous time commitment in order to meet his financial obligations, then that is what must be done, and the individual is justified in not being able to make an impact elsewhere. A mother whose husband has abandoned her, or a father whose hours at work were cut in half due to stagnant economic conditions, or a recent college graduate unable to find a desired job with good pay—these and plenty of other situations are extremely common and understandable. However, an individual is not justified who would otherwise be able to dedicate resources to fighting for liberty, were it not for the bondage he has placed himself under through unnecessary expenditures and an unwise management of his income. King Benjamin, speaking in reference to the sharing of resources with those in need, taught the pattern that applies here: those blessed to be stewards over sufficient resources, whether to give to the poor, dedicate to the cause of liberty, or use in other noble pursuits, and who instead "withhold [their] substance" (or misuse it, perhaps) are told that they face condemnation and that their substance "shall perish with [them]" (Mosiah 4:22–23). Those who are poor and thus unable to help the needy (or in this context use their resources to advance the cause of liberty) are counseled to "say in your hearts that: I give not because I have not, but if I had I would give"

(Mosiah 4:24). As King Benjamin said, those who have this attitude remain guiltless (see Mosiah 4:25) and are spared the condemnation reserved for those who were not wise stewards of what they were given.

Whether in debt or simply living paycheck to paycheck, a person who is financially dependent on another person falls short of his full potential in being able to enjoy his liberties and dedicate the time to defend them. Both the individual who is accountable to a creditor and the individual whose livelihood is entirely dependent upon the next payment from his employer lack the freedom with which to significantly impact the world around them. To counteract this trend, and regardless of circumstances, individuals should live beneath their level of income so as to have some amount of financial flexibility with extra money. As President Heber J. Grant said, "If there is any one thing that will bring peace and contentment into the human heart, and into the family, it is to live within our means."[30] From there, a portion of that income should be dedicated to savings for future financial security, unforeseeable expenditures, or operating capital with which to engage in important causes. Elder L. Tom Perry taught that "After paying your tithing of 10 percent to the Lord, you pay yourself a predetermined amount directly into savings."[31] Only by consistently setting aside a certain amount of money can a person accumulate the capital needed to become truly financially free, and thus better able to promote the cause of liberty.

Even those in financial bondage to a creditor or dependent upon their next paycheck can still enjoy a degree of liberty and find ways to be engaged in the process of defending and increasing it. However, it is the independent individual who is best able to make a difference, since both free time and money are required to run for office, support a worthy candidate, distribute educational literature, attend a rally, file a lawsuit, conduct research, organize a protest, or any number of other activities. Attaining that independence should be the goal of every liberty-minded individual.

ENTREPRENEURIALISM

Financial independence can come through various means, but it is closely linked to entrepreneurialism—the pursuit of innovation and production by a person taking a risk and working hard in order to yield a profit. Despite the prominence of "Corporate America" and the overwhelming attention large companies receive, it is the small businesses that are the backbone of the economy. In fact, self-employed entrepreneurs account for 78 percent of US businesses and their total revenue is almost $1 trillion per year.[32] Every day an average of 2,356 people either leave their existing job or bring themselves out of unemployment by starting a new business. Surprisingly, these businesses account for 99 percent of all employers in the country and employ half of everybody in the private sector.[33] While not all entrepreneurs succeed, and some go into debt as part of pursuing their financial independence, many are able to generate enough revenue to work independently of an employer and grow large enough to employ others.

Interestingly, many entrepreneurs start their own businessbecause of the lure of independence itself: being their own boss, determining the direction they will follow, and implementing whatever ideas they think best. Surveys consistently suggest that the primary reason somebody starts a small business is to avoid having a boss.[34] Another reason that closely follows that independence is the flexibility afforded by not having to warm a desk chair for hours on end each day; many entrepreneurs enjoy the easier work/life balance that comes through being able to set their own schedule.[35] One survey of entrepreneurs yielded the following list of ten reasons why they liked running their own business:

> You control your own destiny
> You can find your own work/life balance
> You choose the people you work with
> You take on the risk—and reap the rewards
> You can challenge yourself
> You can follow your passion
> You can get things done faster
> You can connect with your clients
> You can give back to your community
> You feel pride in building something of your own [36]

Many of these items have a close correlation to the political independence that comes in part by pursuing the responsibility of financial freedom. To illustrate this point, consider the opposite of each point just listed:

You cannot control your own destiny

You cannot find your own work/life balance

You are told who to work with

You assume no risk and therefore reap no rewards

You live in mediocrity, unable to challenge yourself

You are told what to do, rather than following your passion

You are dependent upon others for getting things done

You are a cog in a machine and are of no individual value to the client

You are dependent upon others in your community to support you

You have no sense of stewardship nor pride in your accomplishments

These opposites are symptoms of financial bondage, part of which can come from being entirely dependent upon an employer—one who may not share your interests, ideas, or initiative. Entrepreneurialism can allow a person to break free from this bondage and begin to chart his own course, unrestrained from the demands and dependencies of others. Individuals who create their own business are often able to enjoy a much greater ability to manage their time, resources, and priorities. It is by taking advantage of that inherently independent financial condition that they are then able to more effectively work toward a more general independence in their lives. Independent business owners have the ability, if they so choose, to participate in activities unrelated to work that will help secure their own independence and that of others as well—as was the case with the statesmen of the founding generation.

Thomas Jefferson's inclusion of the "pursuit of happiness" as an unalienable right listed in the Declaration of Independence holds special meaning for many entrepreneurs who look at a desk job with disdain and want to experience the thrill of complete financial independence. An apocryphal quote attributed to Benjamin Franklin suggests a reason why: "The Declaration only guarantees you the *right* to pursue happiness. You have to catch it yourself." While an employee is more regimented in how they can catch opportunities in pursuit of their own happiness, an entrepreneur actively chases after and attempts to catch them. As the employee is in many cases "acted upon" by his employer, an entrepreneur is more freely able to "act."

The spiritual component of entrepreneurialism is no less significant. A necessary characteristic of one's God-given agency is the ability and opportunity to act independent of external coercion. As President

David O. McKay said: "If man is to be rewarded for righteousness and punished for evil, then common justice demands that he be given the power of independent action. . . . If he were coerced to do right at all times, or were helplessly enticed to commit sin, he would merit neither a blessing for the first nor punishment for the second."[37] As independence and risk increase, so does the corresponding opportunity or blessing. Reducing the direction of or dependence upon an employer allows a person to possess greater power of independent action. "God gave unto man that he should act for himself" (2 Nephi 2:16), and few people understand that responsibility (and its potential reward) greater than an entrepreneur does.

Circumstances may prevent a person from being a "full-time" entrepreneur, as might some career paths. However, entrepreneurialism is not so much a destination as it is a process and a mindset. Even an individual working a nine-to-five job for another employer can still have an entrepreneurial attitude. For example, he can look for innovative ways to solve existing problems within the company he works for, helping to maximize efficiency, save resources, and inspire a higher rate of production amongst his coworkers. By applying this entrepreneurial spirit to an employer-employee relationship, that individual will likely be given increasing opportunities and responsibilities by the employer, thus allowing him to become more independent. Additionally, even those with a mundane nine-to-five job can explore other business opportunities that can be managed on one's lunch hour, nights, weekends, and so on. Home-based business ideas abound, and the Internet makes such an opportunity even more feasible. Establishing several sources of income, whether active (for example, working at an hourly rate) or passive (for example, selling products on a website) is an important goal that will also help in pursuing financial independence. This arrangement is beneficial in cases where the person loses his main source of revenue by being fired, for example; having all of one's eggs in a single basket is never a good idea.

"Entrepreneurs are particularly independent," as one business owner commented. "We throw off bosses like the colonists threw off the king. No matter how risky starting a business seems, to us it's the route to 'life, liberty, and the pursuit of happiness.'"[38] The drive for independence over dependence and production over consumerism is at the heart of entrepreneurialism—as it is with the cause of liberty. It is a passion that can often result in failure but permeates a person's life and applies to areas other than just business. While owning a business can often lead to financial freedom, simply having the desire for and dedication to pursuing ownership, innovation, and independence will result in positive changes that can bring the individual out of financial bondage and place him or her in a position to more freely act with his or her time, talents, and resources for the benefit of others.

Thomas Paine succinctly captured the connection between the independence that financial freedom brings and the more general, political independence that comes along with it. He wrote: "Those who expect to reap the blessings of freedom, must, like men, undergo the fatigue of supporting it."[39] Supporting liberty is most likely to be done by those individuals who can afford the time and money necessary to make a significant and lasting impact. The key players in America's founding generation (many of whom were entrepreneurs) were able to "mutually pledge to each other [their] lives, [their] fortunes, and [their] sacred honor" largely because of financial circumstances that enabled them to put their lives on hold, almost completely, for weeks, months, and even years at a time. Fatigue, indeed—reaping the blessings of freedom is something that neither the "summer soldier" nor "sunshine patriot"[40] are able to effectively do, for those who must labor to make ends meet lack the time, energy, and resources to be fully engaged in the fight.

Those who seek to liberate themselves from financial bondage, create wealth, and innovate and produce, obtain their reward of financial freedom after taking on great risk. Along with its many benefits, both temporal and spiritual, this freedom brings with it the flexibility necessary to be "anxiously engaged in a good cause" (D&C 58:27), whether political or otherwise. Most important, and at a minimum, being free from debt allows an individual to enjoy peace of mind and allows a family to have more harmony in their home.

SUGGESTIONS

The following suggestions, taken from a talk by President N. Eldon Tanner,[41] are offered on how to better fulfill the responsibility of becoming financially free:

1. PAY AN HONEST TITHING.

Tithing is not a donation or gift given to God, but rather the payment of a debt. Just as a person becomes more independent by working his way out of financial bondage, so too does the person become more independent (or, a better steward) by consistently complying with the commandment to tithe on the resources with which he is blessed. The promised blessings are both temporal and spiritual; one who prays for help in pursuing financial freedom should have as his first priority the payment of tithing so as to qualify for additional blessings that might be given as a result. When that financial obligation to God has been discharged, he is bound to fulfill his promises (see D&C 82:10).

2. LIVE ON LESS THAN YOU EARN.

"Money can be an obedient servant but a harsh taskmaster," taught President Tanner. Becoming disciplined in matters of finance is a character trait that will help in other areas of life as well. Taming your appetite, avoiding the temptation to spend money that you don't have, and delaying gratification until a later time brings strength, resolve, and peace. Adjusting your budget such that you do not spend more than you earn will allow you to pay off any existing debt, save for a future need, and becoming increasingly independent.

3. LEARN TO DISTINGUISH BETWEEN NEEDS AND WANTS.

Perhaps the most helpful strategy to accomplish this step is to avoid advertising wherever possible. Americans see up to five thousand ads per day[42] and are thus constantly bombarded with enticements to purchase something they don't already have. Look for ways to reduce exposure to consumer temptation, such as an ad-blocking plugin for your Internet browser (for example, the "Ad Block" plugin), watching any television programs on a recorded device so you can skip through commercials, or watching them online where fewer ads are shown, reading books instead of magazines that are filled with ads, and so on. Minimizing the exposure to the clutter of consumeristic messages will better allow a person to rationally and methodically think about his purchases, and better distinguish between a need and a want.

Consider also the following counsel from President Kimball, suggesting an emphasized focus on something that truly is a need: "Many people spend most of their time working in the service of a self-image that includes sufficient money, stocks, bonds, investment portfolios, property, credit cards, furnishings, automobiles, and the like to guarantee carnal security throughout, it is hoped, a long and happy life. Forgotten is the fact that our assignment is to use these many resources in our families and quorums to build up the kingdom of God."[43] Being a righteous steward of the resources you have been blessed with requires using them in a way that is pleasing to God.

4. DEVELOP AND LIVE WITHIN A BUDGET.

As the saying goes, "those who don't learn from the past are condemned to repeat it." With finances, those who do not track and account for their spending will be unable to effectively make changes in the future that will help them correct poor choices or better save for future needs. Just as a steward is accountable for his actions and must later return and report to his master, so too must we manage our resources wisely through a budget and other accounting best practices to understand how they are being used, and more importantly, how we can better use them. Becoming financially free rarely happens accidentally—one must plan, sacrifice, and work hard based on a specific budget in order to free himself from bondage and become independent.

5. GET A FINANCIAL EDUCATION.

Few people have a solid educational foundation on which to base good financial decisions. A 2008 survey conducted by Harvard Business School and Dartmouth College professors concluded that "Americans are financially illiterate,"[44] suggesting that practice does not make perfect when it comes to earning and spending money. Many seem to fear learning about financial topics and consider it like swallowing a bitter pill, but it should be treated more like an immunization from bad financial decisions in the future.

A good first step is to review the material in "One for the Money— Guide to Family Finance," published by the LDS Church and accessible online. Many people in the bondage of debt have had good success with Dave Ramsey's programs found at www.daveramsey.com. Another option is Robert Kiyosaki's "Rich Dad Poor Dad" material found at www.richdad.com. Ask your local bank or credit union if they have resources for increasing financial literacy, and spend time searching for answers to your questions online from a variety of sources to ensure that you can better understand the topic, and filter out incorrect information. Increasing your understanding of financial topics will improve your ability to make better decisions that will more quickly lead to your financial freedom.

NOTES

1. N. Eldon Tanner, "Constancy amid Change," *Ensign*, June 1982, 4.
2. Benjamin Franklin, *The Works of Dr. Benjamin Franklin* (London: William Walker, Otley, 1840), 277.
3. Gordon B. Hinckley, "To the Boys and to the Men," *Ensign*, Nov. 1998.
4. To be hanged, drawn and quartered was the penalty in England for those convicted of high treason. Convicts were fastened to a wooden panel and drawn by horse to the place of execution, where they were hanged (almost to the point of death), disemboweled, beheaded, and quartered (chopped into four pieces). Their remains were often displayed in prominent places across the country, ostensibly as a warning to sympathetic rebels who would be treated the same if caught and convicted.
5. "A Dozen Alarming Consumer Debt Statistics," *Economy Watch*, May 23, 2011, accessed May 12, 2012, http://www.economywatch.com/economy-business-and-finance-news/a-dozen-alarming-consumer-debt-statistics.21-05.html.
6. Megan Maloney, "Spending Spiritually," *Religion & Liberty, Acton Institute*, vol. 14, no. 3.
7. Joseph B. Wirthlin, "Earthly Debts, Heavenly Debts," *Ensign*, May 2004, 40-41; emphasis added.
8. J. Reuben Clark, *Improvement Era*, Jun. 1938, 328.
9. Thomas S. Monson, "Guiding Principles of Personal and Family Welfare," Ensign, Sep. 1986.
10. Ezra Taft Benson, *God, Family, Country: Our Three Great Loyalties* (Salt Lake City: Deseret Book, 1984), 408.
11. Gordon B. Hinckley, "To the Boys and Men," *Ensign*, Oct. 1998.
12. Quoted in LeRoi C. Snow, "The Lord's Way Out of Bondage," *Improvement Era*, July 1938, No. 7, 439.
13. In Conference Report, Apr. 1907, 7.

14. J. Thomas Fyans, "Employment Challenges in the 1980s," *Ensign*, May 1982, 82.

15. In Utah, where a majority of citizens are members of the Church, the average consumer debt (excluding a mortgage) per person is over $15,000 and the average revolving debt per person is over $7,000. See "Consumer Credit Conditions: Utah," Federal Reserve Bank of San Francisco, accessed May 12, 2012, http://www.frbsf.org/publications/community/consumer-credit-conditions/ConsumerCredit_UT-11A3.pdf.

16. Gordon B. Hinckley, "The State of the Church," *Ensign*, May 1991.

17. Quoted in J. Golden Kimball, "The Gift of Prophecy," in Conference Report, Oct. 1930, 58.

18. See "Builder blasts speculators," *Deseret News*, August 29, 2006, accessed May 12, 2012, http://www.deseretnews.com/article/645196879/Builder-blasts-speculators.html.

19. See "Multilevel marketing is top scam," *Deseret News*, March 19, 2008, accessed May 12, 2012, http://www.deseretnews.com/article/695262703/Multilevel-marketing-is-top-scam.html.

20. See "LDS official: Don't let trust blind you to scams," *Salt Lake Tribune,* February 15, 2012, accessed May 12, 2012, http://www.sltrib.com/sltrib/money/53514946-79/fraud-utah-church-event.html.csp.

21. Forbes magazine listed Salt Lake City as the most "vain" city in the nation based on percentage of plastic surgeons relative to the population at large. See "Salt Lake City leads nation for vanity, Forbes says," *Deseret News*, December 18, 2007, accessed May 12, 2012, http://www.deseretnews.com/article/695237037/Salt-Lake-City-leads-nation-for-vanity-Forbes-says.html.

22. The Church's pamphlet on financial management titled *All Is Safety Gathered In* states, in part: "Spending less money than you make is essential to your financial security. Avoid debt, with the exception of buying a modest home or paying for education or other vital needs. Save money to purchase what you need. If you are in debt, pay it off as quickly as possible."

23. Robert D. Hales, "A Gospel Vision of Welfare: Faith in Action," *Basic Principles of Welfare and Self-Reliance* (2009), 1.

24. "Debt stress causing health problems, poll finds," *Associated Press*, June 9, 2008, accessed May 12, 2012, http://www.msnbc.msn.com/id/25060719/ns/health-mental_health/t/debt-stress-causing-health-problems-poll-finds/.

25. Ezra Taft Benson, "Pay Thy Debt, and Live," in Conference Report, April 1957.

26. "Advertisers Will Spend $500 Billion in 2011," eMarketer, September 6, 2011, accessed May 12, 2012, http://www.emarketer.com/blog/index.php/tag/worldwide-ad-spending/.

27. GDP is Gross Domestic Product, or the value of all goods and services sold in a given year.

28. Jerry Goodis, quoted in Joyce Nelson, "As the brain tunes out, the TV admen tune in," *Globe and Mail*, Apr. 16, 1983, 10.

29. John O'Shaughnessy and Nicholas J. O'Shaughnessy, *Persuasion in Advertising* (London: Routledge, 2004), ix.

30. Heber J. Grant, Quoted in G. Homer Durham, ed., *Gospel Standards: Selections From the Sermons and Writings of Heber J. Grant* (Salt Lake City: Improvement Era, 1941), 111.

31. L. Tom Perry, "Becoming Self-Reliant," *Ensign*, Nov. 1991, 66.

32. See "Nonemployer Statistics," US Census Bureau, http://www.census.gov/econ/nonemployer/.

33. "Frequently Asked Questions," US Small Business Administration, accessed May 2, 2012, http://web.sba.gov/faqs/faqindex.cfm?areaID=24.

34. See, for example, "A Typical Entrepreneur's Aspirations." Bloomberg, November 6, 2009, accessed May 2, 2012, http://www.businessweek.com/smallbiz/content/nov2009/sb2009114_400060.htm?campaign_id=rss_topStories.

35. "Independence 'key benefit' to being entrepreneur," Startups, February 1, 2007, accessed May 2, 2012, http://www.startups.co.uk/independence-key-benefit-to-being-entrepreneur.html.

36. "Top 10 Reasons to Run Your Own Business," Inc., January 21, 2011, accessed May 12, 2012, http://www.inc.com/guides/201101/top-10-reasons-to-run-your-own-business.html.

37. David O. McKay, "Free Agency—A Divine Gift," *Improvement Era*, May 1950, 366.

38. Rhonda Abrams, "Strategies: Independence day, your way," *USA Today*, June 29, 2007, accessed May 12, 2012, http://www.usatoday.com/money/smallbusiness/columnist/abrams/2007-06-29-independence_N.htm.

39. Thomas Paine, The American Crisis (London: R. Carlile, 1819), 63.

40. Ibid., 11.

41. N. Eldon Tanner, "Constancy Amid Change," *Ensign*, Nov. 1979.

42. "Anywhere the Eye Can See, It's Likely to See an Ad," *New York Times*, January 15, 2007, accessed May 12, 2012, http://www.nytimes.com/2007/01/15/business/media/15everywhere.html.

43. Quoted in Tanner, "Constancy."

44. "Befuddled by debt? You're not alone," *CNN*, February 26, 2008, accessed May 12, 2012, http://money.cnn.com/2008/02/26/pf/financial_illiteracy/index.htm.

WELFARE AND CHARITY

The government seems too anxious to give, give, give to the poor, to the aged, to the schools, to everyone, and blinded people feel they are getting something, whereas they pay it to the government so that the government can after great overhead expense return a part of it to the people. And every time a gift returns to the people—a so-called gift—it comes with fetters binding and tying and enslaving. For every block of funds given to the people, they lose a bigger block of liberty.[1]

—Spencer W. Kimball

If we can prevent the government from wasting the labors of the people, under the pretense of taking care of them, they must become happy.[2]

—Thomas Jefferson

QUESTIONS TO PONDER

1. Does the government's involvement in welfare help or hurt the poor?

2. Would there be more or less poverty if you were not taxed to fund the welfare system and could instead choose how much you would donate and to whom?

3. To whom do your money and possessions actually belong?

4. If you were to experience severe financial difficulty, would it be morally justifiable to rely on a government "social safety net"?

ot long ago, most Americans wanted the government to leave them alone. In today's entitlement society, many people want the government to care for them from cradle to grave, regardless of whatever impact that desire might have on others. Rather than a world of responsible, independent people looking for opportunities to help their neighbors, one prevailing concern has become how to get the most government "benefits" possible. Gaming the system to produce a nice profit is not an uncommon activity. The shift from independence to dependence has been gradual but firm, like flaxen cords turning into strong cords around our necks (see 2 Nephi 2:22).

The view held by most of the patriots of the founding generation was that government is generally destructive and had historically been, and ever would be, the greatest threat to individual liberty. Through checks and balances, a structure of federalism, and a diffusion of political power, they attempted to restrain and decentralize government. Save for the staunch nationalists like Alexander Hamilton, they recognized that an activist, intrusive state would always (and aggressively) violate the rights of those who lived under its jurisdiction.

While this general sentiment was shared by many of the colonists, it was supplemented by a corresponding recognition of the responsibility to provide for one's self, one's family, and others in need. The dual responsibility of both welfare and charity is one that only an independent person can fully realize; we cannot care for ourselves if we lack the knowledge and resources necessary to do so. From the earliest days of America, this was recognized and encouraged. Governor John Winthrop, the Puritan lawyer who helped establish the Massachusetts Bay Colony in 1630, delivered a sermon while en route to North America titled "A Model of Christian Charity," in which is found the famous "city upon a hill" remark. The portion preceding that well-known quote conveys this principle:

> Now the only way to avoid this shipwreck [of suffering God's wrath for not fulfilling our obligations], and to provide for our posterity, is to follow the counsel of Micah, to do justly, to love mercy, to walk humbly with our God. For this end, we must be knit together, in this work, as one man. We must entertain each other in brotherly affection. We must be willing to abridge ourselves of our superfluities, for the supply of others' necessities. We must uphold a familiar commerce together in all meekness,

gentleness, patience and liberality. We must delight in each other; make others' conditions our own; rejoice together, mourn together, labor and suffer together, always having before our eyes our commission and community in the work, as members of the same body. So shall we keep the unity of the spirit in the bond of peace.[3]

Winthrop was advocating a strong community built of individuals who fulfilled their responsibilities relating to welfare and charity, taking care of themselves and one another as changing circumstances required. The different colonies dealt with poverty in distinct ways. Virginia, Connecticut, Massachusetts, and Rhode Island each passed colonial "poor laws" which used a taxation-based model for attending to the needs of the impoverished. The first session of the Rhode Island legislature, for example, declared that the management of the needs of the poor would be taken care of by appointed persons who would tax and collect the money to care for the poor "according to the provisions of the law of England."[4] The Elizabethan Poor Law was enacted in 1601 by the English Parliament and served as a model for many of the colonial poor laws. Others, such as New Amsterdam, encouraged an ecclesiastical response to the needy; officers of the Dutch Reformed Church in this colony raised needed funds through voluntary contributions, which were then disbursed to the destitute.

Eventually, all colonial governments came to rely on the taxation-based model, though the local townships were responsible for the collection and use of funds. Over the course of several decades, however, social welfare policies increasingly escalated to higher levels of government. In the early seventeen hundreds, management of assistance for the needy began to emerge at the colony level—demonstrating how early America was not necessarily the utopia of liberty some think it to have been.[5] Other methods were often employed to defray costs, such as requiring shipmasters to post a bond for each person they brought to the colonies, should any of them become a "public charge" (dependent on welfare). Coming from a society where "poor laws" were commonplace, and coupled with a religious heritage that emphasized the responsibility of caring not only for one's self and family but also for the needy, colonists largely recognized and acted upon the obligation to help the members of their community who were not able to care for themselves. A complementary attitude emphasized the importance of work; the religious concept of having a "calling" in life made work a sacred act. Hard work was a virtue, and idleness was a sin. Because of these dual beliefs, little sympathy existed for any "sturdy beggars"—individuals fit and able to work, but who chose to beg for help instead. Cotton Mather, the prolific Puritan minister, had this to say on the subject: "For those who indulge themselves in idleness, the express command of God unto us is, that we should let them starve."[6]

As the colonies united to declare independence, fought a revolution, and began to confederate, they universally recognized that care for the poor was not a task for the general government. Writing in the Federalist,[45] James Madison made clear the separation of powers between the differing levels of government:

> The powers delegated by the proposed Constitution to the federal government, are few and defined. Those which are to remain in the State governments are numerous and indefinite. The former will be exercised principally on external objects, as war, peace, negotiation, and foreign commerce; with which last the power of taxation will, for the most part, be connected. The powers reserved to the several States will extend to all the objects which, in the ordinary course of affairs, concern the lives, liberties, and properties of the people, and the internal order, improvement, and prosperity of the State.[7]

When debating a proposed welfare bill in Congress in 1794, Madison spoke on the floor of the House of Representatives in firm opposition, noting that he "could not undertake to lay [a] finger on that article in the Federal Constitution which granted a right to Congress of expending, on objects of benevolence, the money of their constituents."[8] Decades later, President Franklin Pierce maintained the same position when vetoing a bill that would have given land to the states in order to build institutions for the insane. "I cannot find any authority in the Constitution for making the Federal Government the great almoner of public charity throughout the United States. To do so would . . . be contrary to the letter and spirit of the Constitution and subversive of the whole theory upon which the Union of these States is founded."[9] Despite the existence of government anti-poverty programs from the earliest colonial settlements, it was heavily supplemented by private charity—just as it is today.[10] When he toured America, the French political historian Alexis de Tocqueville observed the marked contrast from the pervasive welfare states in Europe where "the state almost exclusively undertakes to supply bread to the hungry, assistance and shelter to the sick, work to the idle, and to act as the sole reliever of all kinds of misery."[11] Though they tolerated and generally thought justified the taxation-based support of the needy at a local governmental level, Americans still recognized the responsibility of working and caring for themselves and providing aid to the needy.

Is this a sentiment shared by Americans in the twenty-first century? A few statistics might suggest that attitudes toward work and welfare are not what they once were. In 2011, social welfare entitlement payouts made up 35 percent of Americans' wages and salaries, up from 21 percent in 2000 and 10 percent in 1960.[12] This large amount of money funneled through the government affects all Americans through confiscatory taxation and offers a benefit to the 48.5 percent of Americans who, according to the 2010 Census, live in a household that receives some form of government aid.[13] In that same year, a poll of one thousand Americans found that 58 percent believed that a good work ethic would not pay off, and only 26 percent believed it was still possible for just about anyone in America to work hard and generate wealth.[14] The Protestant work ethic that once infused American society, recognized by a host of historians and sociologists, has largely disintegrated. Two centuries ago, de Tocqueville observed:

> The citizen of the United States is taught from his earliest infancy to rely on his own exertions in order to resist the evils and difficulties of life; he looks upon social authority with an eye of mistrust and anxiety and he only claims its assistance when he is quite unable to shift without it.

The degree to which we have strayed from this ignored but superior trend can largely be attributed to the individual neglect of welfare and charity. These complementary responsibilities must together be implemented in order to counteract the encroachments of the welfare state, where taxation-based programs are enacted and enforced to care for those who allegedly wouldn't be cared for otherwise. The responsibility of welfare requires that an individual provide for himself along with those under his stewardship: a spouse, children, elderly parents, and so on. Church leaders have unanimously declared that "by divine design, fathers . . . are responsible to provide the necessities of life . . . for their families."[15] Numerous scriptures reaffirm the doctrinal importance of working and caring for one's self and family. For example, the Apostle Paul stated that those who do not so provide have "denied the faith" and are "worse than an infidel" (1 Timothy 5:8). The Lord has said that "thou shalt not be idle," adding that idlers "shall not eat the bread nor wear the garments of the laborer" (D&C 42:42)—a divine condemnation of what has become so common in the welfare state. Those who do not properly provide are liable to lose their position or membership in the Church (see D&C 75:29). King Benjamin taught his people that they should not "suffer your children that they go hungry" (Mosiah 4:14). Perhaps the most straightforward commentary comes from God's initial instruction to Adam: "In the sweat of thy face shalt thou eat bread" (Genesis 3:19). We are commanded of God to "provide for [our] own family" (D&C 75:28) and consider work to be, as President Heber J. Grant said, "the ruling principle" in our lives.[16]

The second responsibility, that of charity, is quite related—rather than meeting the needs of family members, one helps to meet the needs of others outside his immediate stewardship. "A man filled with the love of God," taught the Prophet Joseph Smith, "is not content with blessing his family alone, but ranges through the whole world, anxious to bless the whole human race."[17] While few would dispute the personal responsibility to take care of one's self and family members, there is not as clear a recognition of the responsibility to care for others outside our family. The scriptural record, however, is quite clear on this responsibility. King Benjamin counseled his people to "succor those that stand in need of your succor" and to "administer of your substance unto him that standeth in need" (Mosiah 4:16). Jacob taught his people to be "familiar with all and free with your substance" (Jacob 2:17). Amulek labeled as hypocritical apostates the alleged followers of Christ who would "turn away the needy, and the naked, and visit not the sick and afflicted, and impart of your substance, if ye have, to those who stand in need" (Alma 34:28). In this dispensation, the Lord reintroduced the law of consecration, which requires imparting of our substance to those in need as part of building up the kingdom of God on the earth. The purpose of this law, which is both temporal and spiritual, is not only to care for the poor and needy (D&C 42:30), but more important to foster industry and unity:

And you are to be equal, or in other words, you are to have equal claims on the properties, for the benefit of managing the concerns of your stewardships, every man according to his wants and his needs, inasmuch as his wants are just—

And all this for the benefit of the church of the living God, that every man may improve upon his talent, that every man may gain other talents, yea, even an hundred fold, to be cast into the Lord's storehouse, to become the common property of the whole church—

Every man seeking the interest of his neighbor, and doing all things with an eye single to the glory of God. (D&C 82:17–19)

All individuals, but especially Latter-day Saints, have the responsibility of taking care of their own needs, and to the extent possible, helping to meet the needs of others outside of their immediate stewardship. The reason behind this responsibility is self-evident when one considers the alternative. Without any government welfare programs, as should ideally be the case, and without a society comprised of individuals willing to help one another, what would the poor do? How would they get by? Would they wither away and die, or would they do whatever it takes to survive? Many would no doubt turn to theft, whether turning into criminals themselves, or delegating that criminality to a centralized body such as the government to take others' property on their behalf. Thus, the failure to take care of one's self and one's neighbors produces, in the aggregate, an environment in which those in need look for whatever ways they can to obtain what they need. The unwillingness to freely give of such resources results in a scenario where those resources are forcibly taken from us.

God has said in plain and emphatic terms that "ye must visit the poor and the needy and administer to their relief" (D&C 44:6). Every person is a steward over his property (D&C 42:32) and "unto whom much is given much is required" (D&C 82:3). While taxation-based methods of caring for the poor have long existed and are considered appropriate and adequate by many, they violate the fundamental components of how charity must be carried out. Welfare and charity are only properly based on love, work, and an individual's voluntary willingness to freely share of the resources in his possession. Elder Joseph B. Wirthlin makes clear the significance of this dual responsibility:

At the final day the Savior will not ask about the nature of our callings. He will not inquire about our material possessions or fame. He will ask if we ministered to the sick, gave food and drink to the hungry, visited those in prison, or gave succor to the weak. When we reach out to assist the least of Heavenly Father's children, we do it unto Him. That is the essence of the gospel of Jesus Christ.[18]

THE WELFARE STATE

It is generally recognized that the modern-day welfare state has become rife with abuse and wasteful spending. Despite this obvious assumption, few people and politicians demonstrate any commitment to cutting the budget for these government "anti-poverty" programs. In helping individuals to understand why private, voluntary charity is principled and preferable to the state-managed alternative, it is often useful to provide some examples demonstrating the consequences these programs have produced.

Perhaps the most well-known government welfare program is Social Security, one which has taken $14 trillion from taxpayers since its inception in 1937, and which has doled out over $11 trillion.[19] In 2009, seven hundred bureaucrat executives tasked with overseeing this albatross of an agency gathered in Phoenix, Arizona, for a lavish three-day party.[20] The total expense of the "conference," held at a time when the economy was at a low and tens of millions of Americans were unemployed, was $700,000. With a performance from a motivational dance company, an excursion to a local casino, and a relaxing weekend in thirty-nine acres of lush gardens with swimming pools and a golf course, this excess is a horrible mismanagement of the money taken from taxpayers to allegedly care for those in need. While this indulgence may be maddening, what the politicians have done is worse: every dollar taken from individuals for the purpose of funding the Social Security system has been diverted to other projects and programs these politicians wanted to fund.[21] In place of the Social Security funds, these politicians have placed treasury bonds—in other words, government IOUs.

The abuse is not relegated only to one or a few of the eighty[22] social welfare programs administered by the federal government. It is a systemic side effect of government wealth redistribution. Unemployment insurance, for example, is likewise leaking its illegitimately obtained money; in 2010 alone, an estimated $17 billion was fraudulently obtained by people who were either never eligible for the program or who became employed yet continued to collect checks.[23] Taxpayer dollars used to fund the infamous "stimulus" package championed by Barack Obama have also, unsurprisingly, been susceptible to theft (setting aside the fact that they were initially obtained by taxation, which is legalized theft). One aspect of the stimulus, an incentive for people to make their homes more energy efficient in order to lower their utility bills, has "misspent" $5 billion, with some going to lobbyists, consultants, and lawyers who performed little to no work for the easy money.[24] The money taken from taxpayers to allegedly fund projects to benefit society at large have in many cases simply lined the pockets of a well-connected few.

This systemic mismanagement results in untold waste that often goes unreported and sometimes makes the news in a startling fashion. Consider the example of Anthony Garcia, a convicted killer in a Los Angeles jail. Between 2008 and 2010, Garcia received more than $30,000 in unemployment insurance while in prison.[25] Amanda Clayton also had access to money she did not need. Clayton won the Michigan State Lottery, netting $1 million as a prize, yet she continued to collect food stamps from the government.[26] Despite owning two homes and a new car, she received $200 per month in food assistance from the state of Michigan as part of a program meant to benefit low-income residents. When asked if she had a "right" to the welfare money she was collecting despite her recent wealth, she replied: "I mean, I kinda do. . . . I have no income and I have bills to pay. I have two houses." Another wealthy woman living off of her neighbors resides in a 2,500-square-foot home on a waterfront property, complete with gardens and a boat dock, which is valued at $1.2 million.[27] As of December 2011, the woman had been collecting welfare payments since 2003 while living in this home; she received more than $1,200 a month in public housing vouchers, cash each month from both the federal and state governments for a disability, and food stamps.

Far too many examples could be provided, enough to fill this book and more. One exchange summarizes them all, and drives home the inefficiency and ineffectiveness of getting government involved in welfare and charity. On June 1, 2011, the Subcommittee on Regulatory

Affairs, Stimulus Oversight and Government Spending of the House of Representatives Committee on Oversight and Government Reform held a hearing on the issue of "Duplication, Overlap, and Inefficiencies in Federal Welfare Programs."[28] Patricia Dalton, the chief operating officer of the General Accountability Office (GAO)—an independent, nonpartisan agency serving as a "congressional watchdog" to investigate how the federal government spends taxpayer dollars—was at the meeting to testify. The chairman of the subcommittee noted conflicting reports regarding just how many federal welfare programs even exist. When he asked Dalton for a total number of such programs as well as their success rates, she stated that she couldn't provide an answer because the GAO couldn't identify all of the programs in the various federal departments and agencies, nor could they determine how much they cost. The chairman pressed further, asking Dalton to "hazard a guess" as to what percentage of existing programs are accomplishing the purposes for which they were created. Dalton declined to even attempt an answer. She agreed with the chairman's statement that "it would be good to have a number of how many programs there are, what exactly are we spending, and what are we getting for that money" but stated that the GAO—the governmental body tasked with investigating and reporting this very type of thing—did not know and was unable to find out.

It is a repeatedly proven truism that individuals manage their money better than the government ever could. Taking money from taxpayers (under the threat or actual use of coercion) to help those in need may sound good on paper, but in practice has been a massive failure. At the federal level alone, $16 trillion has been spent since the government declared war on poverty in 1964[29]—and yet the number of people dependent upon the government continues to rise. The existence of these programs enables lazy people to become "sturdy beggars," taking advantage of a system where the qualifications are loosened over time to accommodate more and more people. Even those who have legitimate needs and are not necessarily exploiting the welfare system can be harmed by their participation in it. Those dependent upon others and who are able to receive a consistent amount of cash become disincentivized to change their circumstances and are not held accountable by those whose property has been taken to help that individual.

As the modern welfare state rose to prominence during the

administration of President Franklin D. Roosevelt, the passage of numerous welfare programs was accompanied with an ominous warning from Roosevelt. It seems both hypocritical, coming from a politician who promoted such programs so heavily, and prophetic, given the matching results we witness today. In his 1935 State of the Union address, Roosevelt said:

> The lessons of history, confirmed by the evidence immediately before me, show conclusively that continued dependence upon relief induces a spiritual disintegration fundamentally destructive to the national fibre. To dole out relief in this way is to administer a narcotic, a subtle destroyer of the human spirit.[30]

Roosevelt's observation was right, despite his actions to the contrary. Part of the disintegration he mentions is the way in which the economic distortions of government aid subsidize poor choices. In 1935, the percentage of births to first-time, unmarried mothers was just over 8 percent;[31] today, the number hovers around 40 percent.[32] In 1935, the divorce rate was 1.7 for every thousand people,[33] whereas today it has doubled.[34] In the 1930s, economic conditions necessitated many mothers working outside the home to supplement the family's income, but even with that factor, just 16 percent of married women with children were absent from their homes during the day.[35] Today, 69 percent of married mothers leave their homes to work.[36] Family dynamics are altered, socioeconomic statuses are distorted, and financial decisions are manipulated, all through the presence of and participation in a system that rewards poor choices and subsidizes bad decisions.

Part of the problem lies in the existing and heavy use of welfare programs, which encourage the very thing they aim to prevent. By offering food, housing, and cash payments to individuals in a certain economic category, people who otherwise would not be in that category will gravitate to it because of the "free" items being offered. Further, individuals who otherwise would be cautious in their family planning and life choices throw caution to the wind when they know that should they fall on hard times, the government will be there to bail them out. With over thirteen hundred different "benefits" offered by the federal government alone,[37] market forces are pushed aside and individuals lose important incentives to become educated, learn a skill, live responsibly, and work hard. Mark Owen, an economics professor at Northwood

University, drives home the hypocritical subsidization of the poor and needy:

> Government programs have not only created dependency, but have allowed people to escape the social norms that were the result of centuries of successful social behavior. The welfare state put in place a series of incentives that broke people free of the restraints of personal discipline. Before the advent of the full-blown welfare state, an out of wedlock birth was a familial disaster. The moral constraints of the time had some very good economic reasoning within it. Without a father, a single mother would have an extremely difficult time providing for the child, and her fitness for marriage would come into question for many suitors. The result was most likely to be either extreme poverty, an additional burden on the mother's parents, or adoption for the child. When the government steps in and subsidizes behaviors that in previous generations would have resulted in great hardship or even death, a sort of social Gresham's Law takes place where bad behavior chases out the good. Why have a father and husband around when the state will assure your financial situation? Why find a new job when you can collect unemployment for some time? The changes in societal incentives have resulted in a change in societal rules.[38]

The law of the harvest—you reap what you sow—must once again be made to govern our actions. We must face the consequences of our choices, and where help is needed, friends, family, neighbors, churches, and other non-governmental institutions should be looked to for assistance. The modern welfare state has a poor track record: it has cost tens of trillions of dollars, it has exacerbated the problems it was allegedly intended to alleviate, it operates based on the illegitimate confiscation of property from taxpayers, and it disincentivizes people from fulfilling their innate responsibility to care for themselves and charitably care for others. News stories are produced almost daily that point to corruption, waste, and inefficiency within the current system. Reasonable people must ask if there's a better way. In asking that question, it's important to understand how private charity could (and does) work. One compelling story demonstrates the blessings and miracles that can attend one's choosing to fulfill these responsibilities personally while also relying on other people in times of need.

ZEKE'S STORY

January 31, 2011, started out as a typical Sunday for one Utah family but quickly collapsed into a life-changing crisis.[39] Seven-week-old Zeke became clammy, cold, and repeatedly vomited anything he ate. Zeke was unable to sleep all night, continued to throw up, and had a temperature six degrees below normal the following morning. At a doctor visit the next day, Zeke's mother, Jenn, learned that he had both a heart murmur and Respiratory Syncytial Virus (RSV). Zeke's body immediately began to shut down—he turned white and his lips turned blue within minutes at the doctor's office. Rushed in an ambulance to the nearest hospital, Zeke was stabilized and then life-flighted to the children's hospital, where Jenn heard the words that would change her family's lives: her baby boy had been born with a series of congenital heart defects.

Zeke's initial hospital stay lasted three weeks to recover from RSV. Because of the sickness, open-heart surgery was inadvisable, and so another procedure was performed to further stabilize the performance of his tiny, defective heart. After several weeks of recuperation and quarantine at home, Zeke returned to the hospital so doctors could determine possible options for surgery. In preparation for his MRI, Zeke was given anesthesia and had a negative reaction, causing him to stop breathing. He was successfully stabilized and remained in the cardiac intensive care unit for his first surgery two days later. After a couple of more weeks in the hospital, Zeke was sent home only to return two weeks later with signs of heart failure. Doctors determined that the pressure on his lungs was extremely high, as was the risk of total heart failure. Unfortunately, little Zeke was not considered a candidate for a heart transplant because of the high blood pressure surging through his lungs, which also needed replacement.

Further surgery was postponed, first because of a cold and then because of pneumonia. With the window of time for surgery closing, Zeke's parents were counseled on how to cope with losing a child. Fortunately, with the help of antibiotics, Zeke was able to become well enough for surgery the second time, which was performed on May twenty-fifth—almost four months after the initial manifestations of his illness. The result of that surgery was a miracle, with everybody on the medical staff (including the surgeon) expressing their surprise at how well Zeke did. In the following months, Zeke grew and progressed extremely well, to the profound gratitude of his parents.

This story is perhaps not unique, since many people deal with unforeseen medical complications. But Zeke's situation is further complicated since his parents, Royal and Jenn, did not have medical insurance. These young parents had a small family—Zeke was their third child—and had recently become owners of a small ice cream business. Prior to Zeke's sickness, they had been working hard to pay down their debt and live frugally—in only one and a half more years, their debt would be paid off completely, and they were then planning to obtain insurance. Unfortunately, crisis hit before that milestone was achieved—a circumstance they now clearly recognize as being too risky to ever repeat. As the bills rapidly began to pile up—at a rate averaging $10,000 every day—Jenn said, "I felt like I was in the eye of a tornado. Standing still, while my world was being turned upside down. I knew we were financially ruined. I wasn't sure if my son would live. I felt overwhelmed, uneducated, disconnected, and exhausted. Yet strangely I also felt lifted and strengthened by the outpouring of love we received from family, friends, and total strangers."

That outpouring came quickly. Family friends organized an online fund-raiser that resulted in donations from around the world. Checks came in the mail on a daily basis. Roughly $20,000 was donated to the family—money which Royal says was "considered sacred and used carefully." Even months later, a $500 check came in the mail on the very day that Jenn had to spend $200 on medication at the pharmacy. "I was moved to tears that people still cared and thought about us after the initial crisis had passed," she says.

Even at this point, the story is not entirely unique, since many people who are uninsured still deal with unforeseen medical complications and are able to somehow find financial relief. But Royal and Jenn were unwilling to forcibly shoulder their burden onto others' backs by accepting government assistance. Royal says that they told every doctor, pilot, nurse, cardiologist, and surgeon that they did not have insurance but planned to pay for everything out of pocket and would not accept government assistance. "I'm not completely ignorant," he says. "I know that we were facing hundreds of thousands of dollars in medical bills, but I wanted every person helping my son to do it of their free will, knowing that they were going to be paid back by an ice cream man."

Despite their intentions, Royal and Jenn were referred to a case-worker who provided a variety of forms that would have allowed them to receive government aid. After regular visits, including taking them to a class explaining in detail how they could take advantage of the welfare system, the caseworker became irritated with the couple's persistent rejections. "Every time we sat down to fill out the forms, it just felt so wrong," says Jenn. "Whenever we considered whether to use government aid, I felt confused. Others often see it as the light at the end of the tunnel. Royal and I both felt clouded by it."

Instead, they requested to pursue the charity option through the hospital, hoping to be given discounts or waived fees due to their circumstances. The caseworker became angry, asking the couple why they would take other people's money when the government would pay for it "for free." Royal and Jenn recognized that government assistance was not in fact free, and they told the worker that they wanted no part in a system that uses unjust coercion. "I feel better about being responsible for our debt than I would by stealing it from my neighbors, through the government, and making them pay for it without having a choice," says Jenn. She and her husband stuck to their convictions, even in the face of almost everybody—the doctors included—calling them crazy for refusing what was readily available to them.

Blessings and miracles poured in, financial and otherwise. Interviewed separately, both Royal and Jenn responded that the greatest blessing received had been peace. Royal said that "Both Jenn and I have been at peace with each other, Zeke's medical situation, our finances, our business, our family, friends, and our future." Jenn agreed: "I have always felt at peace even though our financial outlook is still unknown. I never felt peace while putting a pen to the government aid forms. I felt overwhelming peace when I threw those forms in the trash."

Peace only goes so far, though. They still had tens of thousands of dollars in medical bills, with the dollar amount rising hourly. For a short time they were accepted by the hospital's charity fund, only to be cut off soon thereafter when the administrators learned that they had refused to first apply to receive government welfare. Only those who were denied by the government could apply to the hospital's private fund. Jenn then felt prompted to seek out private insurance, something Royal thought not worth her time. Zeke's preexisting (and costly!) condition clearly meant immediate rejection from any insurance agency.

Yet Jenn persisted and found a supportive insurance agent who helped her write letters and actually talk to a committee of underwriters. After one week, the insurance company miraculously offered a policy to their family, even with Zeke's situation and his parents' views regarding government welfare. Their corporate charity went further: the standard fifteen-day waiting period was waived, leaving them only with one (expensive) week of medical bills to resolve. Jenn describes the moment she was told that they would be insured:

> When the insurance agent told me over the phone that we would be insured, and that the plan would be back-dated to February 7th, I sat in silence completely paralyzed as to what I was hearing. I could do nothing but sob. As I squeaked out a "thank you" I wished there were more words in the English language to help me express what I was feeling. I heard the agent say to people in the background, "she's crying." For a few moments, all business formalities stopped. We were just people on the phone—not employees trying to make a sale or customers trying to milk a system. It was pure; it was human; it was amazing.

The babysitting, help with their business, financial contributions, meals, and so many other methods of service offered for this family created an opportunity for true charity. "It was very overwhelming to see the love that others were so freely willing to give," Royal says. "I've never felt so close to understanding the Atonement as when I couldn't do what I was supposed (and trying!) to do on my own, and others offered to help us because they loved me and my family." Jenn believes that this circumstance would not have happened had they accepted government assistance: "I feel that our decision not to use government welfare has really spread the beauty of true charity," she says. "Those who have given to us feel fulfilled and appreciated for giving, while we feel humbled and grateful that family, friends, and even complete strangers would want to sacrifice their resources to help us. That relationship simply doesn't exist when a person in need gets a handout from the government at the taxpayers' expense."

High medical bills, no insurance, and a reliance upon God rather than government make Royal and Jenn's situation rare and thus makes their story quite compelling. They still have a lot of debt to deal with, but it is manageable enough that their lives can move forward. Early on, Royal decided to heed the advice from the familiar hymn: "Do what is right; let the consequence follow." Their firm belief that it is not right to participate in a system of government welfare meant that for them, doing what is right required relying on the charity of others who were willing to fulfill the responsibility to provide for their own welfare, and then look after the welfare of others. "I've learned that if you put your faith in God instead of the government, everything will work out somehow," concludes Jenn.

SOCIAL SAFETY NETS

Zeke's story demonstrates that individuals fulfilling their responsibility can provide support for those in need, even in the absence of (or refusal to use) government programs. It shows that even with such tax-funded programs in place, individuals are still able and willing to give—even in cases where the financial misfortune is partially or entirely of one's own making. Imagine if the programs (and the taxes) were removed: people would have much more money available to help others in need, with whom they could individually identify, hold accountable, and share that sacred experience. The "sturdy beggars" would be forced to work, not finding anybody willing to voluntarily finance their laziness. Those abusing the system to profit at taxpayers' expense would have no system to abuse, and thus would be made to recognize and work on their own responsibility of personal welfare. The truly needy would be more visible to those able to help, and private institutions would raise funds more easily since individuals would no longer be taxed to finance a bloated, inefficient system.

Supporters of government-managed "anti-poverty" programs often recognize the waste and corruption easily evident in the current system, yet contend that the programs are still needed as a sort of "social safety net" to help provide for and look after those among us who are disabled, diseased, and downtrodden. Most people agree with this and thus accept government's intervention into what otherwise would be a private, voluntary charity system. "Although there are occasional political debates about these parts of the original American welfare state," writes one political scientist reviewing government welfare programs, "they are for the most part uncontroversial and politically stable."[40] Simply put, most people are willing to be taxed to know that such programs

95

exist for the truly needy and feel absolved of doing anything about it on an individual basis.

Yet the willingness to be taxed for that purpose does not make the tax morally acceptable, since it is likewise imposed upon others who may not consent. Further, it does not justify the existence and methods of government anti-poverty programs, which have consistently grown more costly, less efficient, and cultivated dependence by those who participate. Elder Robert D. Hales put it bluntly: "The Lord rejects such welfare programs."[41] He further described the effects of such programs, noting that they are "destined to trample initiative, undermine family responsibility, foster divisiveness, and erect barriers to equity, opportunity, and fellowship." There is a better way—one that is, as President Kimball said, "the gospel in action."[42] That way is the very thing demonstrated in Zeke's story: private, voluntary charity from friends, family, neighbors, and others committed to their responsibility to be charitable and who saw a need and acted to help.

Perhaps the most important reason to fulfill the personal responsibility of welfare and charity is to benefit from the spiritual side effects produced. When both giver and receiver have a direct connection one to another, then as President Marion G. Romney said, "There is an interdependence between those who have and those who have not. The process of giving exalts the poor and humbles the rich. In the process, both are sanctified."[43] Asked about the blessings he saw from choosing to rely for assistance on family, friends, and those directly connected to him, Zeke's father Royal replied: "I now have a stronger desire to establish Zion than I have ever had before." This is one more witness of the very principle taught by Elder Hales: the Lord's welfare plan "sanctifies both givers and receivers and prepares a Zion people."[44]

Being a Zion people means being not only united, but equal. The prophet Enoch taught his people and persuaded them to repent, ultimately helping create a society of Saints dedicated to living righteously. "And the Lord called his people Zion, because they were of one heart and one mind, and dwelt in righteousness; and there was no poor among them" (Moses 7:18). Thus, while unity is a well-known component of a celestial community, so too is equality. When Joseph Smith received a revelation regarding the establishment of a storehouse for the poor, God stated its purpose: "That you may be equal in the bonds of heavenly things, yea, and earthly things also, for the obtaining of heavenly things. For if ye are not equal in earthly things ye cannot be equal in obtaining heavenly things" (D&C 78:5–6).

Speaking to the Saints in his day, Paul provided some potent instructions as to how best to help the poor and become equal: "For I mean not that other men be eased, and ye burdened: But by an equality, that now at this time your abundance may be a supply for their want, that their abundance also may be a supply for your want: that there may be equality" (2 Corinthians 8:13–14). These verses fly in the face of conventional (and socialist) wisdom, which states that men should be equal in terms of possessions and opportunity. They instead teach that welfare and charity are reciprocal responsibilities; while at times we can take care of ourselves and others, sometimes others are needed to help take care of us. In other words, we achieve equality not through making sure that each person has the same amount and type of things as everybody else, but by freely offering resources, talents, and time to others in need. No middlemen need be involved, for the most rewarding and uplifting forms of charity are those which allow giver and receiver to both benefit through their intimate exchange of one's abundance becoming another's supply.

Perhaps not every story of true need would have as happy an ending as Zeke's if individuals acted upon their responsibility and got government out of the game of welfare. It would be an imperfect process, as it is now even with scores of government programs. Building Zion, however, is predicated on a few core activities, one of which is the free offering of the resources over which we have been made stewards to benefit those around us who currently stand in need. Unity and equality cannot and will not ever be achieved by funneling funds through a bureaucracy tasked with coercively taxing and spending others' money. Social safety nets are needed, of course, for as Jesus said "ye have the poor always with you" (Matthew 26:11). But the true and proper social safety net is each of us working together to build Zion. One of the only real social safety nets that can be found in the historical record is that of the city of Enoch, where by adhering to celestial principles (including voluntary charity, love, service, and so on) they were able to eradicate poverty in their community. Advocates of a social safety net should therefore turn away from government programs (given their illegitimate source of funds, poor results, and awful side effects) and look to implement policies and practices based on the principles found in Zion.

Being dependent upon others for our care may be necessary in some circumstances, but generally is a condition that should be avoided. We are counseled to "act for [our]selves and not to be acted upon" (2 Nephi 2:26), implying that independence should be our goal. Yet even some of those who are "anxiously engaged in a good cause" doing "many things of their own free will" (D&C 58:27) may only act when supported and served by those around them. "The Family: A Proclamation to the World" notes that husbands and wives are to "love and care for each other and for their children," "help one another as equal partners," and that "extended families should lend support when needed."[45] Thus, while in many ways independence is a noble goal, the fullest realization of being a righteous steward implies not only independence, but also *inter*dependence. The dual responsibilities of welfare (taking care of ourselves and those within our stewardship) and charity (taking care of others outside our immediate stewardship) support this very idea, namely, that we are to serve, support, and cooperate with one another.

Marriage is an example of this important interdependence between people, also serving as a microcosm for what should be done on a larger scale between all of God's children. "In the little kingdom of a family," writes Elder Bruce C. Hafen, "each spouse freely gives something the other does not have and without which neither can be complete and return to God's presence. Spouses are not a soloist with an accompanist, nor are they two solos. They are the interdependent parts of a duet, singing together in harmony at a level where no solo can go."[46] As the Proclamation similarly states, spouses support and serve one another while each works to fulfill his or her primary responsibilities. Each looks after his or her welfare and duties, serves the other spouse, and is also rendered service by that spouse. This interdependence is, through welfare and charity, to be found between all people. Paul taught that as members of the "body of Christ," we are all given diverse talents and resources with which to serve one another.

> And the eye cannot say unto the hand, I have no need of thee: nor again the head to the feet, I have no need of you.
>
> Nay, much more those members of the body, which seem to be more feeble, are necessary. . . .
>
> That there should be no schism in the body; but that the members should have the same care one for another.
>
> And whether one member suffer, all the members suffer with

it; or one member be honoured, all the members rejoice with it.
(1 Corinthians 12:21–22, 25–26)

The body of Christ is the true social safety net; God intends for us to support ourselves and serve one another. Rather than reducing those in need to a government-issue ID that "entitles" them to a certain amount of monetary support, we are to connect with, serve, and love those who have "hands which hang down" (see D&C 81:5) with a weight greater than they can bear. As President Thomas S. Monson has taught, "we are surrounded by those in need of our attention, our encouragement, our support, our comfort, our kindness—be they family members, friends, acquaintances, or strangers. We are the Lord's hands here upon the earth, with the mandate to serve and to lift His children. He is dependent on each of us."[47]

Interdependence means working together. The government's involvement into what should be an individual and personal relationship between the giver and recipient distorts and ultimately destroys the shared bond that is strengthened by sacrifice and service. Rather than building Zion, the government's programs build Babylon by enabling indolence, dependence, and greed. Even in the midst of taxpayer-financed welfare programs, people are generally very generous and willing to help those in need, as Zeke's story and many others demonstrate. This is a good start, but private and proper charity must move from playing defense to going on the offense against the government's intervention. To do this, we must ensure that the fibers of the real social safety net are strong enough to catch those who would otherwise fall by collectively fulfilling our personal responsibilities of welfare and charity. If we are quick to fulfill these responsibilities, we can save others before they turn to the government.

Suggestions

The following suggestions are offered on how to better fulfill the responsibilities of welfare and charity:

1. Pay an honest tithe.

The law of the tithe is a temporal and a spiritual commandment with temporal and spiritual benefits. The Lord commands his people to tithe, adding the following promise to those who obey: "prove me now herewith, saith the Lord of hosts, if I will not open you the windows of heaven, and pour you out a blessing, that there shall not be room enough to receive it" (Malachi 3:10). By demonstrating to God that you are being a wise steward of the resources he has blessed you with, your stewardship will increase with the increased blessings referenced in this verse.

In his April 1975 general conference address, which has since been turned into the financial management pamphlet "One For the Money" distributed by the Church, Elder Marvin J. Ashton said: "Paying tithing promptly to Him who does not come to check up each month will teach us to be more honest with those physically closer at hand."[48] If personal welfare and charity are your priorities, they will be made easier by first committing to pay your tithing.

2. Develop new skills.

To increase your stewardship and acquire the resources necessary to provide for your family and help others in need, education is the basic and first step. In a competitive environment where many people are applying for the same position or trying to court a potential client, it's important that you stand out and can offer a variety of talents to develop different streams of income. Stay-at-home mothers can develop home-based or online businesses, working fathers can look for freelance opportunities on the side, and everybody can and should continually receive more education to increase their earning potential. Acquiring unique skills can also help avoid prolonged unemployment.

3. Create a budget.

Being a wise steward requires being ready and able to give an account of that stewardship. To ensure that the resources you have been blessed with are appropriately used, detailed records should be kept of how much income you receive, how it should be spent, and what priority each expenditure should be given. By tracking income and expenses, a family will better be able to ensure that their needs are being met, their wants are being saved for, and that they are setting aside money for savings and charity along the way.

4. SACRIFICE, SAVE, AND AVOID DEBT.

To prioritize things such as tithing, savings, and charity, instant gratification must give way to delayed gratification. Unnecessary items often need to be deferred until later so that one's resources can be better used in the short term. Our self-indulgent, materialistic society of extreme consumerism offers many enticing products and services, and people often incur substantial amounts of debt in pursuit of things they don't need. As Elder L. Tom Perry has taught:

> The current cries we hear coming from the great and spacious building tempt us to compete for ownership of things in this world. We think we need a larger home, with a three-car garage, a recreational vehicle parked next to it. We long for designer clothes, extra TV sets . . . the latest model computers and the newest car. Often these items are purchased with borrowed money, without giving any thought to providing for our future needs. The result of this instant gratification is overloaded bankruptcy courts and families that are far too preoccupied with their financial burdens.

Suffering exists in our own neighborhoods and around the world, which can be alleviated in part by our contributions and service. To ignore the divine mandate and important responsibility of charity by using up all of our resources on ourselves implies a failure in our stewardship and a refusal to succor the weak, as we have been commanded to do. Moroni spoke of this very thing: "For behold, ye do love money, and your substance, and your fine apparel, and the adorning of your churches, more than ye love the poor and the needy, the sick and the afflicted" (Mormon 8:37). Families must sacrifice and save, where necessary, to get (and stay) out of debt, and to build up a reserve that can be used to benefit others' lives.

5. RENDER SERVICE.

Not all charity requires money. Often the greatest acts of service come by offering labor rather than goods, such as helping to plant a garden, clean a room, repair an appliance, babysit some children, or simply showing love in a thoughtful visit. As Elder Jeffrey R. Holland said, "To worthy causes and needy people, we can give time if we don't have money, and we can give love when our time runs out."[49] While sharing of our abundance is important to alleviate hunger, sickness, and poverty, it is only one aspect of being charitable toward those in need. Look for opportunities to serve in whatever form they may come. Organizations such as the Red Cross or United Way and websites such as www.justserve.org can help you find opportunities near your area where you can help someone in need.

NOTES

1. Edward L. Kimball and Andrew E. Kimball, Jr., *Spencer W. Kimball* (Salt Lake City: Bookcraft, 1979), 352–53.
2. Foley, *The Jefferson Cyclopedia*, 320.
3. Ellen Mackay Hutchinson and Edmund Clarence Stedman, eds., *A Library of American Literature,* vol. 1 (New York: Charles L. Webster, 1892), 306.
4. Walter I. Trattner, *From Poor Law to Welfare State: A History of Social Welfare in America* (New York: Simon and Schuster, 1999), 17.
5. Ibid, 22.
6. Ibid.
7. Clinton Rossiter, ed., *The Federalist Papers* (New York: Mentor, 1999), 260.
8. Annals of the Congress of the United States, 1789–1824 3rd Congress, 1st session, p. 170, 1794-01-10.
9. James D. Richardson, ed., *A Compilation of the Messages and Papers of the Presidents*, vol. 5 (Bureau of National Literature and Art, 1907), 249.
10. Americans gave over $290 billion to charities in 2010. See "Americans dig deep to give more to charities," *Christian Science Monitor*, June 20, 2011, accessed May 12, 2012, http://www.csmonitor.com/World/Making-a-difference/Change-Agent/2011/0620/Americans-dig-deep-to-give-more-to-charities.
11. de Tocqueville, *Democracy*, 375.
12. "Welfare State: Handouts Make Up One-Third of U.S. Wages," *CNBC*, March 8, 2011, accessed May 2, 2012, http://www.cnbc.com/id/41969508/Welfare_State_Handouts_Make_Up_One_Third_of_U_S_Wages.

13. "Nearly Half of U.S. Lives in Household Receiving Government Benefit," The Wall Street Journal, October 5, 2011, accessed May 2, 2012, http://blogs.wsj.com/economics/2011/10/05/nearly-half-of-households-receive-some-government-benefit/

14. "Most Americans Don't Believe Hard Work Can Get You Rich," *Rasmussen Reports*, September 30, 2010, accessed May 2, 2012, http://www.rasmussenreports.com/public_content/business/general_business/september_2010/most_americans_don_t_believe_hard_work_can_get_you_rich.

15. "The Family: A Proclamation to the World," *Ensign*, Nov. 1995.

16. Heber J. Grant, in Conference Report, Oct. 1936, 3.

17. B. H. Roberts, ed., *History of the Church of Jesus Christ of Latter-day Saints*, vol. 4 (Salt Lake City: Deseret Book, 1978), 226–27.

18. Joseph B. Wirthlin, "The Great Commandment," *Ensign*, Nov. 2007, 31.

19. "Frequently Asked Questions," Social Security Online, accessed May 12, 2012, http://www.socialsecurity.gov/history/hfaq.html.

20. "Social Security Execs Boogie Down at Lavish Phoenix Conference," ABC, July 15, 2009, accessed May 2, 2012, http://abcnews.go.com/Blotter/story?id=8084663.

21. "Social Security IOUs stashed away," the *Washington Times*, March 16, 2010, accessed May 2, 2012, http://www.washingtontimes.com/news/2010/mar/16/social-security-ious-stashed-away-in-wva/.

22. "Rep. Jim Jordan presses to reform the volume of welfare programs," PolitiFact, March 22, 2011, accessed May 2, 2012, http://www.politifact.com/ohio/statements/2011/apr/05/jim-jordan/rep-jim-jordan-presses-reform-numerous-welfare-pro/.

23. "Unemployment payments fraud worth $17B per year," CBS, July 3, 2011, accessed May 2, 2012, http://www.cbsnews.com/stories/2011/07/03/national/main20076594.shtml.

24. "Stimulus funds for W. Virginia's handicapped and poor instead goes for lobbying, consulting," The Center for Public Integrity, July 6, 2011, accessed May 2, 2012, http://www.iwatchnews.org/2011/07/06/5120/stimulus-funds-w-virginias-handicapped-and-poor-instead-goes-lobbying-consulting.

25. "Report: Convicted killer received unemployment checks while in jail," Fox News, March 4, 2012, accessed May 12, 2012, http://www.foxnews.com/us/2012/03/04/report-convicted-killer-received-unemployment-checks-while-in-jail/.

26. "Lottery winner on food stamps even after $1 million jackpot," Yahoo, March 7, 2012, accessed May 12, 2012, http://news.yahoo.com/blogs/sideshow/michigan-woman-still-collecting-food-stamps-winning-1-201751693.html.

27. "Feds: Seattle welfare recipient lives in million dollar home," King 5,

December 2, 2011, accessed May 2, 2012, http://www.king5.com/news/local/Feds--Seattle-welfare-recipient-lived-in-million-dollar-home-134943613.html.

28. "Federal Government Cannot Identify How Many Government Welfare Programs Exist, Much Less Whether They Are Working," The Carleson Center for Public Policy, accessed May 2, 2012, http://theccpp.org/2011/09/federal-government-cannot-identify-how-many-government-welfare-programs-exist-much-less-whether-they.html.

29. "Obama to Spend $10.3 Trillion on Welfare: Uncovering the Full Cost of Means-Tested Welfare or Aid to the Poor," The Heritage Foundation, September 16, 2009, accessed May 2, 2012, http://www.heritage.org/Research/Reports/2009/09/Obama-to-Spend-103-Trillion-on-Welfare-Uncovering-the-Full-Cost-of-Means-Tested-Welfare-or-Aid-to-the-Poor

30. Richard Polenberg, *The Era of Franklin D. Roosevelt 1933-1945: A Brief History with Documents* (Boston: Bedford, 2000), 51.

31. "Trends in Premarital Childbearing 1930 to 1994," US Census Bureau, October 1999, accessed May 2, 2012, http://www.census.gov/prod/99pubs/p23-197.pdf.

32. "Unmarried Childbearing," CDC, accessed May 2, 2012, http://www.cdc.gov/nchs/fastats/unmarry.htm.

33. "Vital Statistics of the United States 1965, vol. 3" *US Department of Health, Education, and Welfare* (Washington: US Government Printing Office, 1968), 2–5.

34. "Births, Marriages, Divorces and Deaths: Provisional Data for 2009," *National Vital Statistics Reports*, vol. 58, no. 25, Aug. 27, 2010.

35. "The Economics of Middle-Income Family Life: Working Women During the Great Depression," *The Journal of American History*, vol. 65, no. 1, June 1978, 60–74.

36. "Employment Characteristics of Families, 2010," Bureau of Labor Statistics, March 24, 2011, accessed May 2, 2012, http://www.bls.gov/news.release/famee.nr0.htm.

37. See the "Browse by Category" section of www.benefits.gov for a numeric listing of each category's benefits.

38. "The Welfare State: Shredding Society," LewRockwell.com, February 7, 2007, accessed May 2, 2012, http://www.lewrockwell.com/orig8/owen1.html.

39. The details in this story were obtained in an interview with the parents in this family, who are friends of the author. For privacy reasons, their last name and location are not included.

40. Steven Teles, *Whose Welfare? AFDC and Elite Politics* (Lawrence: University Press of Kansas, 1994), 1.

41. Robert D. Hales, "Welfare Principles to Guide Our Lives: An Eternal Plan for the Welfare of Men's Souls," *Ensign*, May 1986, 28.

42. Spencer W. Kimball, "Welfare Services: The Gospel in Action," *Ensign*, Nov. 1977, 76.
43. Marion G. Romney, in Conference Report, Oct. 1982.
44. Hales, "Welfare Principles."
45. "The Family: A Proclamation to the World," *Ensign*, Nov. 1995.
46. "Crossing Thresholds and Becoming Equal Partners," *Ensign*, Aug. 2007, 28.
47. Thomas S. Monson, "What Have I Done for Someone Today?" *Ensign*, Nov. 2009, 86.
48. Marvin J. Ashton, "One For the Money," The Church of Jesus Christ of Latter-day Saints (Salt Lake City: Intellectual Reserve, Inc., 2006), 3.
49. Jeffrey R. Holland, "A Handful of Meal and a Little Oil," *Ensign*, May 1996.

PREPAREDNESS AND SELF-RELIANCE

Many more people could ride out the storm-tossed waves in their economic lives if they had their year's supply of food and clothing and were debt-free. Today we find that many have followed this counsel in reverse: they have at least a year's supply of debt and are food-free.[1]

—President Thomas S. Monson

The purpose of both temporal and spiritual self-reliance is to get ourselves on higher ground so that we can lift others in need.[2]

—Elder Robert D. Hales

We feel the need to emphasize with greater clarity the obligation for members of the Church to become more independent and self reliant.[3]

—President Gordon B. Hinckley

QUESTIONS TO PONDER

1. If your primary source of income stopped, would you be able to feed and provide for your family?

2. Are you more like one of the wise virgins in Christ's parable, or one of the foolish?

3. What spiritual benefits can result from having food storage and becoming prepared for the future?

4. How is your independence threatened by not being prepared for emergencies?

5. Should the government help those who can't help themselves?

A PLENTY, A FAMINE

Sold into slavery by his jealous and scheming brothers, Joseph was at one point cast into prison. His father, Jacob, later named Israel, taught Joseph from an early age to follow God and heed his commandments. This obedience proved beneficial to Joseph during his incarceration, as he was able to correctly interpret the dreams of two of Pharaoh's servants. When Pharaoh later had a troubling dream of his own, one of those servants remembered Joseph and suggested his services to Pharaoh.

The king of Egypt then sent for Joseph, and inquired as to whether he possessed such a power to understand and interpret dreams. "It is not in me," Joseph said. "God shall give Pharaoh an answer of peace" (Genesis 41:16). Pharaoh then recounted his dreams to Joseph, describing seven healthy kine (cattle) and seven sickly ones, along with seven hearty ears of grain and another seven that were thin and withering. "God hath shewed Pharaoh what he is about to do," replied Joseph (Genesis 41:25). He then proceeded to tell the king of Egypt that there would be seven years of prosperity and production where an abundance of food would be grown. Following that period, seven years of a "very grievous" famine would follow. Upon offering the interpretation, Joseph counseled Pharaoh to prepare for the famine during the time of plenty: "let them gather all the food of those good years that come, and lay up corn under the hand of Pharaoh, and let them keep food in the cities" (Genesis 41:35).

Latter-day prophets have often referenced this story since the gospel's restoration to encourage preparedness, laying up in store for times of trial ahead. For example, the First Presidency in 1942 stated:

> We renew the counsel given to the Saints from the days of Brigham Young until now—be honest, truthful, industrious, frugal, thrifty. In the day of plenty, prepare for the day of scarcity. The principle of the fat and lean kine is as applicable today as it was in the days when, on the banks of the Nile, Joseph interpreted Pharaoh's dream. Officials now warn us, and warn again, that scant days are coming.[4]

As noted, this counsel started back in the days of Brother Brigham. Interestingly, much of the prophetic warning voice came not from

Brigham Young, the prophet, but from Elder Heber C. Kimball—recognized by the Saints at that time as having the gift of prophecy. Brigham himself recognized this, who on several occasions admitted, "I am not a visionary man, neither am I given much to prophesying. When I want any of that done I call on brother Heber—he is my Prophet, he loves to prophesy, and I love to hear him."[5] For his part, Elder Kimball downplayed the flattery of being considered a prophet, though noted that "people all the time are telling me that I am."[6] Still, the prophesies came—many dealing with future events and the calamities that would befall the Saints. "Will you be slack, brethren, and let the evil come upon us," he asked, "when we forewarn you of the future events that are coming?" He continued, also referencing Joseph's interpretation of Pharaoh's dream: "We are telling of what the prophets have said—of what the Lord has said to Joseph. Wake up, now, wake up, O Israel, and lay up your grain and your stores. I tell you that there is trouble coming upon the world."[7]

The symbolism of the seven years of plenty and seven years of famine has a more recent application—and an interesting one. During President Hinckley's time as prophet, he mentioned Pharaoh's dream only three times in general conference. The first instance was in the October 1998 session, where he prefaced his remarks by saying "I wish to speak to you about temporal matters." He then paraphrased the dream recorded in Genesis, and then stated: "Now, brethren, I want to make it very clear that I am not prophesying, that I am not predicting years of famine in the future. But I am suggesting that the time has come to get our houses in order."[8] "There is a portent of stormy weather ahead to which we had better give heed," he further warned. Standing alone, this reference to Pharaoh's dream is fairly innocuous, though important still. A prophet's suggestion that we prepare for hard times ahead is significant, though not really uncommon—such has been the message of prophets for a long time. However, just a few days shy of exactly *seven* years later, President Hinckley again referenced the dream in a talk about preparedness during the priesthood session of the October 2005 general conference: "Let us never lose sight of the dream of Pharaoh concerning the fat cattle and the lean, the full ears of corn, and the blasted ears; the meaning of which was interpreted by Joseph to indicate years of plenty and years of scarcity."[9] Many have speculated that despite his disclaimer in 1998 of not offering a prophecy, that

President Hinckley nevertheless had signaled the beginning of seven years of plenty, which would conclude in 2005, to be followed by seven years of famine ending in 2012.

The third and final mention of this dream by President Hinckley was in a conference address just weeks after the 9/11 attacks (and thus falling chronologically between the other two references), where he stated: "I do not know what the future holds. I do not wish to sound negative, but I wish to remind you of the warnings of scripture and the teachings of the prophets which we have had constantly before us. I cannot forget the great lesson of Pharaoh's dream of the fat and lean kine and of the full and withered stalks of corn."[10] It is quite possible, if not likely, that these references do not suggest anything more than the message they contain, and that a latter-day time line of seven years of plenty and seven years of famine has not yet begun, if it will at all. Even so, the counsel has long been clear: "prepare every needful thing" (D&C 109:8).

The counsel to prepare is so significant in these latter-days that the Lord saw fit to include it in the preface to the Doctrine and Covenants, as a sort of introduction to what the purpose of the following revelations would be. Many revelations had been given to Joseph Smith prior to this one, but as the publication process for the 1833 Book of Commandments[11] began, the Lord gave Joseph a preface (see D&C 1:6) to be included as an inspired introduction to the revelations compiled in the book. The entirety of this revelation revolves around warning of future events and declaring God's purpose in bringing to pass the restoration of all things. One verse conveys the theme of the entire chapter of scripture, with God telling his children: "Prepare ye, prepare ye for that which is to come" (D&C 1:12).

What is "to come?" Before his death, Jesus told his disciples that the events preceding his second coming would include "wars, and rumors of wars" (Joseph Smith—Matthew 1:28), "famines, and pestilences, and earthquakes" (JSM 1:29), the fulfillment of the "abomination of desolation" (JSM 1:32), and astrological changes: "the sun shall be darkened, and the moon shall not give her light, and the stars shall fall from heaven, and the powers of heaven shall be shaken" (JSM 1:33). Similar signs are recorded elsewhere in scripture in even more detail: "there shall be weeping and wailing" (D&C 29:15); "there shall be a great hailstorm sent forth to destroy the crops of the earth" (D&C

29:16); "God will send forth flies upon the face of the earth, which shall take hold of the inhabitants thereof, and shall eat their flesh, and shall cause maggots to come in upon them" (D&C 29:18); and "their flesh shall fall from off their bones, and their eyes from their sockets" (D&C 29:19). Such a gruesome warning emphasizes just how dreadful the "great and dreadful day of the Lord" (Malachi 4:5) will be for those not prepared to meet God.

The divine mandate to prepare for that which is to come makes clear our responsibility. An overall preparedness plan includes both spiritual and temporal components; one does not fully ready himself for the Lord's return by canning wheat and packing a seventy-two-hour kit. This chapter will focus specifically on the temporal aspect of preparedness, however, since our ability to claim and maintain our individual liberty during our time on the earth necessitates being independent—in times of plenty as well as in times of proverbial famine. One cannot be free while simultaneously being a burden on others.

Whether preparing for latter-day conditions which will come upon us "as a whirlwind" (D&C 112:24) and will "not be stayed until the Lord come" (D&C 97:23), or preparing for more common occurrences of financial trouble such as unemployment, unforeseen medical needs, or a natural disaster, the responsibility to become self-reliant requires action in the short term for weathering events in the long term. Consistency is key, for one does not know when disaster may strike—we must always be ready. President Spencer W. Kimball commented on the difficulty of maintaining such a state of preparedness as follows:

> Do we lose faith, do we lose patience, do we lose hope, do we get weary in waiting, because the day is long and the event delayed? It is difficult to be prepared for an event so long delayed. Many have found it too difficult and they slumber without due preparation. Hundreds of thousands of us today are in this position. Confidence has been dulled and patience worn thin. It is so hard to wait and be prepared always. But we cannot allow ourselves to slumber.[12]

A well-known example of what slumbering does when disaster strikes comes from the story of the flood during Noah's time. Hearing an old man ramble on for over a century (see Moses 8:17) about an impending flood[13] must have sounded odd when the solid, dry ground and clear blue sky gave no hint of danger. Elder Neal A. Maxwell observed: "It has been asked, and well it might be, how many of us would have jeered, or at least been privately amused, by the sight of Noah building his ark. Presumably, the laughter and heedlessness continued until it began to rain—and kept raining! How wet some people must have been before Noah's ark suddenly seemed the only sane act in an insane, bewildering situation!"[14] Consider how the parents in Noah's day must have felt as they frantically gathered their families to the highest spot of land they could find, and as the waters continued to rise, having to ultimately look their children in the eyes and apologize for not having listened to Noah's warning voice. The example Noah's story provides has plenty of application to our day; prophets have consistently warned of future times of calamity and conflict, calling for God's people to prepare. Jesus, again teaching his disciples, also referenced this story in connection to preparing for future events:

> But as it was in the days of Noah, so it shall be also at the coming of the Son of Man;
>
> For it shall be with them, as it was in the days which were before the flood; for until the day that Noah entered into the ark they were eating and drinking, marrying and giving in marriage;
>
> And knew not until the flood came, and took them all away; so shall also the coming of the Son of Man be. (JSM 1:41–43)

Jesus further taught his followers to "watch, therefore, for you know not at what hour your Lord doth come" (JSM 1:46). Merely watching is insufficient, of course, so he added on the need to prepare: "be ye also ready, for in such an hour as ye think not, the Son of Man cometh" (JSM 1:48). Protecting our life, liberty, and property requires preparing for future events that may put them in jeopardy. Joseph's interpretation of Pharaoh's dream has direct relevance to our day, as has been made clear on numerous occasions by modern prophets. "We are constantly charged with preparation in time of plenty against want in time of need," noted President J. Reuben Clark.[15] Whether in times of plenty or times of famine, the consistent counsel to be ready for whatever may come cannot be ignored by those who wish to be free.

FOOLISH OR WISE?

These teachings by Jesus were repeated and simplified in the parable of the ten virgins, emphasizing the need to be ready for future anticipated events. In the Jewish culture, it was customary for a bridegroom to come at night to the bride's house where her bridesmaids were attending to her. When the bridegroom's arrival was announced, the maids would go to meet him with oil-filled lamps to illuminate his path toward the house and his bride-to-be.

Christ's parable tells of ten virgins serving as maids, each with oiled lamps at the ready. Five were foolish and did not have extra oil on hand, while five were wise and carried extra vessels of oil. The bridegroom's arrival came later than anticipated, and all of the virgins "slumbered and slept" (Matthew 25:5) as a result of the late hour. Finally, the call came and the virgins were told to go out and meet the arriving bridegroom. The foolish virgins had run out of oil but could not get any from their wise counterparts, and thus were unable to meet the bridegroom and go in with him to the marriage ceremony. Desperate to be a part of the much-anticipated proceedings, the foolish virgins petitioned the bridegroom to let them enter. The response: "I know you not" (Matthew 25:12). The lesson to be drawn from this parable is clear and familiar: "Watch therefore, for ye know neither the day nor the hour wherein the Son of man cometh" (Matthew 25:13).

While this parable primarily relates to being spiritually ready for Christ's second coming, one can and should draw temporal lessons as well. After all, God has made clear that to him even temporal things are spiritual in nature (see D&C 29:31–35). Prophetic counsel has repeatedly reaffirmed that becoming ready for the return of Christ requires both spiritual and temporal preparedness. "We need to make both temporal and spiritual preparation for the events prophesied at the time of the Second Coming," according to Elder Dallin H. Oaks.[16] The counsel to have food storage, financial savings, and a self-reliant lifestyle has been consistently given to the Saints since the Church's nineteenth century migration to Utah. Like the virgin maids waiting with filled lamps and anxious for the bridegroom's arrival, we as members of the Church have been warned to be ready for Christ's coming. Elder James E. Talmage taught: "In mercy the Lord warns and forewarns. He sees the coming storm, knows the forces operating to produce it, and calls aloud through His prophets, advises, counsels, exhorts, even commands—that we prepare for what is about to befall and take shelter while yet there is time."[17]

It is important to note that the virgins in Christ's parable represent members of his Church who knew of his coming and were (at least to varying degrees) prepared for his arrival. Those who were not adequately prepared were not labeled as wicked or slothful, but foolish. Elder Bruce R. McConkie clarified this distinction: "Not good and bad, not righteous and wicked, but wise and foolish. That is, all of them have accepted the invitation to meet the Bridegroom; all are members of the Church . . . but only five are valiant therein."[18] These foolish virgins apparently felt entitled to enter in with the bridegroom, even going so far as to trim their empty lamps once they had been notified of his arrival. Elder Lynn G. Robbins notes that "They all thought they were ready. Outwardly, they all appeared prepared."[19] Believing that all was well, the foolish virgins (or members of the Church) perhaps expected to be forgiven and included, despite not being fully prepared as they had been told. Elder Robbins further states:

> The fact that the five foolish virgins knocked, expecting to enter the marriage supper, indicates one of two things: (1) they thought they could prepare themselves after the Bridegroom came, or (2) knowing that they at first had not been prepared to enter, they were hoping for mercy. Either way, the door was shut.[20]

How disheartening it must have felt for the foolish virgins to be rejected by the very person they were waiting to see. How unfortunate was their unwillingness to make themselves fully ready, preparing for a circumstance in which the bridegroom's arrival was later than anticipated. We too have been taught to make ourselves ready—not only for Christ's arrival, but also for circumstances along the way that are unexpected and potentially burdensome. For whatever reason, however, decades of prophetic encouragement have failed to produce an adequate response from the Saints; estimates suggest that only 10–20 percent of American Latter-day Saints are anywhere close to being adequately prepared with food storage.[21] President Ezra Taft Benson commented on this trend, rebuking the foolish among us who fail to prepare:

> Too often we bask in our comfortable complacency and rationalize that the ravages of war, economic disaster, famine, and

earthquake cannot happen here. Those who believe this are either not acquainted with the revelations of the Lord, or they do not believe them. Those who smugly think these calamities will not happen, that they somehow will be set aside because of the righteousness of the Saints, are deceived and will rue the day they harbored such a delusion.[22]

Like the unprepared virgins whose actions prevented them from enjoying the very experience they had anticipated, many Saints unwisely delay their preparations. As President Henry B. Eyring once noted, we often put off until tomorrow what we would rather not do today, expecting that we will still be able to do it tomorrow:

> Because the Lord is kind, He calls servants to warn people of danger. That call to warn is made harder and more important by the fact that the warnings of most worth are about dangers that people don't yet think are real. . . . It's easy to say, "The time isn't right." But there is danger in procrastination.[23]

The effects of such foolish procrastination are readily evident in the common turmoils of life on earth. The Savior's Second Coming will be preceded by a volley of so-called "natural" disasters, but such disasters are already fairly commonplace. In the years since 2000, between twenty thousand and thirty thousand earthquakes have occurred worldwide each year, with at least one earthquake larger than an 8.0 on the Richter Scale occurring almost every year.[24] In 2011, there were fourteen weather-related disasters in the United States that each exceeded $1 billion in damage estimates.[25] The year prior, 2010, was the deadliest year in more than a generation in terms of natural disasters, with earthquakes, heat waves, floods, volcanoes, super typhoons, blizzards, landslides and droughts killing at least a quarter million people throughout the world in that year alone.[26] This high death toll cannot solely be blamed on nature's random happenings, however. Experts argue that poor construction and development practices, as well as residential location choices, make earthquakes and other disasters more dangerous than they otherwise would be. As an example, the earthquake that struck Haiti in January 2010 killed over 220,000 people—most of whom lived in densely populated, poorly built shanties. In February, an earthquake five hundred times stronger occurred in Chile, where it was less populated and buildings were better constructed. That larger earthquake caused fewer than one thousand deaths.[27]

"It's a form of suicide, isn't it?" observed one professor of geological sciences in response.[28] "We build houses that kill ourselves (in earthquakes). We build houses in flood zones that drown ourselves. It's our fault for not anticipating these things." This may be a bitter pill to swallow for those who are affected by an unexpected disaster, but to some extent his observation is correct. Primary children learn in a popular song about a wise man building a house upon a rock (which, when the rains and floods came, stood still) and a foolish man building his upon the sand (which washed away). While the implications of the lyrics are spiritual, the temporal application is obvious. If a person builds a house on a beautiful coastline which years later is swallowed up in a turbulent storm by crashing waves, was that person wise or foolish? Like the virgins who failed to perform certain actions that would allow them to be better prepared for unanticipated circumstances, those who unnecessarily expose themselves to risk are foolish.

This foolishness is used to justify government programs that tax the wise and foolish together, to benefit both those in true need and the foolish who should have known better. Through such government redistribution of wealth, those choosing to wisely live in a safer location are required to subsidize those who did not prepare for emergencies, and even worse, those who intentionally place themselves in harm's way. The foolish virgins in Christ's parable asked their wise counterparts for some oil and were denied this last-minute bailout, yet the government today takes from the "haves" and gives to the "have-nots" anyway.

As with other illegitimate government interventions, the existence of programs that pay people after they've suffered from a disaster creates a moral hazard that alters individual behavior, as people shirk their responsibility to be prepared and self-reliant, believing (whether consciously or not) that they will be taken care of should something go wrong. Rather than taking precaution when determining where to live, what to purchase, and how (or if) to prepare, many people throw caution to the wind and expect to be saved by somebody else. Though they did not carry extra vessels of oil in preparation for a long wait, the foolish virgins at least had oil-filled lamps. Many people today would not even meet that basic benchmark.

The government has not always subsidized the foolish. A couple of notable examples stand out and are worth mentioning. In 1794, when

Congress was considering the appropriation of $15,000 for the relief of French refugees who had fled Haiti during its violent revolution, James Madison arose and declared: "I could not undertake to lay [my] finger on that article in the Federal Constitution which granted a right to Congress of expending, on objects of benevolence, the money of their constituents . . . Charity is no part of the legislative duty of the government."[29] A century later, President Grover Cleveland vetoed a bill that would have dispensed money to suffering farmers in the West. Affirming that the Constitution granted no such authority, and that individuals were far more altruistic and efficient in their charity than government could be, he wrote:

> The friendliness and charity of our countrymen can always be relied upon to relieve their fellow-citizens in misfortune. This has been repeatedly and quite lately demonstrated. Federal aid in such cases encourages the expectation of paternal care on the part of the Government and weakens the sturdiness of our national character, while it prevents the indulgence among our people of that kindly sentiment and conduct which strengthens the bonds of a common brotherhood.[30]

Though these examples are in the minority compared to a consistent violation of the Constitution, individual liberty, and basic principles of self-reliance, others have thankfully objected over the years to the government's "paternal care." Preparedness is a personal responsibility, and deferring emergency-related assistance to the government leads people to reject this duty and expect that if trouble arises, others will provide for them. This foolish behavior is not consistent with God's law, including the "law of the harvest" which dictates that "whatsoever a man soweth, that shall he also reap" (Galatians 6:7). Commenting on this trend, President Howard W. Hunter declared:

> There appears to me to be a trend to shift responsibility for life and its processes from the individual to the state. In this shift there is a basic violation of the Law of the Harvest, or the law of justice. The attitude of "something for nothing" is encouraged. The government is often looked to as the source of wealth. There is the feeling that the government should step in and take care of one's needs, one's emergencies, and one's future. . . .
> What is the real cause of this trend toward the welfare state,

toward more socialism? In the last analysis, in my judgment, it is personal unrighteousness. When people do not use their freedoms responsibly and righteously, they will gradually lose these freedoms.

If man will not recognize the inequalities around him and voluntarily, through the gospel plan, come to the aid of his brother, . . . he will find that through "a democratic process" he will be forced to come to the aid of his brother. The government will take from the "haves" and give to the "have nots." Both have lost their freedom. Those who "have," lost their freedom to give voluntarily of their own free will and in the way they desire. Those who "have not" lost their freedom because they did not earn what they received. They got "something for nothing," and they will neither appreciate the gift nor the giver of the gift.

Under this climate, people gradually become blind to what has happened and to the vital freedoms which they have lost.[31]

The foolish who do not prepare have assumed a significant risk that at any time might result in disaster. President Benson once observed that "a famine in this land of one year's duration could wipe out a large percentage of slothful members, including some ward and stake officers. Yet we cannot say we have not been warned."[32] We must be prepared for calamities of any size; while food storage would help a family survive during a long famine, it can also feed them during prolonged unemployment, for example. In preparing for the unexpected, we must remember that the events for which we are preparing are just that: unexpected. It is impossible to know what tragedies might occur in the future, so steps must be taken to be as ready as possible so that we can help ourselves and those around us.

The wise and the foolish alike must be accountable; each of God's children is a steward and is responsible for preparing for emergencies, both large and small. This preparation should not be a one-time action, for Christ's commandment to "watch" requires that one consistently prepare for times of famine while in a time of plenty. "Be faithful, praying always," God said, "having your lamps trimmed and burning, and oil with you, that you may be ready at the coming of the Bridegroom" (D&C 33:17).

PROVIDENT LIVING

Liberty implies being *at* liberty to do something. It is closely connected to agency, which means being able to *act* rather than being acted upon. The importance of being prepared for emergencies and living a self-reliant lifestyle becomes clearer when framed in this way. Imagine a tornado in which a person's home is destroyed, and every possession is either carried away in the wind or ruined. Imagine further that this person had no significant financial savings and thus is completely unprepared for the emergency situation he now finds himself in. This state of necessary dependency upon others is at odds with being an independent agent who enjoys and uses his individual liberty; his actions are now dictated not by his desires and long-term priorities, but by external circumstances that act upon him.

Preparing for such emergencies allows a person to maintain his independence even amid significant trials and financial difficulties. Further, it allows an individual the flexibility to make decisions that are better in the long run. Had Esau been better prepared, for example, he might have gotten a better bargain for his mess of pottage because he would not have been so desperate (see Genesis 25:29–34). The various actions one can take in order to prepare for the future—acquire food storage, accumulate financial savings, learn first aid and emergency response, and so on—are necessary in order to be independent and maintain liberty. Freedom requires *being* free, and the foolish who fail to prepare are, in times of emergency, forced into a condition of diminished freedom.

Many who are unfamiliar with general preparedness practices often (and incorrectly) believe that their purpose is to ready the individual primarily for an Armageddon-like calamity where the world is proverbially turned upside down and everybody is left to fend for themselves. Given that Jesus warned his disciples (and by extension, each of us) to watch and prepare for such an eventuality, this belief is not completely wrong. However, the statistical probability of experiencing a significant life-altering disaster is relatively low. Of course, this depends upon a large number of factors, primarily the location where one chooses to live. Take California, for example. A recent study indicated that the state stands more than a 99 percent chance of having a magnitude 6.7 or larger earthquake within the next thirty years.[33] Living near a fault line increases the likelihood of being more severely impacted by such a quake. In conjunction with those odds, consider the more common occurrences that will play out in the lives of California's thirty-eight million current residents over the next three decades: unemployment, vandalism, theft, medical complications, the death of a family member, the birth of an unexpected child, or economic turmoil such as high inflation, along with thousands of other circumstances which may jeopardize one's financial stability, health, and general well-being. Despite the likelihood of a large disaster, coupled with the even greater likelihood of life's common curveballs, few people actually take the steps necessary to be prepared. Dr. Howard Kunreuther, professor of decision sciences and public policy at The Wharton School, suggests a reason as to why this is:

> There are only so many things people can worry about at any point in time, and we often use decision rules that suggest if the likelihood of a devastating event is perceived low enough, then we prefer not to think about it. It is psychologically bothersome to pay attention to the possibility of suffering emotionally and financially from a natural catastrophe. Someone living in an area where earthquakes or hurricanes are frequent would rather consider the beauty of the mountains or the coastline.[34]

In short, people think that even though emergencies both large and small occur daily, they probably won't happen to them. They prioritize other pursuits over preparing for times of proverbial famine, and therefore risk endangering their ability to freely act in the future—a condition which would be especially helpful in times of emergency so as to help others in need. While there are many ways to correct this deception and begin to fulfill the responsibility of being prepared for the future, perhaps the best strategy is to incorporate preparedness-related activities into daily life. Rather than saving up for large purchases like dozens of buckets of wheat, or hundreds of rounds of ammunition, or a large tent, this approach would imply changing daily spending habits and financial priorities. Instead of simply becoming prepared for the future through infrequent purchases, trainings, and practices, those who choose to follow this daily model would be prepared in the present. The general pattern observed by Dr. Kunreuther would thus be avoided—individuals would not consider preparing for the future as being psychologically bothersome, since it would be a natural and thus somewhat subconscious part of their life.

This method of becoming prepared has been termed "provident living" by Church leaders, and it encompasses more than simply acquiring supplies during times of plenty to later be used in times of famine. It entails being a frugal steward of one's resources, both setting aside storage and savings for possible future needs while wisely providing for current needs. As Elder Robert D. Hales has said, provident living means, "joyfully living within our means, being content with what we have, avoiding excessive debt, and diligently saving and preparing for rainy-day emergencies. When we live providently, we can provide for ourselves and our families and also follow the Savior's example to serve and bless others."[35] Provident living recognizes that merely storing goods to weather a future storm is insufficient. Recall that the virgins in Christ's parable did not turn off their lamps to save oil, with a plan to light them back up as the bridegroom arrived. Their lamps were constantly lit, using oil along the way, requiring them to have sufficient on hand for both short and long term needs. Similarly, a person living providently accommodates both immediate and future needs by living frugally and preparing for unexpected future needs.

Provident living provides opportunities to experience life in ways that otherwise would be missed. Lessons learned from sacrifice, service, delayed gratification, saving for a "rainy day," gardening, repairing and caring for one's property, and other activities included in a "provident" lifestyle are priceless and commonplace when practiced daily. On this topic President Kimball suggested that we "refer to all the components of personal and family preparedness, not in relation to holocaust or disaster, but in cultivating a lifestyle that is on a day-to-day basis its own reward."[36] Preparing for the future is essential and laying up in store against a potential time of need is wise. When one prepares for emergencies in a sporadic way, provident living is abandoned in favor of a simple checklist of "to dos." Those who follow this model think not in terms of how preparing might bless their life now, but rather how preparing might make their life less miserable later. Bishop Victor L. Brown articulated the opposing ideal, namely, that "personal and family preparedness should be a way of provident living, an orderly approach to using the resources, gifts, and talents the Lord shares with us. So the first step is to teach our people to be self-reliant and independent through proper preparation for daily life."[37] Righteous stewards of God's resources don't save some of those resources for a future time and then carry on "eat[ing], drink[ing], and be[ing] merry" (see 2 Nephi 28:8). They adapt their lives to be constantly prepared for whatever might come, while enjoying and wisely using the resources they've been blessed with.

Provident living is neither defeatist nor alarmist. This type of individual is not so concerned with last days events as he is with present day events. Instead of being preoccupied by Armageddon, he works on his garden. By living in a frugal and self-reliant manner, one can prepare for the future while *enjoying* the present—after all, as President Hinckley once quipped, "Life is to be enjoyed, not just endured."[38] President Benson taught that "I believe a man should prepare for the worst while working for the best."[39] Likewise, President Wilford Woodruff once said "I would live as if [the Second Coming] were to be tomorrow—but I am still planting cherry trees!"[40] Approaching preparedness with this frame of mind places the person in a state of constant readiness for whatever may come. Describing some of the events preceding his return, Christ noted, "All things shall be in commotion; and surely, men's hearts shall fail them; for fear shall come upon all people" (D&C 88:91). On another occasion he gave the antidote: "if ye are prepared ye shall not fear" (D&C 38:30). A provident life is one that encourages the individual to become both temporally, spiritually, and emotionally prepared for times of trial.

Perhaps the most important reason to incorporate the actions of preparedness into one's daily life is the increased independence that comes as a result. The responsibility to be prepared for the future requires accumulating resources and skills in the short term that may be of future use, should the need ever arise. Following a provident living model, those resources are used and replenished routinely, and the skills are continuously applied and enhanced over time. In the long run, those who are regularly practicing preparedness become far more independent than those who bought and stored food, and perhaps learned CPR or how to use a ham radio. Independence requires action—being able to take care of one's own needs and respond to others' needs as well. For example, an individual who has stored a large quantity of wheat in his basement but has never used it is far less independent than the individual who has grown his own wheat, owns both an electric and manual grinder, and has used wheat in a variety of recipes over the years. By taking advantage of frequent opportunities to use the resources and practice the skills that would be needed in an emergency scenario, those living providently become much more self-reliant and are better able to help themselves and those around them.

SELF-RELIANCE

Brigham Young once taught: "Instead of searching after what the Lord is going to do for us, let us inquire what we can do for ourselves."[41] Likewise, Elder L. Tom Perry said that "the Lord only helps those who are willing to help themselves. He expects His children to be self-reliant to the degree they can be."[42] If even God should not be petitioned for things we can do for ourselves, than the government's emergency and welfare programs should likewise be set aside in favor of individual initiative and independent action. Even the institutional Church should not be looked to as a source of assistance when one can and should take care of himself wherever possible. In 1980, President Ezra Taft Benson noted that due to the then-existing economic difficulties of increasing taxes and inflation, some Church members were soliciting financial help from their bishops for house payments, car loans, and utilities. He then stated:

> Unfortunately, there has been fostered in the minds of some an expectation that when we experience hard times, when we have been unwise and extravagant with our resources and have lived beyond our means, we should look to either the Church or government to bail us out. Forgotten by some of our members is an underlying principle of the Church welfare plan that "no true Latter-day Saint will, while physically able, voluntarily shift from himself the burden of his own support."[43]

That principle has been consistently taught by the Church, as also noted in the same address by President Benson: "For over forty years, in a spirit of love, members of the Church have been counseled to be thrifty and self-reliant; to avoid debt; pay tithes and a generous fast offering; be industrious; and have sufficient food, clothing, and fuel on hand to last at least one year."[44] President Monson has noted that self-reliance "is an essential element in our spiritual as well as our temporal well-being."[45] Self-reliance is a core purpose and goal of the gospel. When the First Presidency established the Church's welfare program in 1936, they declared: "The aim of the Church is to help the people to help themselves. Work is to be re-enthroned as the ruling principle of the lives of our Church membership."[46] Working, or acting, is the primary component of becoming self-reliant. It is also based upon God's gift of agency, which offers to each individual the opportunity and blessing of independent action and personal accountability. God's children are made stewards over the resources with which he blesses them (see D&C 104:13, 17), and are then commanded to work (see Genesis 3:19, D&C 82:18) and take care of themselves and those within their stewardship. Self-reliance, being directly connected to the eternal principle of agency, thus "becomes a fundamental truth in the gospel plan," as President Romney taught.[47]

Becoming self-reliant allows a person to provide for himself both in times of plenty and times of famine. By being able to produce and cook food, mend clothes, repair appliances, build items, and so on, that individual can act in times of need rather than being acted upon by the circumstances around him. Further, and most importantly, in being able to independently act the self-reliant individual can come to the aid of others. As the First Presidency recently taught, God "has lovingly commanded us to 'prepare every needful thing' (see D&C 109:8) so that, should adversity come, we may care for ourselves and our neighbors and support bishops as they care for others."[48] A self-reliant individual has the independence and resources necessary to reach out and assist others, since he is not dependent upon anybody else for his food, shelter, or other necessities. The story of the good Samaritan shows how a person who fulfills the responsibility of preparedness and self-reliance is at liberty to help others in need. How many people today have the supplies and finances necessary to give aid and comfort to a suffering stranger for a week? The Samaritan in Jesus's story was in a position to help because he had the resources necessary to do so. Without those resources, he could have done little more than offer words and prayers of support.

In a study of more than five hundred emergencies, the Disaster Research Center at the University of Delaware observed that contrary to popular opinion, people in general did not panic after widespread disaster. Rather, their findings showed that people consistently work to help themselves and their neighbors.[49] While certainly beneficial when responding to immediate issues such as an injury, displacement from loved ones, or some other danger, this willingness to help cannot satisfy ongoing needs unless the resources exist to do so. Those who face such adversity will quickly need food, water, shelter, energy, protection, and emotional support. The images from Hurricane Katrina highlight what can occur in an intense disaster in just a short period. Tens of thousands were unprepared, stranded in the local football stadium and convention center, and entirely dependent upon government assistance for basic needs. Reports of rampant drug use, fights, rape, and filthy living conditions spread quickly as the situation worsened and time wore on. Looting, violence, and other criminal activity intensified in New Orleans as emergency responders focused on bigger issues, and victims were unable to defend themselves and their property. One tourist asked a police officer for assistance and was told, "Go to hell—it's every man for himself."[50] Truer words were never spoken, and that circumstance coupled with a completely unprepared people resulted in chaos, disease, death, and complete dependence. As the government inefficiently responded to the aftermath of the hurricane, a report was ordered to determine what went wrong and how to fix it in the future. "Hurricane Katrina: A Nation Still Unprepared" was the result of a special report by the US Senate's Committee on Homeland Security and Governmental Affairs.[51] The conclusion was quite obvious: the government at all levels was not prepared, even years after the events of 9/11, to respond to a disaster. But the report focused only on governmental entities, assuming that they are responsible for protecting, feeding, and sheltering those in need. In truth, the governments with jurisdiction over New Orleans were not prepared for the disaster because the *individuals* living in New Orleans were not prepared.

Suggesting that such individuals should become self-reliant and work to take care of themselves can sometimes be misinterpreted to mean something neither intended nor ideal. To many people, especially those who think they don't have the means and skills to do so, being self-reliant can sound harsh and unsympathetic. Relying on one's self, like other terms and practices connected to the gospel, must be properly defined and contextualized to be best understood and practiced. Lacking that context, one might be led to think that "self-reliance" means what it appears to suggest: relying only on one's self, and nobody else—including God. This isolationist interpretation is at odds with the way in which

Church leaders use the term. Youth are taught in the "For the Strength of Youth" manual, for example, "Self-reliance does not mean that you must be able to do all things on your own. To be truly self-reliant, you must learn how to work with others and turn to the Lord for His help and strength."[52] Elder Bruce R. McConkie explained it this way:

> Properly understood and practiced, self-reliance is a desirable saintly virtue; when it leaves the Lord out of the picture, however, it becomes a vice that leads men from the paths of righteousness. The saints, for instance, should have confidence in their own abilities, efforts, and judgments to make a living, to increase in faith and the attributes of godliness, to work out their salvation, to pass all the tests of this mortal probation. They should know that the Lord has not placed his children in positions beyond their capacities to cope with, that the normal trials and tribulations of life are part of the eternal system. . . .
>
> But with it all, man of himself is not wholly self-sufficient. He is not to trust solely in his own strength, nor in the arm of flesh. The Lord is his Counselor and Deliverer, upon whom he must rely for guidance, direction, and inspiration. If the great Creator had not stepped forward to redeem the creatures of his creating, the whole plan of salvation would be void and the most perfect manifestations of self-reliance would have no worth.[53]

Self-reliance refers to the independence that we should pursue temporally, in regards to God's other children. We are taught, for example, neither to be in bondage to others (see D&C 101:79) nor dependent upon them (see D&C 78:13-14). But it does not suggest that one should seek independence from the Lord. In fact, the opposite situation is a natural byproduct of a provident lifestyle that embraces self-reliance; those who seek to become wise stewards of the resources God has given them recognize and respect the Master to whom they are accountable as his agents. Each individual is a steward and is therefore responsible for the resources given by God:

> It is wisdom in me; therefore, a commandment I give unto you, that ye shall organize yourselves and appoint every man his stewardship;
>
> That every man may give an account unto me of the stewardship which is appointed unto him.
>
> For it is expedient that I, the Lord, should make every man

accountable, as a steward over earthly blessings, which I have made and prepared for my creatures. (D&C 104:11–13)

As stewards, we are accountable to our Master. Because God is our master, we have claim upon him when we lack the resources, knowledge, or ability to accomplish any given task. Those who seek to become wise stewards do so while recognizing their responsibility to become independent in relation to others, while also being dependent upon God, as Elder McConkie said, for guidance, direction, and inspiration.

Preparing for the future and becoming self-reliant in the present has many important benefits, both temporal and spiritual. The independence that results from freely acting rather than being acted upon allows individual liberty to flourish. Conversely, failing to prepare for unexpected life events may result in bondage and thus decreased liberty. As Elder L. Tom Perry taught: "Whenever we get into situations which threaten our self-reliance, we will find our freedoms threatened as well. If we increase our dependence on anything or anyone except the Lord, we will find an immediate decrease in our freedom to act."[54] President Heber J. Grant similarly stated: "Nothing destroys the individuality of a man, a woman, or a child as much as the failure to be self-reliant."[55]

Emergencies happen frequently, and when victims are unable to care for themselves, they become dependent on the aid of others. These victims, especially in extreme cases such as devastating natural disasters, often cry out for government assistance—thus implicitly endorsing the forcible confiscation of property from prepared people to be redistributed to the unprepared. To counteract this unfortunately common trend, the liberty-minded individual must not only prepare to maintain independence in an emergency—creating a more "provident" lifestyle, acquiring the necessary resources and skills—but also be ready to help others in exigent circumstances. Further, as we pursue this path we must encourage others to act likewise. Responding to the needs of unprepared people, whether it be unemployment-related expenses during a recession or life-altering changes resulting from an earthquake, requires a larger group of prepared people who are ready and able to freely offer the resources and skills needed to help those in need. The responsibility to become prepared and self-reliant is therefore not only a personal responsibility, but also an interpersonal one; we need to prepare to help not only ourselves, but potentially help others within our stewardship and sphere of influence.

SUGGESTIONS

The following suggestions are offered on how to better fulfill the responsibility of becoming prepared and self-reliant:

1. BUILD A SEVENTY-TWO-HOUR KIT.

When beginning to prepare for emergencies, it is often best to smart small and work your way to larger purchases and plans. Focus first on putting together a seventy-two-hour kit (sometimes called a "bugout bag") that is customized for your needs and circumstances. Avoid buying a prepackaged kit that will have items you'll never use, and which usually will not include things that you would want in the event of an emergency. In addition to basic items such as a hygiene kit, money, matches, essential medications, and so on, be sure to include food, water, and clothing appropriate for the upcoming season. Make sure to rotate these items out at least every six months.

Spend time searching online to find different suggestions of what to include, and make your kit personal to you. See http://connorboyack .com/drop/bugout.pdf for one example. Keep each person's kit in an accessible and memorable location so that the kits can quickly be retrieved in the event of an evacuation or other emergency. Also be sure that the kit is inside a container that can easily be transported, such as a lightweight hiking backpack.

2. ACQUIRE A SHORT-TERM FOOD STORAGE SUPPLY.

It's easy to store buckets of wheat. It's not easy to work that wheat into your diet. If the time comes when you're eating off of your food storage, you're going to want food that you actually want to eat, and that won't make life miserable for you. Take an inventory of what foods you regularly purchase and eat, and simply buy extra of those same items. Over time you'll essentially have your own mini grocery store in your pantry by having on hand the various items you regularly would go to the store to purchase. As you use each item, you can then replenish it with a new one, allowing you to rotate through your short-term food storage supply. In the event of an emergency, you'll then have access to normal food that will provide a sense of familiarity in your life while other circumstances might be more chaotic and stressful. You'll appreciate having some of your favorite crackers on hand when life is tough as opposed to only wheat, oats, and beans. There are many resources online that can help you prioritize what you should add to your storage, such as www.foodstoragemadeeasy.net or www.thesurvivalmom.com.

Don't forget to include water in your food storage plans. The general rule is to store one gallon per person per day to cover consumption, cooking, and hygiene during an emergency situation. Many types of food require water to prepare, so those who fail to include water in their storage will be unable to use what they had intended to eat. See http://connorboyack.com/drop/water.pdf for tips on how to store and purify water.

3. BUILD A LONG-TERM FOOD STORAGE SUPPLY.

As convenient as it is to store food you regularly eat, it often does not have a very long shelf life. Part of a well-rounded food storage supply therefore includes some of the "basics" intended for long term needs—wheat, oats, rice, beans, pasta, and so on. For maximum shelf life (up to three decades), store this food in a cool, dark, and dry place (such as a basement), ideally in sealed Mylar bags or number-ten metal cans with oxygen absorbers included.

Another long-term option is to store either dehydrated or freeze-dried food, which also lasts a very long time when stored in optimal conditions. The benefit of this approach is that the food is usually a ready-made meal that simply needs water and heat in order to be ready to eat. It's important to store a variety of foods so that if/when you must use the food, you don't quickly get tired of eating the same thing each day.

It's important to know how to use these stored goods should the time ever come to consistently use them. The information at websites such as www.everydayfoodstorage.net and www.simplylivingsmart.com, as well as others, can help you find recipes and ideas to use your long-term goods in meals that you and your family will enjoy.

4. DON'T GO INTO DEBT TO BECOME PREPARED.

The purpose of becoming prepared is to become independent and able to freely act in almost any circumstance. Going into debt to purchase preparedness items is therefore a hypocritical action, for one should not pursue independence through financial dependence. President Benson taught that "You do not need to go into debt, may I add, to obtain a year's supply. Plan to build up your food supply just as you would a savings account."[56] Similarly, the First Presidency recently stated: "We ask that you be wise as you store food and water and build your savings. Do not go to extremes; it is not prudent, for example, to go into debt to establish your food storage all at once. With careful planning, you can, over time, establish a home storage supply and a financial reserve."[57]

5. LEARN SELF-RELIANCE SKILLS.

Becoming self-reliant requires being generally independent, and thus capable of "getting by" without too much outside assistance. To work toward that goal, it's important to receive training on a variety of things such as gardening, cooking, sewing, first aid, mechanical repair, construction, physical fitness, electronics, plumbing, and so on. Learning these skills can be as simple as asking somebody who has experience with them, or more formal instruction can be sought from specialized courses or online material. As with any new skills, it's especially important to practice and gain personal experience so that if an emergency happens, you don't have to put much thought into using these skills, as they will be second nature to you.

NOTES

1. "That Noble Gift—Love at Home," *Church News*, May 12, 2001, 7.
2. Robert D. Hales, "Coming to Ourselves: The Sacrament, the Temple, and Sacrifice in Service," *Ensign*, Apr. 2012.
3. Gordon B. Hinckley, Regional Representatives' Seminar, Apr. 1, 1983.
4. In Conference Report, Apr. 1942, 88–97.
5. Stanley B. Kimball, *Heber C. Kimball: Mormon Patriarch and Pioneer* (Champaign: University of Illinois Press, 1981), 283.
6. Ibid.
7. G. D. Watt, ed., *Journal of Discourses*, vol. 4 (Liverpool: S. W. Richards, 1857), 338–9.
8. Gordon B. Hinckley, "To the Boys and to the Men," *Ensign*, Nov. 1998.
9. Gordon B. Hinckley, "If Ye Are Prepared Ye Shall Not Fear," *Ensign*, Nov. 2005.
10. Gordon B. Hinckley, "The Times in Which We Live," *Ensign*, Nov. 2001.
11. The Doctrine and Covenants was first published in 1835 as a later version of the Book of Commandments, which had been partially printed in 1833. This earlier book contained 65 early revelations to

Church leaders including Joseph Smith, Jr., and Oliver Cowdery. Before many copies of the book could be printed, however, the printing press and most of the printed copies were destroyed by a mob in Missouri.

12. Spencer W. Kimball, *Faith Precedes the Miracle* (Salt Lake City: Deseret Book, 1972), 253–56.

13. President Benson once stated that "The revelation to produce and store food may be as essential to our temporal welfare today as boarding the ark was to the people in the days of Noah." See Ezra Taft Benson, "Prepare for the Days of Tribulation," *Ensign*, Nov. 1980, 33.

14. Neal A. Maxwell, For the Power is in Them . . . (Salt Lake City: Deseret Book, 1970), 20.

15. J. Reuben Clark, *The Improvement Era*, Sep. 1961, 632.

16. Dallin H. Oaks, "Preparation for the Second Coming," *Ensign*, Apr. 2004.

17. James E. Talmage, The Parables of James E. Talmage (Salt Lake City: Deseret Book Company, 1973), 50.

18. Bruce R. McConkie, *Doctrinal New Testament Commentary*, vol. 1 (Salt Lake City: Deseret Book Company, 1973), 685.

19. Lynn G. Robbins, "Oil in Our Lamps," *Ensign*, June 2007, 47.

20. Ibid.

21. A 1959 sampling, reported in the Improvement Era, stated that "approximately 80 percent of our active Melchizedek Priesthood holders do not have on hand the essentials that will preserve life for one year." In 1975, Bishop H. Burke Peterson highlighted a Utah State University study regarding the Saint's food storage preparations, noting that only 18 percent had a year's supply of grains, and "on the average, about 30 percent of the Church had a two-month supply of food; the remainder had little or none." A few years later, in the First Presidency message in the September 1986 *Ensign*, President Monson stated: "Recent surveys of Church members have shown a serious erosion in the number of families who have a year's supply of life's necessities. Most members plan to do it. Too few have begun." Sources and more information can be found in Neil H. Leash, *Prophetic Statements on Food Storage for Latter-day Saints* (Springville, UT: Cedar Fort, 1999), 111–12.

22. Ezra Taft Benson, "Prepare for the Days of Tribulation," *Ensign*, Nov. 1980, 34.

23. Henry B. Eyring, "Let Us Raise Our Voice of Warning," *Ensign*, Jan. 2009

24. "Earthquake Facts and Statistics," USGS, accessed May 2, 2012, http://earthquake.usgs.gov/earthquakes/eqarchives/year/eqstats.php.

25. "Extreme Weather Statistics," NOAA, accessed May 2, 2012, http://www.noaa.gov/extreme2011/.

26. "2010's world gone wild: Quakes, floods, blizzards," Associated Press,

December 19, 2010, accessed May 2, 2012, http://www.msnbc.msn. com/id/40739667/ns/us_news-2010_year_in_review/t/s-world-gone-wild-quakes-floods-blizzards/.

27. Ibid.

28. Ibid.

29. Annals of Congress, House of Representatives, 3rd Congress, 1st Session, 169–70, http://memory.loc.gov/cgi-bin/ ampage?collId=llac&fileName=004/llac004.db&recNum=82.

30. Fred L. Israel and J. F. Watts, eds., *Presidential Documents: The Speeches, Proclamations, and Policies That Have Shaped the Nation from Washington to Clinton* (New York: Routledge, 2000), 165.

31. Howard W. Hunter, "The Law of the Harvest," BYU Devotional, Mar. 8, 1966.

32. Ezra Taft Benson, in Conference Report, April 1965.

33. "California Has More Than 99 percent Chance Of A Big Earthquake Within 30 Years, Report Shows," *Science Daily*, April 14, 2008, accessed May 12, 2012, http://www.sciencedaily.com/ releases/2008/04/080414203459.htm.

34. Howard Kunreuther, quoted in "Flirting with Natural Disasters: Why Companies Risk It All," FM Global, August 2010, accessed May 12, 2012, http://www.fmglobal.com/assets/pdf/P10168.pdf.

35. Robert D. Hales, "Becoming Provident Providers Temporally and Spiritually," *Ensign*, Apr. 2009.

36. Spencer W. Kimball, "Welfare Services: The Gospel in Action," *Ensign*, Nov. 1977

37. Victor L. Brown, "Welfare Services Essentials: The Bishops Storehouse," *Ensign*, Oct. 1976.

38. Gordon B. Hinckley, "Stand True and Faithful," *Ensign*, May 1996, 91.

39. Quoted in Mark E. Petersen, "Ezra Taft Benson: 'A Habit of Integrity'," *Ensign*, Oct. 1974.

40. In Conference Report, April 1950, 105.

41. John A. Widtsoe, ed., *Discourses of Brigham Young* (Salt Lake City: Deseret Book, 1941), 293.

42. L. Tom Perry, "Becoming Self-Reliant," *Ensign*, Oct. 1991.

43. Marion G. Romney, In Conference Report, Oct. 1973, 106.

44. Ibid.

45. Thomas S. Monson, "Guiding Principles of Personal and Family Welfare," *Ensign*, Sep. 1986, 3.

46. In Conference Report, Oct. 1936, 3.

47. Marion G. Romney, "Principles of Temporal Salvation," *Ensign*, Apr. 1981.

48. First Presidency, *All Is Safely Gathered In: Family Home Storage* (2007).

49. "How Self Reliance Can Get You Through Any Disaster," *Popular*

Mechanics, September 11, 2009, accessed May 12, 2012, http://www.popularmechanics.com/outdoors/survival/tips/4330416.

50. "Explosion Rocks New Orleans, Mayor Nagin Fuming," *NewsMax*, September 2, 2005, accessed May 12, 2012, http://archive.newsmax.com/archives/articles/2005/9/2/84908.shtml.

51. "Hurricane Katrina: A Nation Still Unprepared," *Special Report of the Committee on Homeland Security and Governmental Affairs* (Washington DC: US Government Printing Office, 2006).

52. First Presidency, *For the Strength of Youth* (Salt Lake City: The Church of Jesus Christ of Latter-day Saints, 2011), 41.

53. Bruce R. McConkie, *Mormon Doctrine* (Salt Lake City: Deseret Book, 1966), 701–2.

54. Perry, "Becoming."

55. Heber J. Grant, *Relief Society Magazine*, Oct. 1937, 627.

56. Ezra Taft Benson, "Prepare for the Days of Tribulation," *Ensign*, Nov. 1980, 33.

57. First Presidency, *All Is Safely Gathered In: Family Home Storage* (2007).

EDUCATION

By preventing a free market in education, a handful of social engineers, backed by the industries that profit from compulsory schooling—teacher colleges, textbook publishers, materials suppliers, and others—has ensured that most of our children will not have an education, even though they may be thoroughly schooled.[1]

—John Taylor Gatto

The best means of forming a manly, virtuous and happy people, will be found in the right education of youth. Without this foundation, every other means, in my opinion, must fail.[2]

—George Washington

What spectacle can be more edifying or more seasonable than that of Liberty and Learning, each leaning on the other for their mutual and surest support?[3]

—James Madison

QUESTIONS TO PONDER

1. Can a person who does not understand his rights defend them when they're being violated?

2. If you've finished school, what are you doing to continue your education?

3. Are you familiar with the US Constitution, and could you recognize which bills or laws are unconstitutional?

4. If you were asked to explain the various threats to individual liberty—the people funding, advocating, and popularizing them—could you do it?

*I*n his book *The Moral Basis of a Free Society*, Elder H. Verlan Andersen emphasizes the importance of education as it relates to defending individual liberty:

> One who knows not what his rights are can never know when they are taken and is unable to defend them. He is like a man who believes he owns a piece of ground which his neighbor also claims, but he doesn't know its boundaries. The neighbor continues to encroach further and further onto land he suspects is his, but since he is never certain where the boundary is, he cannot check the advance. Until he takes a firm position and says: "this far and no further," there is no line.[4]

If an individual does not know his rights are being violated, how can he defend them? These violations may be easier to discern, even for the uneducated person, when they are bold and carried out publicly. But when they occur incrementally and subtly, an individual who does not adequately understand his rights and the proper boundaries around them will be unable to do anything about it. Without the information necessary to appropriately act, he will be acted upon by those who wish to do him harm.

For this reason, education is one of the most fundamental components of enjoying and defending individual liberty. Thomas Jefferson, the individual who perhaps best understood and exemplified this connection between education and liberty, observed that "If a nation expects to be ignorant and free, in a state of civilization, it expects what never was and never will be."[5] In other words, a society of uneducated individuals will not be successful in restraining their government and maintaining their liberty. In his farewell address, President Andrew Jackson emphasized this connection: "But you must remember, my fellow-citizens, that eternal vigilance by the people is the price of liberty: and that you must pay the price if you wish to secure the blessing. It behooves you, therefore, to be watchful in your states, as well as in the federal government."[6] Those who don't know what to vigilantly watch out for cannot pay the "price" of liberty, and therefore will likely lose it. Only an informed citizenry can check the illegitimate advances of the state.

If education is necessary to maintain liberty, then institutional ignorance is necessary to maintain bondage. This adverse relationship is readily apparent in the influential writings of Frederick Douglass, a slave-turned-statesman whose passionate abolitionist writings swayed the minds of many regarding the depravity of slavery. In his autobiography, Douglass repeatedly illustrated the need of slaveholders to keep their slaves ignorant and illiterate in order to maintain control over them. For example, he writes:

> It is perfectly well understood at the south, that to educate a slave is to make him discontented with slavery, and to invest him with a power which shall open to him the treasures of freedom; and since the object of the slaveholder is to maintain complete authority over his slave, his constant vigilance is exercised to prevent everything which militates against, or endangers, the stability of his authority. Education being among the menacing influences, and, perhaps, the most dangerous, is, therefore, the most cautiously guarded against.[7]

Douglass further notes that in almost every state that permitted slavery, "there are laws absolutely prohibitory of education among the slaves. The crime of teaching a slave to read is punishable with severe fines and imprisonment, and, in some instances, with death itself."[8] "God has given [the slave] an intellect," he wrote. "The slaveholder declares it shall not be cultivated."[9] The slave was "carefully deprived of everything that tends in the slightest degree to detract from his value as property." The prospect of an educated slave was a dangerous one for slaveholders who viewed such a condition as "unmanageable,"[10] as Douglass observed.

As Douglass himself secretly learned how to read, he initially felt that his increasing knowledge was "a curse rather than a blessing."[11] "It had given me a view of my wretched condition," he observed, "without the remedy. It opened my eyes to the horrible pit, but to no ladder upon which to get out." Obtaining a better understanding of the depravity of slavery, the psychology behind it, and its pervasiveness throughout America often made him more miserable than he otherwise might have been while still ignorant of the "big picture." Despite the ordeal,

Douglass pressed onward with his self-education and also began teaching other slaves. As he later commented, knowledge was "the pathway from slavery to freedom,"[12] confirmation of Christ's teaching that "ye shall know the truth, and the truth shall make you free" (John 8:32).

While present-day circumstances are thankfully not directly comparable, important lessons should be gleaned from Douglass's observations. Just as the institution of slavery was a depraved, immoral societal trend, so too are the government policies which violate the right to life, liberty, and property of each individual—even when imposed through a majority vote. Latter-day Saints are obligated to learn about and oppose this trend (see D&C 98:10, 134:1) as part of establishing the kingdom of God on the earth, by "awake[ning] to a sense of [our] awful situation" (Ether 8:24), a process that requires an extensive education covering "things both in heaven and in the earth, and under the earth; things which have been, things which are, things which must shortly come to pass; things which are at home, things which are abroad; the wars and the perplexities of the nations, and the judgments which are on the land; and a knowledge also of countries and of kingdoms" (D&C 88:79). We are further counseled to "teach one another" and seek wisdom "out of the best books" (D&C 88:118).

This awakening process can produce many of the same feelings that Douglass himself felt upon realizing the magnitude of the "awful situation," albeit in different degrees than he experienced. For instance, consider the staggering sum of money owed by the United States government. As of now the total federal debt is $16 trillion, with future liabilities (for government programs such as Social Security, Medicare, and Medicaid) weighing in at $118 trillion. That's a total of $134 *trillion*—a colossal number that's easy to say but difficult to comprehend. The following explanations will help contextualize the "awful situation" that this debt has helped create for ourselves and our posterity. If you were to spend $10 million every day, it would take you 273 years to spend just $1 trillion. A four-inch stack of $1,000 bills would be $1 million. To reach $1 billion, the stack would have to be 364 feet high. But to reach $1 trillion, the stack would be 63 miles in height! Of course, visualizing the impact of what a trillion really is still does not convey the magnitude of the federal debt and liabilities, since it would have to be multiplied by 134. It's little wonder why President Ronald Reagan called the trillion number "incomprehensible."[13]

Becoming educated about "the wars and the perplexities of the nations" can also produce feelings of misery and hopelessness. The most conservative reports on the US-instigated military intervention in Iraq estimate that over one hundred thousand Iraqi civilians have been killed.[14] This violence has produced, according to the Iraq government, some five million orphans.[15] Thousands of innocents have similarly been killed in Afghanistan, where the United States government has had its military engaged for over a decade.[16] Remote-controlled drone strikes are occurring in several other countries. In Pakistan, for example, over two thousand people have been reported killed as a result of such aerial strikes, including some 175 children.[17] Hundreds of thousands have been killed, even more have been wounded, and roughly eight million people have been displaced from their homes and families—all through the offensive warfare of the United States government.[18] Nearly $4 trillion has been spent over the past decade in pursuit of such results.[19] Five thousand US soldiers have been prematurely sent to their deaths, and tens of thousands have been wounded[20]—to say nothing of the long-term psychological, social, and spiritual damage inflicted upon those who were spared bodily harm. When President Dwight D. Eisenhower, a former five-star military general, gave his farewell address in 1961, he emphatically warned about what he called the "military-industrial complex"—a "permanent armaments industry of vast proportions" whose existence has "grave implications."[21] The magnitude of this military machine, suggested Eisenhower, must be restrained and tempered appropriately. "In the councils of government," he said, "we must guard against the acquisition of unwarranted influence, whether sought or unsought, by the military-industrial complex. The potential for the disastrous rise of misplaced power exists and will persist." Eisenhower further made clear the imperative of being educated about what this military-industrial complex has done in our name:

> We must never let the weight of this combination endanger our liberties or democratic processes. We should take nothing for granted. Only *an alert and knowledgeable citizenry* can compel the proper meshing of the huge industrial and military machinery of defense with our peaceful methods and goals, so that security and liberty may prosper together.[22]

Awakening to a sense of our awful situation through education, and then being in a position to do something about it, applies to a variety of other issues: the war on drugs and the skyrocketing incarceration rate in America;[23] the downward-spiraling morality of society and the increasing permissiveness of promiscuous behavior;[24] the profound inequality among God's children and the lack of resources in many parts of the world;[25] the oppressiveness of centralized governments and the degree to which the Constitution has been disregarded;[26] and a lengthy list of other issues of great importance. Gaining wisdom through education allows an individual to understand the nature of the problem, which is the first step, so that he can help to fix it. Douglass understandably felt that because of his slavery, this newfound knowledge offered "no ladder upon which to get out." His persistence and motivation to succeed despite these initial feelings of despair helped him to realize that a ladder was there all along, and that he was in fact climbing it. By doing so, Douglass eventually gained his freedom and then became a powerful force in freeing others. Becoming aware of the awful situations around us is not an effort meant to send the student into a paralyzing depression, but rather to enable him to break free of the chains of bondage. Just after writing that God has commanded us to awake to a sense of our awful situation, Moroni noted that he was commanded to write it that each person might "be persuaded to do good continually, that they may come unto the fountain of all righteousness and be saved" (Ether 8:26). Thus, education is itself a ladder "to get out" of ignorance and bondage—even if the hole is deep and the ladder seems to ascend forever.

Education is ennobling and empowering. It arms each person with the knowledge necessary to take action and be an agent unto himself (see 2 Nephi 2:5). It is one of the more fundamental personal responsibilities, for the others all require learning information and skills in order to be fulfilled. Whether working to free ourselves from literal bondage, as in Frederick Douglass's case, or from financial, spiritual, emotional, or political bondage, as is more common in our day, Douglass's prescription is accurate: the knowledge obtained through education is "the pathway from slavery to freedom."

DUMBING US DOWN

That educational pathway from slavery to freedom, like any other path leading to increased liberty and restrained government, is riddled with roadblocks. The educational system itself presents a massive hurdle that must be overcome—individually and collectively—if a thorough and truthful education is to be obtained. The very nature and purpose of the modern public school system in America produces an end result that consistently declines in quality over time. This trend led President Gordon B. Hinckley in the late 1990s to say that it was the "age of utter mediocrity."[27] Fourteen years prior, a government-appointed group called the National Commission on Excellence in Education agreed with President Hinckley's characterization of societal mediocrity. After an eighteen-month study, the commission's report noted: "The educational foundations of our society are presently being eroded by a rising tide of mediocrity that threatens our very future as a Nation and a people."[28] The gravity of the situation was emphasized by the report, which made the following observation:

> If an unfriendly foreign power had attempted to impose on America the mediocre educational performance that exists today, we might well have viewed it as an act of war. As it stands, we have allowed this to happen to ourselves.[29]

Contrasting the results of today's educational system with those of an earlier era offers support for this criticism. In colonial times, literacy soared; John Adams once observed that "A native of America who cannot read and write is as rare an appearance . . . as a Comet or an Earthquake."[30] On top of mastering English, those who received a formal education in early America usually learned several other languages as well. Latin and Greek were taught, and children would learn grammar, history, poetry, and other subjects in those languages. Classical education also stressed the liberal arts, such as grammar, dialectic (logic), and rhetoric (known together as the "trivium"), as well as arithmetic, geometry, music, and astronomy (the "quadrivium"). Looking at the lives of some of the well-known patriots from the founding generation offers examples of the results of this education. As a youth, Thomas Jefferson learned Latin, Greek, and French from Reverend William Douglas, a Scottish clergyman who ran a classical academy. To enter King's

College (now Columbia University) in 1773, Alexander Hamilton was required to already have mastered Greek and Latin grammar, be able to read three orations from Cicero and Virgil's *Aeneid* in the original Latin, and be able to translate the first ten chapters of the Gospel of John from Greek into Latin. James Madison's application to the College of New Jersey (now Princeton) meant he had to be able to "write Latin prose, translate Virgil, Cicero, and the Greek gospels, and [to have] a commensurate knowledge of Latin and Greek grammar."[31] Madison had done that and more, already having read Virgil, Horace, Justinian, Nepos, Caesar, Tacitus, Lucretius, Eutropius, Phaedrus, Herodotus, Thucydides, and Plato, among others.[32] Classical education meant that this material was not learned in college, but *applied* in college; students were required to already have mastered these subjects in their younger years. Noah Webster highlighted the educational trend of the day as follows: "The minds of youth are perpetually led to the history of Greece and Rome or to Great Britain; boys are constantly repeating the declamations of Demosthenes and Cicero or debates upon some political question in the British Parliament."[33]

Several of the founders, including John Adams, attended Harvard. The academic requirements for admission to Harvard University in the 1640s were, simply: "When any scholar is able to read Tully [Cicero] or such like classical Latin author *ex tempore* and make and speak true Latin in verse and prose *suo (ut aiunt) Marte* [by his own power, as they say], and decline perfectly the paradigms of nouns and verbs in the Greek tongue, then may he be admitted into the college, nor shall any claim admission before such qualification."[34] In a world of standardized testing, this educational climate seems antiquated, if not anachronistic. Liberal arts and language were keystones of the education received by students in early America, in contrast to today, and even those who didn't receive a formal education were still exposed to and sought after such source material for their benefit. As the prolific educator and author John Taylor Gatto notes, "Young people in America were expected to make something of themselves, not to prepare themselves to fit into a pre-established hierarchy. Every foreign commentator notes the early training in independence, the remarkable precocity of American youth, their assumption of adult responsibility."[35] In short, individuals in early America generally recognized and fulfilled their individual responsibility of education, seeking learning however and wherever they could—especially in the home.

A century later, and after the educational system had become more structured and formal throughout the country, the academic discipline required of students was still quite rigorous. For example, consider the following selection of questions from an 8th grade final examination given to students in Kansas in 1895.[36] While reviewing the questions (excerpted from a much longer list), ponder how well students of the same age might perform today:

Name the parts of speech and define those that have no modifications.

Find the interest of $512.60 for eight months and eighteen days at 7 percent. [Calculators, of course, had not yet been invented.]

Describe three of the most prominent battles of the Rebellion.

Write ten words frequently mispronounced and indicate pronunciation by use of diacritical marks and by syllabication.

Name and locate the principle trade centers of the US.

Could today's students answer such questions? If not, why not? To be sure, tests in public school today are sometimes equally challenging—though often presented with "multiple choice" answers. Kids today do learn difficult concepts, and receive instruction on a variety of topics. But are they truly learning the material, and more important, are they learning *how* to learn? While experiences vary wildly and though there are always exceptions to the norm, many commentators agree that the educational system of recent decades is consistently producing subpar results as time progresses—this despite all levels of government throwing significant quantities of money at the problem. Though it spends more money per student than any other country, the United States recently ranked thirty-second among other nations for mathematics proficiency and seventeenth place for reading.[37] Results from the 2010 National Assessment of Educational Progress showed that just 13 percent of high school seniors showed solid academic performance in American history.[38]

Statistics are interesting to use in determining whether children are truly receiving an education, but the anecdotal assertions of one student brings the issue sharply to life. Erica Goldson, valedictorian of her high school in New York for the graduating class of 2010, rebuked the system that she had just finished working her way through for not offering a real opportunity to become educated. Conceding that she did in fact learn some things while being required by the very nature of the system to "memorize names, places, and dates to later on forget in order to clear your mind for the next test," she attempted in her speech to draw a contrast between "school" and "education." Speaking to her fellow classmates, school faculty, and guests, she said:

> School is not all that it can be. Right now, it is a place for most people to determine that their goal is to get out as soon as possible.
>
> I am now accomplishing that goal. I am graduating. I should look at this as a positive experience, especially being at the top of my class. However, in retrospect, I cannot say that I am any more intelligent than my peers. I can attest that I am only the best at doing what I am told and working the system. Yet, here I stand, and I am supposed to be proud that I have completed this period of indoctrination. I will leave in the fall to go on to the next phase expected of me, in order to receive a paper document that certifies that I am capable of work. But I contest that I am a human being, a thinker, an adventurer—not a worker. A worker is someone who is trapped within repetition—a slave of the system set up before him. But now, I have successfully shown that I was the best slave. I did what I was told to the extreme.
>
> While others sat in class and doodled to later become great artists, I sat in class to take notes and become a great test-taker. While others would come to class without their homework done because they were reading about an interest of theirs, I never missed an assignment. While others were creating music and writing lyrics, I decided to do extra credit, even though I never needed it. So, I wonder, why did I even want this position? Sure, I earned it, but what will come of it? When I leave educational institutionalism, will I be successful or forever lost? I have no clue about what I want to do with my life; I have no interests because I saw every subject of study as work, and I excelled at every subject just for the purpose of excelling, not learning. And quite frankly, now I'm scared.[39]

Goldson's bold speech gives a true "insider" view of the modern public school system by one who learned and mastered its rules and followed its mandates to the letter. It is an example of what the influential writer H. L. Mencken once cynically observed about the modern American educational system: "The aim . . . is simply to reduce as many individuals as possible to the same safe level, to breed and train a standardized citizenry, to put down dissent and originality."[40] For her part, Goldson agreed: "Between these cinderblock walls, we are all expected to be the same. We are trained to ace every standardized test, and those who deviate and see light through a different lens are worthless to the scheme of public education, and therefore viewed with contempt."

Memorizing and regurgitating facts and data does not instill in students a desire to learn nor does it grant the mechanisms necessary to proactively pursue such a desire. While teachers exist within the school system who sincerely want to inspire and help educate their students, the nature and methods of the system make such goals extremely difficult. The institutionalized and monopolistic school system today does not engender individuality, creativity, and exploration. It is not so much concerned with inspiring youth to independently pursue their own educational paths as it is about homogenizing educational practices and tests into a "conveyor belt" system that churns out consistent results deemed desirable by bureaucrats overseeing the system. Educator and author Oliver DeMille explains the nature and danger of this conveyor belt system:

> [Public schools] are set up like a factory: everyone in the class gets the same education at the same age from the same textbooks, and they are tested the same and graded based upon the same scale regardless of their individual interests, talents or goals.
>
> The goal is to give students the same ideas, and to grade and rank them according to their conformity with these ideas. In this system you go down the factory line, first grade, second grade, third grade, with a factory worker at each station, being assembled with certain parts (the curriculum) at a certain point in a certain way from a common book or manual. Of course, all of the products (students) are fitted with the same parts (called "education") as everyone else on the conveyor belt. When you finish twelfth grade, you get a stamp (diploma) on your forehead signifying that you are a finished product ready to be sold to the job market.[41]

Of course, things don't magically change when students graduate from this educational system and enroll in a college or university. A professor at Dartmouth College who "quickly became aware of the utter bewilderment of entering freshmen"[42] observed in a 1996 op-ed that "they emerge from the near-nullity of K-12 and stroll into the chaos of the Dartmouth curriculum" unprepared for what they are required to already know—let alone what they will be expected to learn. This professor assigned the students in his freshman composition course to read the first half of the then-newly-released book *The Closing of the American Mind* by Allan Bloom—a book that is severely critical of what the modern educational system has become. "They hated it," wrote the professor. He continued:

> Oh, yes, they understood perfectly well what Bloom was saying: that they were ignorant, that they believed in clichés, that their education so far had been dangerous piffle and that what they were about to receive was not likely to be any better.
>
> No wonder they hated it. After all, they were the best and the brightest, Ivy Leaguers with stratospheric SAT scores, the Masters of the Universe. . . .
>
> So I launched into an impromptu oral quiz. Could anyone (in that class of 25 students) say anything about the Mayflower Compact? Complete silence. John Locke? Nope. James Madison? Silentia. Magna Carta? The Spanish Armada? The Battle of Yorktown? The Bull Moose party? Don Giovanni? William James? The Tenth Amendment? Zero. Zilch. Forget it. The embarrassment was acute.[43]

Trained to perform well in tests, many students lose focus on truly learning the material they're being required to review. They are indoctrinated with information (often useless to their future careers and personal interests) in a system that conflates school and education— two things that are not always mutually inclusive. As Gatto notes, the school system so prevalent today "has ensured that most of our children will not have an education, even though they may be thoroughly schooled."[44] To be sure, even within a public school system children can receive a quality education and excel—especially if they have access to caring teachers who buck the bureaucracy and use innovative methods within the system to allow the child to flourish. Even so, the system is stacked against such exceptions; some twenty-five hundred kids drop out of high school each day,[45] and those who survive to the finish line are not necessarily prepared for college or a career. Commenting on recent data showing that only 25 percent of high school graduates possessed the academic skills necessary to pass entry-level college courses, Jack Jennings, president of the Center for Education Policy, observed that even when students "aren't dropping out physically, they are dropping out mentally."[46] The system—a product of some $600 billion spent annually in America for primary and secondary schools[47]—is producing exactly what it was designed by its engineers to produce:[48] a dumbed-down, compliant people who have had their individuality drained out of them by a system that promotes and rewards mediocrity.[49]

Despite the apparent decline in educational quality,[50] many still proceed through the system and graduate with their paper certificates attesting to their test-taking ability. But those who criticize the school system's inability to offer a thorough education have plenty of data to back them up. In the 1990s, a survey was conducted of high school graduates four to eight years out of school, and the participants overwhelmingly stated that they had been well educated during their teen-age years;[51] 68 percent said they had learned math well, 66 percent believed they had been taught to write well, and 78 percent stated that they learned to read well. The high school graduates generally concluded that they had mastered the subjects they were taught. A stark contrast emerges when reviewing the results of employers hiring these high school graduates. Only 30 percent of employers believed that their new hires could read well, 22 percent thought that their employees had adequate math skills, and only 12 percent thought that these high school graduates could write well. Very similar and negative results were reported from colleges and universities surveyed regarding the high school graduates they had accepted for admission. Maturing into adulthood does not solve this general trend, of course. For example, a recent *New York Times* article highlighted some of the educational deficiencies in today's society: "American adults in general do not understand what molecules are (other than that they are really small). Fewer than a third can identify DNA as a key to heredity. Only about 10 percent know what radiation is. One adult American in five thinks the Sun revolves around the Earth, an idea science had abandoned by the seventeenth century."[52]

In her valedictorian speech, Goldson expressed hope for the future despite the school system that hinders educational initiative and independence. "We are thinkers, dreamers, explorers, artists, writers, engineers," she said. "We are anything we want to be—but only if we have an educational system that supports us rather than holds us down. A tree can grow, but only if its roots are given a healthy foundation." These wise words suggest both the problem and the remedy: education—for students both young and old—must have fertile soil in which to grow strong roots. The individual responsibility to receive an education implies that it is up to each person to seek that education however and wherever circumstances permit. Even the most inspiring and effective teachers cannot force a student to learn—the student must have the desire, interest, and ability to acquire, retain, and apply new knowledge. All education is ultimately self-education; a person cannot be forced to learn any more than he can be forced to have faith in God. Thus, a student can personally pursue an education even in a schooling system designed to encourage the memorization and regurgitation of data through mandatory homework, strict teachers, and a required curriculum. Some of the world's brightest minds were either school dropouts, educated only by their parents, or sought an education on their own through books and apprenticeships. A school system designed to dumb down the general population cannot hinder the education of those who understand this personal responsibility and aim to fulfill it, no matter the obstacle. As Elder Russell M. Nelson once said: "in the pursuit of education, individual desire is more influential than institution, and personal faith more forceful than faculty."[53] In the end, it's up to each individual to fulfill this responsibility.

THE GLORY OF GOD

The glory of God is intelligence (D&C 93:36). The liberating laws that God has established, and which he himself obeys,[54] require that we each understand them before being held accountable for them. That is to say, we must know the laws before we can receive blessings from being obedient to them. Each of us, therefore, holds a sacred responsibility to receive an education. Whether these laws are self-evident in nature or conveyed through prophetic revelation, each person must learn them (either intellectually or experientially) on his or her own.

This is not to say, of course, that the process of fulfilling this educational responsibility is an isolated one for each individual. Indeed, education is and always has been an interconnected endeavor, where

God's children reason with and teach one another (see D&C 50:10–12). Professional educators, mentors, leaders, authors, relatives, and many other influences in a person's life can offer exposure to new information, ideas, and insights that will inspire that person to learn. For children, however, the ultimate duty for providing them with educational opportunities lies with the parents. President Ezra Taft Benson counseled:

> Parents, stay close to your children; you cannot delegate your responsibility to the educators no matter how competent they may be. Parents have a duty to train their children, to talk over their problems with them, to discuss what they are learning at school. And it is neither wise nor safe . . . to leave the determination of our educational system and policies exclusively to the professional educators.[55]

While parents are duty-bound to help their children fulfill their own responsibility to receive an education, it is not enough to simply create in the home a microcosm of what the school system has become. "Parents are not simply to teach their children," taught Elder David A. Bednar. "Rather, they are to teach them to understand."[56] More important than inculcating information into a child is fostering attitudes and abilities that will enable that child to learn on his or her own and pursue the passions and intellectual interests that he or she uniquely possesses. Paramount to this teaching process is the use of persuasion and example—a method that recognizes and respects the independence of each individual in pursuing their own education. That educational method, as President Benson taught, "must be based on freedom—never force."[57] It is most successful when a child sees his or her parents as fellow students, learning along the way as the child does the same. Authoritarian attitudes will rarely help cultivate a child's innate desire to learn. Rather, parents should position themselves as mentors, consulting with their child throughout the educational process and helping to point them in the direction of truth. They should be sources of inspiration more than mere information. As President Dieter F. Uchtdorf said, "Education is not so much the filling of a bucket as the lighting of a fire."[58]

Parents and supporting educators alike must remember the purpose and end goal of education: to become like God. For this reason, noted

Elder Russell M. Nelson, "we consider the obtaining of an education to be a religious responsibility."[59] Knowing the quadratic equation, the process of cell division, or how many men signed the Declaration of Independence may be useful and interesting, but a thorough education is one which equips the individual with the capacity and knowledge necessary to one day return to God's presence. As one scripture declares, "It is impossible for a man to be saved in ignorance" (D&C 131:6). Joseph Smith taught the Saints that "Knowledge saves a man, and in the world of spirits a man cannot be exalted but by knowledge."[60] The necessity of learning, along with its eternal implications, is one of the most oft-repeated themes of modern-day revelations.

In the October 1944 general conference, Elder John A. Widtsoe remarked on the educational ends and attitudes of the Saints: "Dominion of the earth will ultimately be in the hands of those who know, and use their powers intelligently," he said. "Therefore, as a people we believe in education—the gathering of knowledge and the training of the mind. The Church itself is really an educational institution. Traditionally, we are an education-loving people."[61] Latter-day Saints are counseled in scripture to pursue an education throughout their lives, leading into the eternities. "Whatever principle of intelligence we attain unto in this life, it will rise with us in the resurrection. And if a person gains more knowledge and intelligence in this life through his diligence and obedience than another, he will have so much the advantage in the world to come" (D&C 130:18–19).

Since the majority of one's education will come during adulthood, it should be plainly evident that formal schooling is not exclusively vital to this process. As President Henry B. Eyring has said, "Our education must never stop." He continued:

> If it ends at the door of the classroom on graduation day, we will fail. And since what we will need to know is hard to discern, we need the help of heaven to know which of the myriad things we could study we would most wisely learn. It also means that we cannot waste time entertaining ourselves when we have the chance to read or to listen to whatever will help us learn what is true and useful. Insatiable curiosity will be our hallmark.[62]

Even those who cannot afford a professionally prepared education are able and encouraged to gain whatever knowledge they can;

intelligence, or the glory of God, is not limited only to those who can pay for it. President Dieter F. Uchtdorf taught:

> If formal education is not available, do not allow that to prevent you from acquiring all the knowledge you can. Under such circumstances, the best books, in a sense, can become your "university"—a classroom that is always open and admits all who apply. Strive to increase your knowledge of all that is "virtuous, lovely, or of good report or praiseworthy." Seek knowledge "by study and also by faith." Seek with a humble spirit and contrite heart. As you apply the spiritual dimension of faith to your study—even of temporal things—you can amplify your intellectual capacity, for "if your eye be single to [God's] glory, your whole [body] shall be filled with light, . . . and [comprehend] all things."[63]

Education is a fundamental component of the moral agency God has given to each of his children. "For behold, ye are free," declared Samuel the Lamanite. "Ye are permitted to act for yourselves; for behold, God hath given unto you a knowledge and he hath made you free" (Helaman 14:30). As we increase our intellectual capacity and learn "things both in heaven and in the earth, and under the earth; things which have been, things which are, things which must shortly come to pass; things which are at home, things which are abroad" (see D&C 88:79–80), we proportionally increase our ability and effectiveness as God's agents on earth. Conversely, those who do not responsibly educate themselves, and who instead willingly remain in ignorance, subject themselves to being placed in bondage by others who know and are able to do more. The opportunities available to an uneducated adult are few and far between. He will likely be paid a low wage (if he can find a job), will probably have to work long hours (or more than one job) to meet his financial obligations, and this financial stress often brings with it decreased time for family and other pursuits outside of work. On the other hand, an educated individual stands a far greater chance of gaining access to a variety of career opportunities that offer a higher wage and more accommodating "perks" allowing for family time, vacation, and opportunity to pursue hobbies and interests outside of work. Thus, an educated person is more free and able to "act" of his own accord, in contrast to the uneducated person who, more often than not, becomes "acted upon" by the circumstances of his environment and whatever limited opportunities he can find.

Those who fulfill the responsibility of receiving an education are also better able to defend their individual liberty. While bloody revolutions are fortunately infrequent, the intellectual political battles that result in lost liberties are ongoing. False ideas of the proper role of government abound, and countering them requires a principled, educated, and active group of individuals who can persuasively demonstrate why certain policies are immoral, illegitimate, or otherwise inadvisable. When reading through essays from the founding generation, one cannot fail to appreciate the brilliant discourse of the enlightened minds that fought the intellectual battle of the Revolution. As just one of countless examples, consider the persuasive success of Thomas Paine's pamphlet *Common Sense*. It remains to this day the bestselling and most widely circulated book in American history relative to the population of the time. Published on January 10, 1776, it articulately argued for colonial America's independence from the Crown. It was so influential that John Adams (who was no fan of Paine's work) later observed: "Without the pen of the author of 'Common Sense,' the sword of Washington would have been raised in vain."[64] The effort to reclaim and maintain individual liberty has been and always will be dependent on the intellectual abilities of those who fight for it.

The founders recognized the connection between education and liberty. They understood that an ignorant populace would be easily duped into surrendering the freedom that had been obtained for them at such great sacrifice. "The most effectual means of preventing the perversion of power into tyranny are," wrote Thomas Jefferson, "to illuminate, as far as practicable, the minds of the people at large, and more especially to give them knowledge of those facts, which history exhibits, that possessed thereby of the experience of other ages and countries, they may be enabled to know ambition under all its shapes, and prompt to exert their natural powers to defeat its purposes."[65] Noah Webster, an extremely educated and liberty-oriented patriot of the founding era, likewise observed: "It is an object of vast magnitude that systems of Education should be adopted and pursued, which may not only diffuse a knowledge of the sciences, but may implant, in the minds of the American youth, the principles of virtue and of liberty and inspire them with just and liberal ideas of government, and with an inviolable attachment to their own country."[66]

Whether seeking to become like God, or building up the kingdom of God on the Earth, or advancing the cause of liberty, the pathway is the same. Education is one of the most basic and essential of responsibilities, and one that is a prerequisite to all other responsibilities. Joseph Smith taught that "God has created man with a mind capable of instruction, and a faculty which may be enlarged in proportion to the heed and diligence given to the light communicated from heaven to the intellect."[67] Light and liberty are inseparably connected. "The glory of God is intelligence, or, in other words, light and truth" (D&C 93:36). That truth, taught Jesus Christ, "shall make you free" (John 8:32). Our educational priorities and processes must be focused on learning about, obeying, and advocating for these liberating truths, including the unalienable rights of each individual and the eternal laws that God has provided to help us one day return to his presence. "If you wish to go where God is," taught Joseph on another occasion, "you must be like God, or possess the principles which God possesses, for if we are not drawing toward God in principle, we are going from Him and drawing towards the devil. . . . As far as we degenerate from God, we descend to the devil and lose knowledge, and without knowledge we cannot be saved."[68] Our ability to become free and follow God requires that we each independently fulfill the personal responsibility of obtaining (and applying) an education—a life-long process with an eternal reward.

SUGGESTIONS

The following suggestions are offered on how to better fulfill the responsibility of receiving an education:

1. DEVELOP A READING LIST OR STUDY PROGRAM.

The founders recognized the benefit to be gained from reading the books of great men and women throughout history. The product of their wisdom is a testament to their educational prowess. The classic literature from which they read helped in more ways than one, as one historian notes:

The classics supplied mixed government theory, the principal basis for the US Constitution. The classics contributed a great deal to the founders' conception of human nature, their understanding of the nature and purpose of virtue, and their appreciation of society's essential role in its production. The classics offered the founders companionship and solace, emotional resources necessary for coping with the deaths and disasters so common in their era. The classics provided the founders with a sense of identity and purpose, assuring them that their exertions were part of a grand universal scheme. The struggles of the Revolutionary and Constitutional periods gave the founders a sense of kinship with the ancients, a thrill of excitement at the opportunity to match their classical heroes' struggles against tyranny and their sage construction of durable republics. In short, the classics supplied a large portion of the founders' intellectual tools.[69]

While textbooks contain a great deal of information (not all of it accurate, truthful, or praiseworthy), they do not offer the student unabridged access to the mind of the person who invented or discovered the information. Learning from others through a fragmented, excerpted process will rarely inspire the student to incorporate and imitate the brilliance of another person. Classical literature and other sources—especially the scriptures—offer a much more inspired and inspiring view of the world and the many "languages, tongues, and people" (D&C 90:15) that are part of it.

A variety of suggested reading lists can be found by searching online. Read book reviews, ask well-read friends, and compile your own list of books you'd like to read. As you read them, consider taking notes or sharing your thoughts with others on a blog or social networking site. Being able to paraphrase what you're learning in your own words will help you internalize the material much more quickly than simply reading through each book.

2. Seek learning "by faith" (D&C 88:118).

After commanding the Saints to explore books for words of wisdom, God noted that education should be obtained both by study and also by faith. This latter component is one that received much attention in early America, including in the early days of the LDS Church (when church-run schools were prevalent), but that has been sidelined by an increasingly secularized educational system. God has been sidelined in public schools, and the bureaucrats often prohibit mere mentions of Jesus Christ.

Whether constrained by such a system or free to incorporate religious instruction and insight into their education through home or private schooling, students are nevertheless always able, regardless of circumstances, to seek learning by faith. President Joseph Fielding Smith taught, for example, "knowledge comes both by reason and by revelation."[70] Prayer and pondering can be employed by anybody desiring to have the mysteries of God unfolded to them. As the Book of Mormon teaches us, learning "is good if [we] hearken unto the counsels of God" (2 Nephi 9:29).

3. Take advantage of free material.

Traditional textbooks are often costly, outdated, and sometimes full of misinformation and bias. Free course content online, while not necessarily completely accurate or free of bias, can allow you to more easily access and review information on a variety of topics. Universities are increasingly putting entire courses online for free, such as MIT and Harvard (see www.edxonline.org), Stanford (itunes.stanford.edu), University of California at Berkeley (webcast.berkeley.edu), and many others. See www.openculture.com/freeonlinecourses for a lengthy of list of other courses and educational material.

The Ludwig von Mises Institute has scores of free books (see www .mises.org/Literature) and also offers an academy to take brief courses from some of their associated professors (academy.mises.org). Historian Tom Woods and other professors also offer some excellent material through Liberty Classroom (www.libertyclassroom.com). The Khan

Academy (www.khanacademy.org) also offers thousands of free educational videos on dozens of topics.

4. ESTABLISH LEARNING BEHAVIORS.

Success in your educational endeavors will be more likely if you develop structural aides to assist you. Consider setting aside daily study time, preferably early in the morning, to consistently allow you to study and ponder your scriptures and other chosen material. Take a class at a local college or other educational institute to expose you to new ideas and perspective. Create a list of new words you would like to learn, or challenge yourself to memorize scriptures, important quotes, or other beneficial information. By consistently challenging yourself you will more quickly and fully learn your chosen material.

5. SEEK OUT MENTORSHIPS AND APPRENTICESHIPS.

Thomas Jefferson's greatness was due in large part to his mentor and fellow statesman, George Wythe. Other founders likewise had their loyal and earnest teachers who inspired and pushed them to excel. Today's educational system has largely shifted away from mentorships and apprenticeships to a format where a variety of specialized teachers instruct and make assignments to large classes of students with whom they can rarely personally connect. Finding a mentor, whether for a child or an adult, allows direct access to a person with the wisdom and willingness to inspire and motivate that person to succeed. Mentors can and should be used in pursuit of a broad, liberal arts education that provides a strong foundation for the rest of that student's life.

General education, while important, cannot adequately prepare those seeking to specialize in a career such as a pianist, podiatrist, or professional pole-vaulter. Many careers require specific training in order to be successful. Apprenticeships can offer dedicated students an opportunity to shadow a person who is already successful in a certain career or hobby, acquiring the skills and insights that can only effectively be taught through dedicated instruction and application. "On the job" training is and always has been more effective and enjoyable than reading about that job in a book.

Adults who are past their age of formal schooling might consider being a mentor for a child other than their own, or where relevant and feasible to their career or professional skill, offer to take on an apprentice.

6. Join like-minded study groups.

Your educational path will be more exciting if you can share it with others who are learning similar things. Consider finding a study group in your area, whether it be a simple book club, a college course you can audit, or an organization that offers classes or social activities that relate to your issue of interest. If no such groups exist where you live, start one! You can also explore online forums to connect with people around the world who share your interests and with whom you can converse about what you're learning.

Notes

1. John Taylor Gatto, *Dumbing Us Down* (Canada: New Society Publishers, 2005), 85.
2. W.W. Abbot, ed., *The Papers of George Washington: Confederation Series*, vol. 2 (Charlottesville, VA: University Press of Virginia, 1992), 183.
3. Ralph Louis Ketcham, *James Madison: A Biography* (Charlottesville, VA: University Press of Virginia, 1990), 658.
4. H. Verlan Anderson, *The Moral Basis of a Free Society* (Orem, UT: Hans V. Andersen, Jr., 1995), 70.
5. Foley, *The Jefferson Cyclopedia*, 274.
6. Edwin Williams, ed., *The Addresses and Messages of the Presidents of the United States, Inaugural, Annual, and Special, from 1789 to 1846*, vol. 2 (New York: Edward Walker, 1849), 957.
7. Frederick Douglass, *My Bondage and My Freedom* (New York: Miller, Orton & Mulligan, 1855), 432.
8. Ibid., 431–32.
9. Ibid., 408.
10. 10 Frederick Douglass, *Narrative of the Life of Frederick Douglass* (Harvard College, 2009), 44.
11. Ibid., 50.
12. Ibid., 44.
13. Richard Reeves, *President Reagan: The Triumph of Imagination* (New York: Simon & Schuster, 2005), 21.
14. Neta C. Crawford, "Civilian Death and Injury in Iraq, 2003–2011," Boston University, September 2011, 1.
15. "Occupation's Toll: 5 Million Iraqi Children Orphaned," AlterNet, December 18, 2007, accessed May 12, 2012, http://www.alternet.org/world/70886/?page=entire.
16. "Afghanistan civilian casualties: year by year, month by month," *The Guardian*, March 12, 2012, accessed May 12, 2012, http://www.guardian.co.uk/news/datablog/2010/aug/10/afghanistan-civilian-casualties-statistics.

17. "Drone War Exposed—the complete picture of CIA strikes in Pakistan," The Bureau of Investigative Journalism, August 10, 2011, accessed May 12, 2012, http://www.thebureauinvestigates.com/2011/08/10/most-complete-picture-yet-of-cia-drone-strikes/.

18. "Cost of war at least $3.7 trillion and counting," Reuters, June 29, 2011, accessed May 12, 2012, http://www.reuters.com/article/2011/06/29/us-usa-war-idUSTRE75S25320110629.

19. Ibid.

20. "Counting the cost of the 9/11 wars," The Guardian, August 22, 2011, accessed May 12, 2012, http://www.guardian.co.uk/world/2011/aug/22/9-11-wars-war-on-terror.

21. Michael S. Mayer The Eisenhower Years (New York: Facts on File, Inc., 2010), 913.

22. Ibid., emphasis added.

23. The "war on drugs" has cost, at the federal level alone, $2.5 trillion to date. As of 2004, drug crimes accounted for 21 percent of state prisoners and 55 percent of all federal prisoners. In 1980, 30,000 people were in jail for drugs, while as of 2008 there were half a million. See Connor Boyack, Latter-day Liberty: A Gospel Approach to Government and Politics (Springville, UT: Cedar Fort, 2011), 224.

24. As one of many data points which might be used in support of this claim, consider the alarming rate at which premarital cohabitation is occurring. "In the late 1960s, only about 10 percent of American couples moved in together first. . . . Today, about 60 percent of couples live together before they first marry." See "Cohabitation before marriage? It's no greater divorce risk," Associated Press, March 22, 2012, accessed May 12, 2012, http://www.csmonitor.com/The-Culture/Family/2012/0322/Cohabitation-before-marriage-It-s-no-greater-divorce-risk.

25. Half of the world lives on $2.50 per day or less. An estimated average of seventeen thousand children die per day from hunger. The world's riches reside in the hands of a comparative few. One's life expectancy in the world's poorest countries is half of what it would be living in the world's richest countries. See Boyack, Latter-day Liberty, 233.

26. Hundreds of millions of innocent people have been murdered by their own government. See Rummel, Death by Government.

27. Gordon B. Hinckley, "Stand Up for Truth," BYU Devotional, September 17, 1996.

28. "A Nation at Risk: The Imperative for Educational Reform," The National Commission on Excellence in Education, April 1983.

29. Ibid.

30. John Adams, The Adams Papers (Cambridge, MA: Harvard University Press, 1977), 120.

31. Carl J. Richard, The Founders and the Classics: Greece, Rome, and the

American Enlightenment (Cambridge, MA: Harvard University Press, 1994), 19.

32. Ibid, 18.

33. Ibid, 13.

34. Ibid, 19.

35. John Taylor Gatto, *The Underground History of American Education* (Oxford: The Oxford Village Press, 2006), 5.

36. "Examination Graduation Questions of Saline County Kansas, April 13, 1895," Smoky Valley Genealogical Society, accessed May 12, 2012, http://skyways.lib.ks.us/genweb/saline/society/exam.html.

37. "Globally Challenged: Are U.S. Students Ready to Compete?," Harvard Kennedy School, August 2011, accessed May 12, 2012, http://www.hks.harvard.edu/pepg/PDF/Papers/PEPG11-03_GloballyChallenged.pdf.

38. "Report: Students don't know much about US history," Associated Press, June 14, 2011, accessed May 12, 2012, http://www.msnbc.msn.com/id/43397386/ns/us_news-life/t/report-students-dont-know-much-about-us-history/.

39. "Coxsackie-Athens High School Valedictory Speech 2010," Erica Goldson, accessed May 12, 2012, http://americaviaerica.blogspot.com/2010/07/coxsackie-athens-valedictorian-speech.html.

40. H. L. Mencken, "The Library" *American Mercury Magazine*, January to April 1924, 504.

41. Oliver DeMille, *A Thomas Jefferson Education: Teaching a Generation of Leaders for the Twenty-First Century* (Cedar City, UT: George Wythe College Press, 2006), 25.

42. Jeffrey Hart, "How to Get a College Education," National Review, September 30, 1996, accessed May 12, 2012, http://old.nationalreview.com/flashback/hart200603131050.asp.

43. Ibid.

44. John Taylor Gatto, *Dumbing Us Down: The Hidden Curriculum of Compulsory Schooling* (Gabriola Island, BC: New Society Publishers, 2005), 85.

45. "The School Drop Out Crisis," Pew Partnership for Civic Change, 2006, accessed May 12, 2012, http://www.pew-partnership.org/pdf/dropout_overview.pdf.

46. "Scores Stagnate at High Schools," *Wall Street Journal*, August 18, 2010, accessed May 12, 2012, http://online.wsj.com/article/SB10001424052748703824304575435831555726858.html?mod=WSJ_WSJ_US_News_3.

47. "Public Education Finances," United States Census Bureau, accessed May 12, 2012, http://www2.census.gov/govs/school/09f33pub.pdf.

48. See John A. Stormer, *None Dare Call it Education* (Florissant, MO: Liberty Bell Press, 1999), 39–50.

49. Boyack, *Latter-day Liberty*, 205–206.

50. See Charles J. Skyes, *Dumbing Down Our Kids* (New York: St. Martin's Press, 1995), 16–24.

51. Ibid, 29.

52. "Scientific Savvy? In U.S., Not Much," *New York Times*, August 30, 2005, accessed May 2, 2012, http://www.nytimes.com/2005/08/30 / science/30profile.html?ex=1125547200&en=631977063d726261 &ei=5070.

53. Russell M. Nelson, "Where Is Wisdom?," *Ensign*, Nov. 1992, 6.

54. Boyack, *Latter-day Liberty*, 37.

55. Ezra Taft Benson, "Three Threatening Dangers" in Conference Report, Oct. 1964.

56. "Understanding is a Wellspring of Life . . . ," Ricks College Campus Education Week Devotional, June 3, 1999, accessed May 12, 2012, http://www2.byui.edu/Presentations/Transcripts/EducationWeek /1999_06_03_Bednar.htm.

57. Ezra Taft Benson, The Red Carpet (Salt Lake City: Bookcraft, 1962), 177.

58. Dieter F. Uchtdorf, "Two Principles for Any Economy," *Ensign*, Oct. 2009.

59. "Where Is Wisdom?," *Ensign*, Nov. 1992, 6.

60. Thomas Ward, ed., *The Latter-day Saints' Millennial Star*, vol. 5 (Liverpool: Thomas Ward, 1845), 91.

61. John A. Widtsoe, "The Returning Soldier," Conference Report, Oct. 1944.

62. Henry B. Eyring, "Education for Real Life," *Ensign*, Oct. 2002.

63. Uchtdorf, "Two Principles for Any Economy."

64. Quoted in Jill Lepore, "The Sharpened Quill," *The New Yorker*, Oct. 16, 2006, http://www.newyorker.com/archive/2006/10/16/061016crbo_books

65. Foley, *The Jefferson Cyclopedia*, 405.

66. Robert Hamlett Bremner, *Children and Youth in America: A Documentary History*, vol. 1, 1600–1865 (Cambridge: Harvard University Press, 1970), 223.

67. B. H. Roberts, *History of the Church of Jesus Christ of Latter-day Saints*, vol. 2 (Salt Lake City: Deseret News, 1904) 8.

68. Roberts, *History of the Church*, vol. 4, 588.

69. Richard, *The Founders and the Classics*, 8.

70. Joseph Fielding Smith, "Educating for a Golden Era of Continuing Righteousness," *A Golden Era of Continuing Education* (Provo, UT: Brigham Young University, 1971), 2.

CIVIC DUTY

The price of freedom has been too high, and the consequences of non-participation are too great for any citizen to feel that they can ignore their responsibility.[1]

—Elder Quentin L. Cook

Cherish, therefore, the spirit of our people, and keep alive their attention. Do not be too severe upon their errors, but reclaim them by enlightening them. If once they become inattentive to the public affairs, you and I, and Congress and Assemblies, Judges and Governors, shall all become wolves.[2]

—Thomas Jefferson

QUESTIONS TO PONDER

1. Is the Constitution "hanging by a thread"? If so, how did it happen?

2. Congress has a 9 percent approval rating[3] but an average reelection rate in the 90–95 percentile for incumbents.[4] Why is this so?

3. Why does most political discussion in the media resort to simple sound bites and talking points?

4. How should we as individuals be involved in the political process?

*T*hroughout the history of The Church of Jesus Christ of Latter-day Saints, Church leaders have repeatedly spoken out on political matters. This has occurred not so much because prophets feel it their duty to opine on controversial topics of temporal relevance, but because the spiritual and temporal elements of our lives are understood by Latter-day Saints to be, at their core, one and the same (see D&C 29:34–35). We have therefore received instructions and commandments regarding our civic duty right alongside similar commandments regarding our spiritual duties as members of the Church. Fulfilling home teaching responsibilities, magnifying our callings, worshipping in the temple, and paying our tithes and offerings are on an equal platform, in some regard, with our responsibility to study, support, and defend the principles of liberty.

President John Taylor spoke of this intertwining of our responsibilities when he said that the Elders of Israel should "understand that they have something to do with the world politically as well as religiously, that it is as much their duty to study correct political principles as well as religious."[5] Further, as Elder Bruce R. McConkie said: "To worship the Lord is to stand valiantly in the cause of truth and righteousness, to let our influence for good be felt in civic, cultural, educational, and governmental fields, and to support those laws and principles which further the Lord's interests on earth." Our responsibility to be engaged in civic matters—to defend individual liberty and uphold one another's agency—is paramount. How else can we battle against the illegitimate interventions of the state except by taking part in the fight? Sidelined observers surrender to the opposition.

This counsel has been consistent since the early days of the gospel's restoration. When open violence broke out against the Church for the first time, the Lord gave Sections 97 and 98 of the Doctrine and Covenants as an anticipatory response to the Saints' natural desire for revenge. On July 20, 1833, an organized mob had destroyed the printing press owned by William W. Phelps, forcefully ejected many Saints from their homes, and tarred and feathered two men on the public square in Independence, Missouri. Verse 9 of Section 98 contains the truism "when the wicked rule the people mourn"—a succinct summary statement of what the early Mormons had to deal with. After this assessment, the Lord provided the following counsel to the Saints: "Wherefore, honest men and wise men should be sought for diligently, and good men and wise men ye should observe to uphold; otherwise whatsoever is less than these cometh of evil" (D&C 98:10).

This, then, is the charge given to the Latter-day Saints in regards to choosing leaders in government: seeking and supporting honesty, wisdom, and goodness (and, of course, opposing the opposites of these traits). A casual analysis of our current political landscape would find few instances of the aforementioned virtues. We seem to be repeating the mistakes of the past, learning for ourselves the truism that has never changed: "when the wicked rule the people mourn." In the end, though, we have ourselves to blame for wicked rulers, for they ascended to and remain in power only with our consent—either directly through voting or indirectly through inaction and apathy.

The leaders of a nation are generally a reflection of the masses over which they rule. A virtuous, liberty-loving people will only tolerate candidates and statesmen whose record and rhetoric match their beliefs and desires. An apathetic populace indifferent to liberty will, on the other hand, allow men and women to rise to power whose selfish desires for power, money, or fame will result in the violation of individual liberty and a host of other evils. Without an awakened and active electorate willing to defend liberty through all means possible, the people will be progressively made to mourn through the entrenched and persistent usurpation of power. President Gordon B. Hinckley's call for principled statesmanship demonstrates this dichotomy:

> We are involved in an intense battle. It is a battle between right and wrong, between truth and error, between the design of the Almighty on the one hand and that of Lucifer on the other. For that reason, we desperately need moral men and women who stand on principle, to be involved in the political process. Otherwise, we abdicate power to those whose designs are almost entirely selfish.[6]

We as a people have reaped what we have historically sewn: corrupt politicians, scandalous back-room deals, oppressive laws, unjust legal codes, and systematic violations of individual liberty are the result of our long-term unwillingness to stand on principle and be involved in the political process. Latter-day Saints, more than any other group of people, must recognize and act on their responsibility to be aware of and engaged in civic affairs.

Four Components of Our Civic Duty

In a 1986 Brigham Young University devotional address, President
Ezra Taft Benson laid out a brief summary of what our civic duty
entails. Prefacing his remarks, President Benson noted that we were
then fast approaching the moment prophesied by Joseph Smith when he
said, "Even this Nation will be on the very verge of crumbling to pieces
and tumbling to the ground and when the constitution is upon the
brink of ruin this people will be the Staff up[on] which the Nation shall
lean, and they shall bear the Constitution away from the very verge
of destruction."[7] The suggestion that Latter-day Saints will play an
important part in restoring the principles embodied in the Constitution
implies that we must first understand what they are, and be adequately
prepared to play our part in their preservation. Latter-day Saints are
under an obligation to support the inspired Constitution[8]—and by
extension, to defend and advance the principles of individual liberty it
was instituted to protect. After rhetorically asking whether we will be
prepared to save the imperiled Constitution, President Benson lists four
things we must each do.

The first item on President Benson's list deals with virtue:

> We must be righteous and moral. We must live the gospel prin-
> ciples—all of them. We have no right to expect a higher degree
> of morality from those who represent us than what we ourselves
> are. To live a higher law means we will not seek to receive what
> we have not earned by our own labor. It means we will remember
> that government owes us nothing. It means we will keep the laws
> of the land. It means we will look to God as our Lawgiver and the
> source of our liberty.[9]

To the outsider it may seem odd that the first listed item for a Latter-
day Saint's civic duty is to live a clean and just life, but here again we
witness the fusion of temporal and spiritual matters into one. While we
should seek a higher standard in morality and virtue, we should still recognize that we are all imperfect people charged with a great responsibility. As President Gordon B. Hinckley taught: "The Lord uses imperfect
people—you and me—to build strong societies. If some of us occasionally stumble, or if our characters may have been slightly flawed in one
way or another, the wonder is the greater that we accomplish so much."[10]

Personal righteousness and morality are not necessary individually in order to understand and defend liberty; anyone can support true political principles and abide by them, even if other aspects of their life are found lacking in virtue. But when immorality becomes a collective characteristic espoused by a majority, then liberty is unlikely to be generally understood, let alone adequately protected. Father Lehi taught that we "are free to choose liberty and eternal life . . . or to choose captivity and death" (2 Nephi 2:27), suggesting that those who violate God's commandments place themselves on a path that leads to bondage, not liberty. "Where the Spirit of the Lord is, there is liberty" (2 Corinthians 3:17), taught the apostle Paul. Conversely, those whose lives are not in accordance with the principles of the gospel will not be as successful in understanding and thus supporting liberty.

President Benson's second recommended item we must do to save the Constitution and support liberty reads as follows:

> We must learn the principles of the Constitution and then abide by its precepts. Have we read the Constitution and pondered it? Are we aware of its principles? Could we defend it? Can we recognize when a law is constitutionally unsound? The Church will not tell us how to do this, but we are admonished to do it.

It should be obvious that one cannot abide by principles, let alone teach them to others, without first knowing and understanding them. In spiritual matters God tells us that we should "first seek to obtain [his] word" (D&C 11:21) before declaring it to others. Similarly, we must be students of the Constitution and the principles of individual liberty before we can teach them to others. Latter-day Saints generally recognize the inspired nature and importance of the Constitution, yet a comparative few likely understand the historical setting in which it was created, the debates and discussions that resulted in its final draft, and the political implications its mandates have for our day. An informed and alert citizenry is the first line of defense against the illegitimate encroachments of the state. Contrast the superficial understanding many have today of proper political principles, and their corresponding unwillingness or inability to support liberty, with the founding generation of which James Madison spoke:

> The freemen of America did not wait till usurped power had strengthened itself by exercise and entangled the question in

precedents. They saw all the consequences in the principle; and they avoided the consequences by denying the principle. We revere this lesson too much soon to forget it.[11]

In other words, an informed and alert citizenry can object to an encroachment when it is first introduced merely on intellectual and philosophical grounds, by being able to observe and point out the violation of principle it would cause. Yet an uninformed populace would not be able to, as President Benson suggested, "recognize when a law is constitutionally unsound." As Thomas Jefferson said: "If a nation expects to be ignorant and free. . . . it expects what never was and never will be."[12] "One who knows not what his rights are," said Elder H. Verlan Andersen, "can never know when they are taken and is unable to defend them."[13]

In section 84 of the Doctrine and Covenants, the Lord says that Zion is under condemnation for treating lightly the revealed scriptures, namely, the Book of Mormon. This condemnation, he said, would remain until we "repent and remember the new covenant, even the Book of Mormon and the former commandments which [he has] given [us], not only to say, but also to do according to that which [he has] written" (D&C 84:57). Here we find application for other divinely inspired documents the Lord has helped to create, such as the Constitution, which themselves carry a charge and obligation to be read and acted upon. Anytime the Lord commands something to be done and we then fail to do our part, we are under condemnation. This leads to President Benson's third suggestion:

> We must become involved in civic affairs. As citizens of this republic, we cannot do our duty and be idle spectators. It is vital that we follow this counsel from the Lord: "Honest men and wise men should be sought for diligently, and good men and wise men ye should observe to uphold; otherwise whatsoever is less than these cometh of evil." (D&C 98:10).
>
> Note the qualities that the Lord demands in those who are to represent us. They must be good, wise, and honest. We must be concerted in our desires and efforts to see men and women represent us who possess all three of these qualities.

Living a clean life and becoming informed are insufficient to actually defend agency and liberty. To fight for these important causes, we must actually *fight*. President Hinckley's statement that we "desperately" need principled people involved in politics reminds us of the consequence of failing to do so: "otherwise, we abdicate power to those whose designs are almost entirely selfish." President Thomas S. Monson painted the gloomy picture of that exact circumstance having come to fruition: "We live in a complex world with currents of conflict everywhere to be found. Political machinations ruin the stability of nations, despots grasp for power, and segments of society seem forever downtrodden, deprived of opportunity, and left with a feeling of failure."[14] This may very well be a manifestation of the Lord's statement that "when the wicked rule the people mourn." God's antidote was made clear, as repeated by President Benson: we should seek out and support leaders who are good, honest, and wise. Doing so requires, of course, that we ourselves embody those characteristics so that we can identify them in others and, without any hypocrisy on our part, hold them accountable to the same standard to which we adhere.

The Lord's admonition to uphold good, honest, and wise men implies not just voting for them at the ballot box and then continuing on with our lives. Consider the story of the Israelites engaged in a long war with the Amalekites. Moses found that by raising his hands with the rod of God, the Israelites prevailed, whereas when he let his hands down they failed. Holding up his hands was a tiring affair, however, so Aaron and Hur each stood by his side and "stayed up his hands" (Exodus 17:12). In supporting leaders for positions of leadership, we should sustain and assist them to the extent possible, so that together we can advance the cause of liberty. Further, our involvement in civic affairs cannot be postponed for later in life; as President Benson noted on another occasion, we must be involved and active right now:

> The Prophet Joseph Smith declared it will be the elders of Israel who will step forward to help save the Constitution, not the Church. And have we elders been warned? Yes, we have. And have we elders been given the guidelines? Yes indeed, we have. And besides, if the Church should ever inaugurate a program, who do you think would be in the forefront to get it moving? It would not be those who were sitting on the sidelines prior to that time or those who were appeasing the enemy. It would be those choice spirits who, not waiting to be "commanded in all things" (D&C 58:26), used their own free will, the counsel of the prophets, and

the Spirit of the Lord as guidelines and who entered the battle "in a good cause" (D&C 58:27) and brought to pass much righteousness in freedom's cause. . . .

Brethren, if we had done our homework and were faithful, we could step forward at this time and help save this country. The fact that most of us are unprepared to do it is an indictment we will have to bear. The longer we wait, the heavier the chains, the deeper the blood, the more the persecution, and the less we can carry out our God-given mandate and worldwide mission. The war in heaven is raging on the earth today. Are you being neutralized in the battle?[15]

Four and a half decades have passed since the Saints were asked this question. Have we improved? Are we passing on even more difficult circumstances and "heavy chains" to our children by neglecting our duty? The need has never been greater to step forward and be actively involved in the developments of our community, state, and nation. As Elder L. Tom Perry has said, "we should use our free agency and be actively engaged in supporting and defending the principles of truth, right, and freedom."[16] Going to vote on Election Day might make us feel like we're involved, but if that is the extent of our involvement in civic affairs, and then we have fallen short of the standard that is required of Latter-day Saints.

President Benson's fourth and final step for fulfilling our civic duty is perhaps the most important: "We must make our influence felt by our vote, our letters, and our advice. We must be wisely informed and let others know how we feel." As we become more politically active in our communities, we will not only become better informed as to the troubles of our day and their possible solutions, but we will have more opportunities to share our knowledge and thoughts with others. We are all on a battlefront in the war of ideas, and even our involvement in civic affairs is not enough to oppose the enemy who is launching his attacks from every angle. Our petitions and votes and campaigns and any other product of our civic involvement will have little impact unless we convince those around us of the virtue of our cause. Without this secondary and supplementary goal, others who will one day take our place will soon overturn our work. Building a structure of good government matters little in the long run if the foundation is weak and rotten. Thus, once informed and engaged, we must persuade and educate others. President Hinckley taught:

I urge you with all the capacity that I have to reach out in a duty that stands beyond the requirements of our everyday lives; that is, to stand strong, even to become a leader in speaking up in behalf of those causes that make our civilization shine and that give comfort and peace to our lives. You can be a leader. You must be a leader.[17]

These words echo those of the Prophet Joseph, who said that "it is our duty to concentrate all our influence to make popular that which is sound and good, and unpopular that which is unsound."[18] Fortunately, speaking up and making our influence felt is far easier today than it was when President Benson mentioned its importance years ago. Elder M. Russell Ballard explains:

Today we have a modern equivalent of the printing press in the Internet. The Internet allows everyone to be a publisher, to have his or her voice heard, and it is revolutionizing society. Before the Internet there were great barriers to printing. It took money, power, influence, and a great amount of time to publish. But today, because of the emergence of what some call "new media," made possible by the Internet, many of those barriers have been removed. New media consists of tools on the Internet that make it possible for nearly anyone to publish or broadcast to either a large or a niche audience . . . . The emergence of new media is facilitating a worldwide conversation on almost every subject, including religion, and nearly everyone can participate. This modern equivalent of the printing press is not reserved only for the elite.[19]

Think of it: a medium of communication that, like the printing press long ago, is "revolutionizing society." Its importance becomes even clearer when we consider the eternal impact of the educational process we're responsible for encouraging in others. As President Harold B. Lee said:

The kingdom of God must be a *continuing revolution against the norms of the society* that fall below the standards that are set for us in the gospel of Jesus Christ. In the field of public life, it must be a continuing revolution against proposals that contradict the fundamental principles as laid down in the Constitution of the United States, which was written by men whom God raised up for this very purpose. If we remember that, *we will be in the forefront of every battle against the things that are tearing down our society.*[20]

The path that God has in mind for us may not involve holding elected office, but being a person of influence can in many ways have a greater effect upon the direction our society is headed. Some of us may be the good, honest, and wise men to be supported for positions of leadership. Others may prefer to support those leaders as they themselves are supporting the principles of individual liberty. President David O. McKay once said that "every loyal member of the Church [should] look down with scorn upon any man or woman who would undermine [the] Constitution."[21] In light of our current political situation, there are, of course, limitless opportunities to look down with scorn[22] upon those who are undermining this divinely inspired document. If our necks become sore from looking downward with derision at so many conniving politicians, then the responsibility we have to find people we can look up to becomes all the more important.

To radiate our positive influence in civic affairs, we must become righteous and moral; as Gandhi said, we must be the change we wish to see in the world. We must dedicate the time and energy necessary to sufficiently understand agency, liberty, and the principles the Constitution was instituted to protect. Then we should become involved in applying those ideas, infusing our political system with their disinfecting simplicity and principled restraints. We must become leaders and work diligently to support good people in positions of leadership, or seek those positions ourselves. And finally, we must radiate our influence by exposing the ideas we know to be true to those who might be impacted and uplifted by our actions, words, and character.

PROPHETIC ENCOURAGEMENT

Our responsibility to be involved in political matters and discharge our civic duty has been repeatedly reaffirmed by leaders of the Church. Half a century ago, President Harold B. Lee noted that "Patriotism and loyalty in defense of the Constitution of the United States is constantly enjoined upon us."[23] A few examples will demonstrate this consistent call for civic engagement. In 1968, the First Presidency said:

> We urge our members to do their civic duty and to assume their responsibilities as individual citizens in seeking solutions to the problems which beset our cities and communities.

With our wide ranging mission, so far as mankind is concerned, Church members cannot ignore the many practical problems that require solution if our families are to live in an environment conducive to spirituality.

Individual Church members . . . should . . . be "anxiously engaged" in good causes, using the principles of the gospel of Jesus Christ as their constant guide.[24]

Five years later, another letter they issued read as follows: "We urge members of the Church and all Americans to begin now to reflect more intently on the meaning and importance of the Constitution, and of adherence to its principles."[25] In 1979, they wrote to "encourage all members, as citizens of the nation, to be actively involved in the political process."[26] In 1987, another letter stated:

We encourage Latter-day Saints throughout the nation to familiarize themselves with the Constitution. They should focus attention on it by reading and studying it. They should ponder the blessings that come through it. They should recommit themselves to its principles and be prepared to defend it and the freedom it provides. (D&C 109:54) . . .

Because some Americans have not kept faith with our Founding Fathers, the Constitution faces severe challenges. Those who do not prize individual freedom are trying to erode its great principles. We believe the Constitution will stand, but it will take the efforts of patriotic and dedicated Americans to uphold it . . . . We, as Latter-day Saints, must be vigilant in doing our part to preserve the Constitution and safeguard the way of life it makes possible.[27]

In 1998, they said:

We wish to reiterate the divine counsel that members "should be anxiously engaged in a good cause, and do many things of their own free will, and bring to pass much righteousness" while using gospel principles as a guide. Therefore, as in the past, we urge members of the Church to be full participants in political, governmental, and community affairs. Members of the church are under special obligation to seek out and then uphold those leaders who are wise, good, and honest.[28]

In 2000 the First Presidency issued a letter to "encourage men and women in the Church to serve in public offices of either election or appointment."[29]

These and a host of other related quotes from Church leaders demonstrate an institutional exhortation to be involved in government and politics. President Hinckley's warning about selfish men acquiring power if we do not get involved (after learning and adhering to principle) has gone mostly unheeded and the consequence he noted—wicked men gaining power—has become more evident. Modern prophets have not been the only ones to warn us of this trend, nor has the connection between inaction and tyranny been a recent one. The Book of Mormon tells the story of two large civilizations—the Nephites and the Jaredites—which rose and fell in the Western Hemisphere. Moroni, commanded by God to summarize their demise and provide for us a lesson, explicitly states that "secret combinations" (conspiring, wicked individuals) caused the destruction of both civilizations. Their ultimate implosion resulted not from a natural disaster, or invasion, or famine, or any other external and unexpected event. Rather, they allowed conspiring tyrants to infest their governments, gain political power, and rule with an iron fist. They sowed seeds of wickedness and disobedience, and reaped the consequences. After recounting these events, Moroni states:

> Wherefore, O ye Gentiles, it is wisdom in God that these things should be shown unto you, that thereby ye may repent of your sins, and suffer not that these murderous combinations shall get above you, which are built up to get power and gain—and the work, yea, even the work of destruction come upon you, yea, even the sword of the justice of the Eternal God shall fall upon you, to your overthrow and destruction if ye shall suffer these things to be.
>
> Wherefore, the Lord commandeth you, when ye shall see these things come among you that ye shall awake to a sense of your awful situation, because of this secret combination which shall be among you; or wo be unto it, because of the blood of them who have been slain; for they cry from the dust for vengeance upon it, and also upon those who built it up.
>
> For it cometh to pass that whoso buildeth it up seeketh to overthrow the freedom of all lands, nations, and countries; and it bringeth to pass the destruction of all people, for it is built up by the devil, who is the father of all lies. (Ether 8:23–25)

Two great civilizations fell because of conspiring, power-lusting, wicked individuals gaining influence and governing as dictators. A cursory review of the world's history easily finds dozens of similar examples, along with their tragic consequences. But the Book of Mormon story in particular, along with its prophetic warning for our own day, must not go unheeded. Said President Hinckley:

> The Book of Mormon narrative is a chronicle of nations long since gone. But in its descriptions of the problems of today's society, it is as current as the morning newspaper and much more definitive, inspired, and inspiring concerning the solutions of those problems.
>
> I know of no other writing which sets forth with such clarity the tragic consequences to societies that follow courses contrary to the commandments of God. Its pages trace the stories of two distinct civilizations that flourished on the Western Hemisphere. Each began as a small nation, its people walking in the fear of the Lord. But with prosperity came growing evils. The people succumbed to the wiles of ambitious and scheming leaders who oppressed them with burdensome taxes, who lulled them with hollow promises, who countenanced and even encouraged loose and lascivious living. These evil schemers led the people into terrible wars that resulted in the death of millions and the final and total extinction of two great civilizations in two different eras.[30]

The last few sentences should sound extremely familiar: scheming leaders, burdensome taxes, hollow (campaign) promises, loose morality, and terrible wars have become a common occurrence in our time. Collusion and corruption are now simply part of doing business in Congress. While it's difficult to pinpoint secret combinations with any certainty and without the benefit of hindsight or investigation, few would deny that such things exist—especially given ample historical evidences and prophetic warnings about our day. One publicly available data point, however, suggests that such circumstances are not altogether "secret," and starkly depicts the consequences of not fulfilling our responsibility to be citizen activists. In 2010, 12,951 registered lobbyists spent a total of $3.5 billion influencing Congress.[31] That amounts to twenty-four lobbyists and $6.5 million for each member of Congress. It also equals over $17 million spent on lobbying for every day Congress was in session. With corporate interests investing so much into securing favorable legislation for themselves, the interests, concerns, and individual rights of the average citizen have been shoved to the backseat—if not kicked off the bus altogether by some politicians. While everybody (including corporations, which are simply organizations of individual citizens) has the right to petition their government, the lucrative revolving door established between Congress and corporate America amounts to little more than bribery. The same companies who benefit from the legislation they seek to have passed help fund the reelection campaigns of the politicians who play along. While this example does not entail the murderous component of historical secret combinations, it does involve power and riches—recall that Moroni said such combinations would be built up in our day "to get power and [monetary] gain."

Moroni indicates that God has commanded us to "awake to a sense of your awful situation." An awakening implies that we are, or were previously, asleep. Two important statements by President Benson touch on this subject, and highlight the consequences of not "awakening."

> It is the devil's desire that the Lord's priesthood stay asleep while the strings of tyranny gradually and quietly entangle us until, like Gulliver, we awake too late and find that while we could have broken each string separately as it was put upon us, our sleepiness permitted enough strings to bind us to make a rope that enslaves us.
>
> For years we have heard of the role the elders could play in saving the Constitution from total destruction. But how can the elders be expected to save it if they have not studied it and are not sure if it is being destroyed or what is destroying it?[32]

While Satan's desire is clear and well known, President Benson also pointed out some of his strategy: "The devil knows that if the elders of Israel should ever wake up, they could step forth and help preserve freedom and extend the gospel. Therefore the devil has concentrated, and to a large extent successfully, in neutralizing much of the priesthood. He has reduced them to sleeping giants."[33] In a world of distraction, instant gratification, and constant competition for our attention, society has largely become indifferent toward our individual responsibility to be involved in civic matters. We have fallen asleep, yet we are commanded to awaken. Two questions arise from this situation: how are we to wake up (and awaken others), and once awake, how do we appropriately discharge our civic duty?

CITIZEN ACTIVISM

Perhaps a question to be considered even before these is whether we are in fact asleep, speaking collectively. Providing an answer to such a question is difficult, since finding a single metric upon which to judge "sleepiness" (political inactivity) is not an easy task. Though it doesn't factor in all the myriad other ways in which we might be involved, the most obvious criteria is voter turnout—how many of us show up to the ballot box to determine which good, honest, and wise men will be elected to a position of power and political influence? Voting in elections is hardly a fulfillment of one's civic duty, yet it nevertheless may be considered a small factor. Viewing the data on voter turnout may therefore shed some light on how well we are participating in a small part of the political process.

A 2005 report by the *Salt Lake Tribune* shows that while the percentage is slowly declining, over 75 percent of residents in Utah County, Utah, are members of the Church.[34] Given its high concentration of Latter-day Saints, this county is the best option for determining the voting activity of Church members. This data is not statistically significant for the entire Church at large, of course, but it still provides some interesting insights if interpreted correctly. Considering general elections only (those which receive significant attention in the media), here are the percentages of voter turnout in Utah County in recent years: 48 percent in 2010; 65 percent in 2008; 44 percent in 2006; 80 percent in 2004; 49 percent in 2002; and 77 percent in 2000. Primary elections produced far less participation: 15 percent in 2010; 10 percent in 2008; 18 percent in 2006; 17 percent in 2004; 8 percent in 2002; and 23 percent in 2000.[35]

Assuming that the 25 percent of Utah County who are not members of the Church did not significantly alter the overall voter turnout, this data shows a dismal rate of participation in something as infrequent and basic as casting a vote on election day. If we Latter-day Saints fail to devote the time and energy required to study the issues and determine which candidates we will support, how will we ever rise to the higher bar of civic duty that has been enjoined upon us? In what may be considered a rebuke in light of this dismal data, President Spencer W. Kimball said: "The only way we can keep our freedom is to work at it. Not some of us. All of us. Not some of the time, but all of the time."[36]

The single data point presented here suggests that the Latter-day Saints are collectively "asleep." Further, reviewing the sizable percentage of straight party-line voters suggests that many of those who even show up to vote are not informed enough about the candidates and issues to make a case-by-case decision on the merits of each. Many Latter-day Saints are simply uninformed and uninvolved—asleep at the proverbial wheel, apathetic to what's going on around them. How, then, does such a person "wake up"?

Scriptures that contain the encouragement to awaken often have a connecting verb suggesting how that process is to be accomplished. Isaiah says to "awake, put on strength" (Isaiah 51:9) and "awake, stand up" (Isaiah 51:17). Paul counseled the Saints to "awake to righteousness, and sin not" (1 Corinthians 15:34). One of Moroni's last recorded verses exhorts us to "awake, and arise from the dust" (Moroni 10:31). Lehi's fatherly rebuke of Laman and Lemuel contains perhaps the most comprehensive example: "Awake, my sons; put on the armor of righteousness. Shake off the chains with which ye are bound, and come forth out of obscurity, and arise from the dust" (2 Nephi 1:23). When the scriptures refer to waking up, this means that the individual has gone through an intellectual and spiritual educational process. His understanding has increased, and what he before did not see is now manifested in plain view. When Jacob preached repentance to his fellow Nephites, he noted that it was "expedient that I should awake you to an awful reality of these things" (2 Nephi 9:47)—in other words, he was interrupting their slumber by bringing an important issue to the forefront of their minds. In King Benjamin's address, he taught his people that they "should awake to a remembrance of the awful situation of those that have fallen into transgression" (Mosiah 2:40). Moroni's warning that we "awake to a sense of [our] awful situation" (Ether 8:24) requires learning about the activities and consequences of the secret combination to which he refers.

While awakening from our slumber is a necessary step, this educational component alone is insufficient. Thus we read in the verses just mentioned, as well as in others, that we need to awake and then arise, stand up, shake off the chains, put on the armor of righteousness, and so on. These are active verbs, referring to actions that we must take after becoming aware and informed of the problems and needs around us. Speaking of the inaction in his own day in reference to priesthood holders within the Church, Elder Wilford L. Woodruff noted: "All the trouble is our eyes have been closed, we have been in a deep sleep; let us wake up and attend to our duty, and make it the first business we do."[37] This reference to "attending to our duty" summarizes the various action verbs previously presented; by fulfilling our personal responsibilities, including those outlined in this book, we complete the "awakening" process.

Like a snoring sleeper who occasionally is jolted into semi-consciousness by an unusual noise, a startling dream, or a spouse jockeying for more of the bedspread, the slumbering electorate has at times engaged in significant outbursts of civic responsibility. During the 2008 presidential campaign, for example, Barack Obama rallied his Democratic base on a package of anti-war, pro-civil liberties policies, which were consistently promoted to contrast George Bush's reckless foreign policy of military adventurism and domestic policy of building a police state. Obama was publicly appalled that Bush was indefinitely detaining individuals accused of being or supporting terrorists, and supported legislation that granted these detainees the right to habeas corpus. His voting base was extremely energized and ready to bury the "Bush Doctrine" in the past. Those same people, however, have remained almost universally silent as the same man who once opposed such abuses has augmented and accelerated them as president. Among other hypocritical reversals of his hollow campaign promises, Obama signed the National Defense Authorization Act of 2011 (NDAA), which purports to grant the president authority to indefinitely detain *American citizens* alleged of somehow supporting terrorists, stripping them of any rights to habeas corpus and denying them their day in court. Further, Obama has now assassinated an American citizen, Anwar al-Awlaki, without any due process at all, and maintains a list of citizens *suspected* of a crime who may likewise be extinguished at one man's order. The supposedly anti-war left fell back asleep when one of their own was placed into power.

The so-called "right" is no different. While Tea Partiers have coalesced around opposition to Obama's health care plan, among other issues, their opposition was altogether absent while the Republican Party was passing Medicare Part D just a few years previous—a massive unfunded liability that has created a $16 trillion burden. Often, however, bursts of opposition form that do not fall on partisan lines. When Congress was considering legislation in January 2012 that would allow private corporations to effectively censor the Internet and shut down websites they perceived to be an economic threat, an overwhelming tidal wave of opposition caused congressmen who had previously supported the bills (SOPA/PIPA) to remove their cosponsorship and speak out against them. Ultimately, the bills were tabled, and the lead sponsor was sent back to the drawing board. When the Federal Drug Administration sought legislation to aggressively expand its regulatory authority in late 2010, a diverse group of people mounted an opposition to some of its more troubling and tyrannical provisions that would have effectively shut down small family farms, farmers markets, and other local, organic alternatives to the multinational food processing giants. While limited success was achieved, the bill ended up passing both houses of Congress and was signed into law by Barack Obama. A similarly diverse coalition rallied two years previously in opposition to the Troubled Assets Relief Program (TARP), which sought to soak the taxpayers to bail out big banks to save them from their own bad decisions. Whether opponents argued on constitutional, ethical, or moral grounds, or for any other reason, an otherwise apathetic people have often responded in great numbers to short-lived but significant political events. This is praiseworthy, but it is simply not enough.

As President Kimball said, we need to be engaged "not some of the time, but all of the time." It is easy to sign a petition, attend a rally, or donate to a cause that receives significant attention and in which many of our friends are participating. What is not as easy, but arguably more important, is the consistent civic duty to observe and oppose violations of individual liberty in the smaller, less noticeable events that occur thousands of times per day. Clearly, this is not a task for one person, nor even a thousand. Through a division of labor—a large group of individuals each focusing on one or more issues of particular interest to them—informed and engaged Americans can ensure that corrupt combinations of power-seeking men, secret or otherwise, do not get "above" us. Individually, this responsibility is impossible; collectively it is far more feasible. Consistency is the key to this effort, for a chain is only as strong as its weakest link.

Due to the constant assault on individual liberty by the state, the chain of citizen activists has, to a large degree, been broken and ineffective. In recent years alone, the government has manufactured or amplified one crisis after another. Never-ending wars half a world away, the burst of the housing bubble, the recession/depression, monumental unemployment, bailouts left and right, the tightening tentacles of the post-9/11 domestic police state, the downgrading of America's credit rating, perpetual budget battles and debt ceiling drama in Congress, and on and on—all of this takes a toll and presents a near-impossible challenge for those few who are willing to consistently and openly object. The blame for all of this ultimately lies with us, of course—especially the so-called "silent majority" who sit contentedly or cowardly on the sidelines when confronted with a civic challenge. Apathetic Americans have helped make America pathetic. This trend must be reversed. The silent majority must become the motivated, vocal majority.

Citizen activists are needed to educate those around them, call attention to problematic legislation or policies, spread news (often that which isn't reported by the "mainstream" media) through social media, organize protests, and generally wake up those around them. We need individuals well informed of their rights, able to point out to others the violation of those rights and what can be done to fight back. We need volunteers to seek out and support good, honest, and wise men for positions of power, willing to invest the time and energy to help ensure that the wicked don't get to rule, so the people won't mourn. Of course, we also need those principled people who are willing, as the First Presidency encouraged in a 2000 letter, to "serve in public offices of either election or appointment."[38] Simply voting on election day is woefully inadequate; daily dedication to defending liberty, in whatever form that might be manifested (depending on one's talents, interests, and life circumstances), is what is required of us. An infrequent and casual flirtation with this essential responsibility has produced the oppressive outcome we witness today. It is an outcome that we must not let stand.

SUGGESTIONS

The following suggestions are offered on how to better fulfill the responsibility of civic duty:

1. LEARN ABOUT LIBERTY.

The principle found in Doctrine and Covenants 11:21—obtaining God's word before sharing it with others—has application to the cause of liberty. One can only defend and share truth with others to the extent that he himself knows it. Thus, before becoming engaged in discussions with others about political issues or civic matters, it is important to become well-versed in the principles of individual liberty and moral agency in order to ensure that a certain law, program, or politician does not undermine these important and eternal principles.

For those who are not yet well versed in the subject of liberty, beginning with *The Law* by Frédéric Bastiat and *Economics in One Lesson* by Henry Hazlitt would be a good start. Latter-day Saints especially will likely benefit from this author's first book, *Latter-day Liberty: A Gospel Approach to Government and Politics* to learn what prophets both ancient and modern have said about the subject. In that book's appendix, a lengthy suggested reading list is provided for those interested in a more in-depth study.

2. BECOME INVOLVED IN YOUR COMMUNITY.

While many people equate doing one's civic duty with voting and other political activities, the best thing that can be done to improve the government is to improve the people it governs. As this book discusses, helping ensure that the government defends and protects individual liberty requires that individuals shoulder their own responsibilities so the government is less tempted to do it for them. Thus, by voluntarily working to build strong communities through service, charity, and industry, fewer people will turn to the government for assistance. Numerous organizations exist that provide opportunities to get involved. In looking for ways to serve, consider supporting institutions that are perhaps lesser known and desperate for help.

Consider running for office, serving in appointed positions, and helping on campaigns and projects. Get to know others who are doing the same, and build a network of like-minded people who believe as you do and want to move the government in the right direction toward individual liberty. As the saying goes, all politics are local—get to know those in your area and team up to advance the cause of liberty together.

3. INCREASE YOUR SPHERE OF INFLUENCE.

Those who understand the principles of individual liberty and moral agency are under an obligation to defend them, in part by educating others as to their importance and nature. Through persuasion, you can invite others to learn about what you yourself have learned, and encourage them to become educated about these ideas and their implications. You can start a blog, share ideas via social media, write op-eds for your local newspaper, begin a podcast, write a book, create videos to share with others, or any number of other avenues for reaching a large number of people. What's most important is that the truths you have come to know are publicized as widely and effectively as possible. As Joseph Smith said, "it is our duty to concentrate all our influence to make popular that which is sound and good."

4. BE A CHANGE AGENT.

Ideas are important and foundational, but action is imperative. Talking about needed changes precedes, but should not replace, actually making those needed changes. Whether running for office, organizing a protest, lobbying for an important cause, or doing other political activity, the idea of individual liberty must be converted into productive activities that will help tear down government power and build up responsible people. As President Hinckley said, "You are good. But it is not enough just to be good. You must be good for something."[39]

NOTES

1. "What E'er Thou Art, Act Well Thy Part," BYU-Idaho devotional, March 4, 2012.
2. Andrew A. Lipscomb, ed., *The Writings of Thomas Jefferson*, vol. 6 (Washington, DC: The Thomas Jefferson Memorial Association, 1905), 58.
3. "Congress' approval rating: How low can it go?," CBS News, November 20, 2011, accessed May 12, 2012, http://www.cbsnews.com/8301-3460_162-57328351/congress-approval-rating-how-low-can-it-go/.

4. "Reelection Rates Over the Years," OpenSecrets.org, accessed May 2, 2012, http://www.opensecrets.org/bigpicture/reelect.php.

5. G. D. Watt, J. V. Long, eds., *Journal of Discourses*, vol. 9 (Liverpool: George Q. Cannon, 1862), 340.

6. Gordon B. Hinckley, *Stand a Little Taller* (Salt Lake City: Eagle Gate Publishers, 2001), 15.

7. Dean C. Jessee, "The Historian's Corner" *BYU Studies*, vol. 19, no. 3, Spring 1979, 392.

8. Hundreds, if not thousands, of quotes from church leaders support this assertion. As one example, President Spencer W. Kimball taught that "Every Latter-day Saint should sustain, honor, and obey the constitutional law of the land in which he lives." In Doctrine and Covenants 98, we read that the Lord "justifies" us in "befriending that law which is the constitutional law of the land," and section 101 teaches that it "should be maintained for the rights and protection of all flesh."

9. Ezra Taft Benson, "The Constitution—A Heavenly Banner," Brigham Young University devotional, Sept. 16, 1986.

10. Gordon B. Hinckley, *Standing for Something* (New York: Three Rivers Press, 2001), 123.

11. William C. Rives, ed., *History of the Life and Times of James Madison*, vol. 1 (Boston: Little, Brown, 1859), 636.

12. Foley, *The Jefferson Cyclopedia*, 274.

13. Andersen, *The Moral Basis of a Free Society*, 70.

14. Thomas S. Monson, "Examples of Righteousness," *Ensign*, May 2008, 65.

15. Ezra Taft Benson, *God, Family, Country: Our Three Great Loyalties* (Salt Lake City: Deseret Book, 1984), 389.

16. L. Tom Perry, "A Meaningful Celebration," *Ensign*, Nov. 1987, 72.

17. Gordon B. Hinckley, "Stand Up for Truth," Brigham Young University devotional, Sep. 17, 1996.

18. B. H. Roberts, ed., *History of the Church of Jesus Christ of Latter-day Saints*, vol. 5 (Salt Lake City: Deseret Book, 1978), 285.

19. M. Russell Ballard, "Sharing the Gospel Using the Internet," *Ensign*, July 2008, 58.

20. Harold B. Lee, "Keep Your Lamp Lighted," in Conference Report, Oct. 1970, 109–12, emphasis added.

21. In *Deseret News*, May 29, 1954, 3.

22. With civility, of course. See "The Mormon Ethic of Civility," LDS Newsroom, October 16, 2009, http://www.mormonnewsroom.org/article/the-mormon-ethic-of-civility.

23. Donald Q. Cannon, ed., *Latter-day Prophets and the United States Constitution* (Provo: Brigham Young University, 1991), 147.

24. Quoted in Spencer W. Kimball, "Living the Gospel in the Home,"

Ensign, May 1978, 100. After quoting this letter a decade later, President Kimball said: "The First Presidency and the Twelve wish to reaffirm this important statement of 1968. We believe this is the wise course to pursue, wherein Church members are urged to do their duties as citizens. The Church of Jesus Christ of Latter-day Saints cannot be committed, as an institution, except on those issues which are determined by the First Presidency and Twelve to be of such a nature that the Church should take an official position concerning them. We believe that to do otherwise would involve the Church, formally and officially, on a sufficient number of issues that the result would be to divert the Church from its basic mission of teaching the restored gospel of the Lord to the world. We earnestly hope Church members will feel their individual responsibilities keenly and pursue them wisely."

25. Cannon, *Prophets*, 152.
26. Quoted in Ezra Taft Benson, "A Witness And A Warning," in Conference Report, Oct. 1979.
27. Cannon, *Prophets*, 208.
28. "First Presidency Urges Citizen Participation," *Ensign*, Apr. 1998, 77.
29. LDS Church News, *Deseret News*, Oct. 28, 2000.
30. Gordon B. Hinckley, "A Testimony Vibrant and True," *Ensign*, Aug. 2005, 4.
31. Lobbying Database, Center for Responsive Politics, accessed May 2, 2012, http://www.opensecrets.org/lobby/index.php.
32. Ezra Taft Benson, *An Enemy Hath Done This* (Salt Lake City: Parliament Publishers, 1969), 313.
33. Ibid, 275.
34. "The Shrinking Majority," *Salt Lake Tribune*, A10, July 24, 2005.
35. Data obtained from "Utah County Election Results Archive," Utah County Clerk/Auditor, accessed May 2, 2012, http://www.utahcountyonline.org/Dept/ClerkAud/Elections/ElectRslts/.
36. Edward L. Kimball, ed., *Teachings of Spencer W. Kimball* (Salt Lake City: Bookcraft, 1982), 405.
37. G. D. Watt, ed., *Journal of Discourses*, vol. 4 (Liverpool: S. W. Richards, 1857), 150.
38. "First Presidency reaffirms political neutrality," *Deseret News*, Oct. 24, 2000.
39. Gordon B. Hinckley, "Stand Up for Truth," Brigham Young University devotional, Sep. 17, 1996.

FOOD PRODUCTION

Cultivators of the earth are the most valuable citizens. They are the most vigorous, the most independent, the most virtuous, and they are tied to their country, and wedded to its liberty and interests, by the most lasting bonds.[1]

—Thomas Jefferson

Ye Latter-day Saints, learn to sustain yourselves, produce everything you need to eat, drink or wear.[2]

—Brigham Young

There are blessings in being close to the soil, in raising your own food even if it is only a garden in your yard and a fruit tree or two. Those families will be fortunate who, in the last days, have an adequate supply of food because of their foresight and ability to produce their own.[3]

—Ezra Taft Benson

QUESTIONS TO PONDER

1. Do you have the exclusive right to eat or drink whatever you please, or do others have the right to prohibit you from consuming certain food?

2. How do you feel knowing that others control what gets put in the food you eat?

3. What benefits would having a garden in your yard bring to you and your family?

4. Can you become independent from others while relying on others to produce the food you eat?

*O*n August 3, 2011, and for the second time in less than a year, federal, state, and municipal law enforcement officers with guns drawn raided Rawesome Foods—a private, members-only organic food cooperative in Venice, California. Owner James Stewart was arrested along with two others present, charged with criminal conspiracy due to "the alleged illegal production and sale of unpasteurized goat milk, goat cheese and other products." The search warrant authorizing the armed raid instructed police to seize any possible evidence of the transportation of these products, including tax records, billing records, emails, receipts, inventory records, along with Stewart's computers, client lists, and other related information. The warrant also authorized police to take samples from any food products they found for laboratory analysis, and discard everything that was "manufactured unlawfully or from unapproved sources." As the raid was executed, government officials proceeded to confiscate the entire inventory of Rawesome's products, valued in the tens of thousands of dollars, and dumped hundreds of gallons of raw milk.

This armed intervention, along with all the legwork over the previous year, was funded by taxpayers and fought by bureaucrats and agents of a variety of levels and agencies of government. The Los Angeles County District Attorney's Office noted that the following were all involved in the year-long sting operation:

> Agencies taking part in the ongoing investigation include the U.S. Food and Drug Administration; the California Franchise Tax Board; the California Department of Food and Agriculture's Milk and Dairy Food Safety Branch and the department's Division of Measurement Standards; the Los Angeles County District Attorney's Office; the Los Angeles County Department of Public Health; the Ventura County Sheriff's Department, the Ventura County Department of Public Health; the Los Angeles Police Department and the Los Angeles Department of Building and Safety.[4]

Drawn weapons, dozens of police officers and government agents, seized contraband, and arrests with felony charges seem like activities associated with the "war on drugs," not the "war on raw milk." Those exchanging the goat cheese contraband were not juvenile delinquents feeding an addiction or adult criminals looking to exploit a banned substance for their personal profile—these were informed and health-conscious adults wanting to eat food as God had provided it. The co-operative nature of Rawesome Foods meant that members were required to sign a contract stating that they understood and accepted the risks of consuming raw foods before even being allowed to enter the property and peruse the selection. Not one member had complained or been harmed by the food, yet the government carried on its war regardless. A manager at Rawesome rightly framed the gravity of the situation: "This is America. How are you going to tell me what I can and cannot eat?"[5]

The Rawesome raids are not the exception to the rule—several similar raids occur each year.[6] The principle violated by these police actions is readily evident to the liberty-minded individual: what authority does the government have to tell an adult what he or she may or may not eat? Further, even if the product is thought by some to be potentially harmful, and if the person signs a waiver explicitly acknowledging that claim and agreeing to hold harmless those offering the product, why should millions of taxpayer dollars, thousands of man hours, and the full force of government be brought to bear against such consenting consumers? "It's very disappointing," said one Rawesome customer, "that in the United States, and especially in California, that I can't feed my family the basic foods that God made and provides."[7]

Given the trend in which California's government has consistently been heading over the years, some might be quick to dismiss this crackdown on milk as being part of the heavy-handed liberal government in that state. But these raids and restrictive laws are found in many other states, and at the federal level as well. Another example comes from the neighboring state of Nevada, where Laura and Monte Bledsoe created an organic, sustainable farm over the course of a few years, attracting over one hundred shareholders to help fund and reap the bounty of their efforts. For the Bledsoes, providing natural food for their family and neighbors had a higher purpose than just filling stomachs. They recognize the beauty of God's creations and the importance of staying connected to the soil, and wanted to share the results of their efforts with

187

others. These noble ideals and the passion and purpose that drove the Bledsoes to produce a large amount of healthy, natural food year-round were forcefully confronted on a cool evening in October 2011. Friends, family, and shareholders gathered at the Bledsoes' Quail Hollow Farm for an annual event which included a large feast incorporating various food and produce from the farm. These invited guests were soon joined by an uninvited guest when the Health Department arrived.[8]

An employee from the Southern Nevada Health District showed up as the meal was beginning to conduct an inspection of the farm and its facilities. Two days prior to this surprise visit, the Bledsoes had received a phone call from this government agency informing them that because their party was considered by the Health Department to be a "public event" (even though it was a private event for invitees only), they would have to apply for a special use permit or face a hefty fine. Eager to see their annual event continue without incident, they complied and sought the permit and paid the required fee. Upon completing the paperwork, however, they were informed that the permit would not be given until an inspection was conducted to verify compliance with all state and federal regulations. Little did the Bledsoes know that the inspector would choose to arrive during the actual event.

Despite bending over backward to comply with regulations and avoid any confrontation with the government officials (including preparing most of the food in a certified kitchen in Las Vegas and renting a certified kitchen trailer to prepare the rest at the farm), the inspector demanded that the party (already in progress) be cancelled. This government agent alleged that some of the food packages did not have labels on them (which is permissible by law under the circumstances which applied to the Bledsoes' event), some of the meat was not USDA certified (obviously, since the meal was intentionally a farm-to-fork process), and that the vegetables prepared in advance were already cut and thus considered by the government to be a "biohazard."

Unfailingly compliant with the government's absurd mandates, the Blesdoes attempted to reason with the inspector and find a way to keep the food and guests together for the meal. The husband asked if they could explicitly make the event a private one by allowing the guests to become part of their club, and thus avoid any possible interpretation of the party being considered a public event—with the intent of avoiding the Health Department's jurisdiction and moving forward with the evening's festivities. This proposal infuriated the inspector's superior who then threatened that if the Bledsoes did not immediately discard their food, the police would be called and the guests would be escorted off of the farm. As the painstakingly prepared fine food was being dumped into the trash can, the family asked if they could save the food for a family dinner another day. Their request was once again denied, and the government agent insulted them by claiming that by doing so, they would be endangering the health of their family. Their last attempt to save the food was a request to give it to the pigs. Again, their request was unilaterally denied. On orders of a low-ranking government bureaucrat, the perfectly healthy, organic, and delicious food was thrown out.

Once informed of the events occurring behind the scene, the guests were justifiably enraged with the government's interventions and refusal to allow them, as consenting and knowledgeable adults, the opportunity to choose what to eat. The crowd was composed of many people who had attended in prior years, and none of them had filed a complaint of any sort against the Bledsoes. No victim existed, no crime was committed, and no sickness had ever resulted from the Bledsoes' agricultural activities. Fortunately, the Bledsoes were quickly instructed by an attorney they had called to assert their constitutional rights and eject the inspector from their property until a search or arrest warrant was brought. The party then continued, albeit with an improvised menu.

Despite the paperwork, permits, and harassment by government agents, the Bledsoes press on in providing for themselves and others a wholesome harvest. This exemplary family fulfills the indispensable responsibility to produce food—a responsibility that is both simple and significant, for individuals who grow and eat their own food can control what it is, how it is grown and stored, and become self-reliant in the process. The Bledsoes' story shows how those who fulfill this responsibility may be attacked and threatened with fines and jail time for daring to consume natural, healthy food without the government's regulatory blessing. The government's claim of authority to dictate to American citizens what they can ingest is an illegitimate and absurd one, yet it is one that is legislated at all levels of government. In an April 2010 response to a lawsuit filed by the Farm-to-Consumer Legal Defense Fund, for example, the United States Food and Drug Administration (FDA) claimed that the assertion that individuals have "a fundamental right to their own bodily and physical health, which includes what foods they do and do not choose to consume for themselves" is incorrect because, says the FDA, individuals "do not have a fundamental right to obtain any food they wish."[9] Ponder that for a moment: the government which derives its legitimate authority from each individual who comprises it has the audacity to tell those individuals that they may not eat anything that does not have the government's approval. For those interested in affirming their natural right to ingest what they please—whether healthy or not—the government's actions seem like part of a sustained assault on their liberty.

THE WAR ON . . . FOOD?

The government's increasing regulation of and enforcement against natural food is found in far more circumstances than the raids that occur each year. Indeed, the infrequent raids are merely a sporadic symptom of a far more prevalent, burdensome, and heavy-handed regulatory apparatus that purports to tell Americans what they can put into their bodies. The steady stream of compounding laws and regulations that are created each year, whether at the federal, state, or local level, increases prices due to compliance costs and protectionist economic policies, alters market behavior by discouraging people from farming, selling, and eating certain foods, and harms the environment by altering the use of certain foods and in some cases, even resulting in the near-extinction of certain food varieties. A few examples will illustrate the effect these regulations can have on food production, distribution, and consumption. They are important to mention in further emphasizing the degree to which the government undermines the personal responsibility of food production, to clarify how significant this circumstance has become. These examples, and many more like them, indicate the negative effect the government can and does have when it illegitimately involves itself in the most basic of daily activities—what people eat.

Under federal regulations, no fresh citrus fruit may be taken outside of Florida without an inspection of the grove it came from within the past thirty days, treatment of the fruit with a decontaminant, a permit issued for the fruit and required to accompany the fruit, and clear markings on the package to indicate that the fruit may not be delivered to other citrus-producing states.[10] This prohibition against a natural fruit and the infringement of individual liberty against the person who might want to purchase some oranges and take them home to a neighboring state has no basis in the Constitution, and yet oddly the USDA claims as its authority the very Commerce Clause intended by the founders to prevent such protectionism by one state against others. Whereas the founders intended this clause to tear down tariff wars between states and provide for the free flow of goods across state borders, today it has been misconstrued and misapplied so as to justify what it was meant to prohibit. This prohibition of citrus in countrywide commerce and the limited shipping options it mandates serve to insulate large citrus companies from competition, thereby increasing the price for the average consumer, as well as restricting the options he might otherwise have through open competition in the citrus marketplace.

A more absurd example comes from the FDA, which in February 2010 sent a letter to Diamond Food regarding the walnuts this company was selling. With thirty-five peer-reviewed, published scientific papers in the US National Library of Medicine's database demonstrating that walnuts can improve vascular health and promote heart function, Diamond Food marketed its walnuts by highlighting some of their relevant health benefits. The FDA claimed in their letter that because of these claims, the walnuts "are drugs" which "are not generally recognized as safe and effective."[11] The government told Diamond Food that they must submit an application for a new drug and await the decision of the agency before continuing to sell their product with the health benefit claims of their walnuts. *Life Extension Magazine*'s William Faloon observed that "This kind of bureaucratic tyranny sends a strong signal to the food industry not to innovate in a way that informs the public about foods that protect against disease. While consumers increasingly reach for healthier dietary choices," Faloon continued, "the federal government wants to deny food companies the ability to convey findings from scientific studies about their products."[12]

While the small farmer and organic food advocates are often made targets of the law, "big agriculture" industrial food giants are often very intertwined with the regulatory agencies that are supposed to be overseeing them and as a result of that cozy relationship, are often exempted from such punishment. For example, the highly controversial company

Monsanto has filled key leadership positions with former USDA and FDA officials, and in turn has had its executives placed in positions of power within these and other food-related government agencies. This has often resulted in favorable policies that punish the small farmer and consumer yet are a financial godsend for the companies involved, such as the effort by Monsanto/FDA/USDA official Michael Taylor to keep information hidden from consumers about the nature of their food. After being employed as a lawyer for Monsanto, a multinational agricultural biotechnology company, Taylor was appointed as the FDA's Deputy Commissioner for Policy. During his time in that office, he defeated a proposed requirement to label genetically modified products, which would have allowed consumers to make an informed decision (likely steering many of them away from Monsanto's genetically modified products[13]). Using his power in government to enforce his edict, Taylor declared natural seeds and genetically modified seeds "substantially equivalent,"[14] thus rejecting the labeling initiative. After his tenure at the FDA, Taylor became a vice president at Monsanto, and then later returned to government as senior advisor to the commissioner of the US Food and Drug Administration.[15] Taylor's example is one of many where the revolving door between regulatory agencies and large "food" companies perpetuates a system that rewards those who do not have the consumer's health and interest most at heart.

While family farmers and local food producers rarely have the resources and time to defend their interests and keep the government's regulatory apparatus away from their healthy, productive enterprise, the large food manufacturing companies have lobbyists, lawyers, and money to ensure that their interests are benefitted by favorable legislation and regulation. To the small farmers suffering from the unfair (government-backed) competition, it is akin to war. Ronnie Cummins, founder of the Organic Consumers Associations frames it this way:

> It is impossible to coexist with a reckless industry that endangers public health, bribes public officials, corrupts scientists, manipulates the media, destroys biodiversity, kills the soil, pollutes the environment, tortures and poisons animals, destabilizes the climate, and economically enslaves the world's 1.5 billion seed-saving small farmers. It's time to take down the Biotech Behemoth, before the living web of biodiversity is terminated.[16]

Healthy, natural foods are being targeted through unfair and burdensome regulation, and even criminalization. But as the quote above illustrates, the battle over food is about far more than what somebody wants to eat—it is about what will even be available to eat in ten, twenty, or thirty years. Entire species of crops are being sent to their extinction through government policies that funnel overwhelming amounts of money to the monopolistic production of a more favored type. The federal government has for many years heavily subsidized the production of corn, for example, in part to drive up the production and use of ethanol in an attempt to pursue "clean energy." Giving these subsidies to farmers alters the marketplace by allowing them to unfairly undersell the competition. Specifically, American corn farmers have over the past two decades flooded the Mexican market with their overabundance of corn, consisting of a small number of hybrid species, which are nearly genetically identical. Beginning in 1994, this subsidy arrangement was found nine years later to have cut in half the price of corn in Mexico, and put 1.3 million Mexican farmers out of a job.[17] These farmers, now able to buy their corn more cheaply from American producers, were effectively forced to give up their business and either look for other work (a daunting task in the impoverished Mexican communities) or become one of the many "illegal immigrants" entering the United States looking for a way to provide for their family.[18] Previous to this government intervention into the food supply, Mexican farmers had maintained hundreds of different varieties of corn. Now, the influx of cheap corn from America has threatened the very existence of many of these ancient genetic forms of corn, since for many farmers it has become cost prohibitive to even plant their own seeds and raise a crop.

Living in such a system—one that is rapidly heading toward more centralization, more control, less genetic diversity, and less health—one's responsibility to counter these trends by growing food becomes clear. The past few decades of government policy have produced an overwhelming burden of regulation, mandates, and market manipulation that threatens one's liberty to eat what one pleases and the ability to freely grow genetically diverse produce. Individuals in first-world countries have overwhelmingly outsourced the production and delivery of their food to corporations, which rarely have their best interests at heart. In shirking the responsibility to grow their own food, or at least purchase it from local, organic farmers with a face and human connection, these individuals lose the ability to answer even the most basic questions about what they consume. Who grew the food being eaten? With what chemicals was it treated? How were the workers treated who harvested, packaged, and transported it? Can those involved in every part of the process for a given type of food be trusted to produce healthy food? While many leave such questions to "the authorities," the examples just listed as well as many others suggest that, contrary to popular belief, the authorities do not have our best interests at heart. We are what we eat, and it is therefore imperative that we know exactly what we are eating. This is nobody's job but our own.

As the Nazis overtook the government through legal means, many Germans resisted the thought that the increasing restrictions would ever apply to them. The incremental targeting and purging of one group after another still was not sufficient to convince some that the government's actions were illegitimate, and closing in on them. Pastor Martin Niemöller, a German Protestant theologian born in 1892, distilled this idea into the following statement:

> First they came for the Socialists, and I did not speak out—
> Because I was not a Socialist.
> Then they came for the Trade Unionists, and I did not speak out—
> Because I was not a Trade Unionist.
> Then they came for the Jews, and I did not speak out—
> Because I wasn't a Jew.
> Then they came for me—and there was no one left to speak for me.[19]

This is not to say in any way that everything the Nazis ultimately did, including the mass extermination of innocent civilians, is comparable to the criminalization and confiscation of food. What can be gleaned from this statement, however, is the trend toward tyranny that inevitably occurs when individuals do not affirm their rights and resist the illegitimate actions of the government which rules over them—even if such actions do not immediately apply to them. While you may not want to drink raw milk, sitting by and doing nothing while raw milk raids occur justifies the practice, establishes a precedent, and inevitably becomes precursor to other forms of restrictions and raids that will someday apply to you. Thus, it becomes incumbent upon each person, even if not directly affected, to oppose the infringement of anybody's individual rights.

When people collectively outsource the production and management of much of their food to a relatively few companies and thus voluntarily shirk their responsibility to at a *minimum* be aware of what they are ingesting, then they allow their very existence—their lives, their liberty, and their pursuit of happiness—to be controlled, to a certain degree, by those who produce and manage that food. Without knowing what they are eating, they allow themselves to become acted upon by others who may not be concerned with the consumer's health and happiness.

The war on food has increased on two fronts since the industrialization of food production, and especially within the past couple of decades. On one side, corporations are pumping "food" full of scientifically concocted ingredients that few can even correctly pronounce, genetically modifying the most important crops in existence, and employing hundreds of lobbyists to secure favorable legislation that stifles the competition comprised of small, family farms often focusing on natural, organic alternatives. On the other side, legislation and bureaucratic regulations from the government regulate the entire food production chain,[20] including family farms and home gardens, claiming the authority to dictate to individuals what they can eat, and what they can offer to other consenting adults who understand and explicitly accept any consequences that might come from eating that food.

This war is part of the "evils and designs which do and will exist in the hearts of conspiring men in the last days" (D&C 89:4), as noted in the section of scripture wherein the Lord offers his health code and instructions on what should or should not be consumed. As with any war, one must either pick sides or abstain altogether and sit on the sidelines. Flanked on different sides by the "enemy" in this case, the liberty-minded individual must decide how best to fulfill the responsibility of food production. At a minimum, he might support farms, government policies, and agricultural practices that respect nature, affirm an individual's right to eat what he pleases, and produce food as naturally as possible. To fully fulfill this responsibility, he might grow his own food (along with keeping chickens, bees, and so on) to be as close to the soil as possible and better able control what he ingests and thus makes a part of his body. The average individual has become so distant from his food that he neither understands nor cares about how it was produced and treated. He makes substantially uninformed decisions about what he eats, and thus implicitly enables the opponents in the war just described.

THE DANGERS OF A DIVISION OF LABOR

The Hawaiian island of Maui features a sugar museum adjacent to Hawaii's largest sugar-processing mill, surrounded by thousands of acres of sugar cane fields. Producing 182,000 tons of raw sugar in 2011, the mill's output accounted for 5 percent of total sugar cane production in the United States.[21] Sugar processed at this facility is only converted to the "raw sugar" state, and from there is shipped to California where it is refined into the commonly recognized white sugar. Afterward, it is transported to New York, where it is then packaged into small packets and shipped across the country. If you were to visit a restaurant nearby the sugar cane museum in Maui, the sugar on your table may have originated from just down the road but would have traveled about ten thousand miles. This is not a rare circumstance—in the modern industrialized food economy, the production, processing, packaging, and distribution of food has created an intricate and fragile network of imports and exports always moving food from one distant location to another.

On average, going from "farm to fork" requires that food travel over four thousand miles.[22] In the process, what a person ends up eating exchanges many hands, is treated, sprayed, cooked, converted, and otherwise processed, and is made to comply with an untold number of bureaucratic regulations. This is a necessary outcome of the industrialization of food, where the economic factors involved in food production and distribution largely determine where, what, and how much food is grown—and how it is modified once produced.

This industrialization of food is not an inherently problematic development in our society—indeed, it has been a fantastic blessing for many people. The typical American meal, prepared at home, now consists of ingredients from at least five separate countries.[23] This is a consequence of a natural division of labor, whereby people in different areas of the world specialize on farming the produce that their climate, skills, and knowledge best allow them to create in large quantities. That output is then exchanged in local and foreign markets for other needed commodities, and the competition between farmers in different areas helps create a wide variety of related offerings (for example, different species of produce) and drives down costs. By growing juicy oranges, a farmer in Florida can still provide for his family the other food he needs. Without this division of labor, each farmer (indeed, each and every individual) would be required to grow and provide for all his or her own food. With it, a carpenter, lawyer, social worker, store clerk, and everybody in any other profession can exchange their products and services for the food they need. Further, a person living in a location where certain foods cannot be grown is able to benefit from the importation of those items from anywhere around the world. As Ludwig von Mises wrote, "Experience teaches man that cooperative action is more efficient and productive than isolated action of self-sufficient individuals."[24] Put more simply, a division of labor and the resulting industrialization of food has largely brought with it cheaper prices, better selection, and focused specialization on increasing both the quantity and quality of food produced.

While a division of labor has its clear and compelling benefits, it is not without its downsides. There is danger in allowing such a division to separate us from the knowledge and skills we are not actively required to use. While produce may be obtained inexpensively at the local grocery store, the skills and knowledge gained through gardening and related home production projects are often worth more than the time and effort invested. In an emergency, such skills would prove invaluable, but more important the existing infrastructure and resources created and maintained during previous years of provident living would allow those skills to be applied to produce the food that could no longer be obtained from a local store, or perhaps would be too costly to purchase in times of scarcity. When an emergency occurs, store shelves are almost immediately cleared of their goods, and only with difficulty or delay are new supplies able to be transported in. "Those families will be fortunate who, in the last days," said President Benson, "have an adequate supply of food because of their foresight and ability to produce their own."[25] President Spencer W. Kimball highlighted the connection between food production and individual liberty when he stated, simply, that "Gardens promote independence." He elaborated: "Should evil times come, many might wish they had filled all their fruit bottles and cultivated a garden in their backyards and planted a few fruit trees and berry bushes and provided for their own commodity needs.

The Lord planned that we would be independent of every creature . . . but . . . should the trucks fail to fill the shelves of the stores, many would go hungry."[26] Gardens and other food production allow individuals to act rather than be acted upon. Bishop Vaughn J. Featherstone echoed President Kimball's remarks: "Raise animals where means and local laws permit. Plant fruit trees, grapevines, berry bushes, and vegetables. You will provide food for your family, much of which can be eaten fresh. Other food you grow can be preserved and included as part of your home storage."[27] The counsel for the Saints to produce food has been consistent and long-standing. President Marion G. Romney prophesied that "We will see the day when we will live on what we produce."[28] It is instructive—and usually quite humbling—to ponder what you can currently produce, and how long you could survive.

President Kimball on another occasion stated: "We encourage you to grow all the food that you feasibly can on your own property. . . . Even those residing in apartments or condominiums can generally grow a little food in pots and planters."[29] Growing "all the food that you feasibly can on your own property" seems like an unreachable goal to many, though Americans in years past embraced this very idea. In the late 1890s, a movement to create school gardens began to build, teaching the youth lessons of self-sufficiency and industry. This effort was eclipsed by the government's encouragement of "liberty gardens" (also referred to as "war gardens") during World War I, in an effort to promote urban and suburban food production to prepare the citizenry for times of scarcity during the war. After the war, and especially during the Depression, home gardening continued to some degree as a means of survival. World War II saw the resurrection of the government's propaganda-fueled gardening effort, this time nicknamed a "victory garden," which by the end of the war had twenty million gardeners producing nearly 40 percent of the nation's total food.[30] As the rapid acceleration of manufacturing technology quickly transformed the industrialization of food, the attention of and desire for home gardening waned.

The last few years, however, have seen a resurgence of this grow-your-own-food movement, with participants expressing various reasons for their involvement. Some want to reduce their energy dependence and create food that doesn't have to travel thousands of miles, while others want to promote a more sustainable and organic agricultural system. Others see no point in having grass in their backyard and want to turn the space into a productive garden to benefit their family, while yet others simply want to assert more control over what they put into their bodies and feel that they cannot trust the manufacturers of mass-produced, imported food. One man who had been unemployed for several months began a garden and intended to turn it into a business. "It makes all the sense in the world for me to get a plot, grow my own food and live," he said. "This is a new reality. And I am actually excited."[31] A man in California who cares for a one-acre garden at the local high school observed that, regarding the students helping at the garden, "There is a positive connection between putting their fingers in the soil and their own mental or spiritual well-being."[32] Whether due to economic, philosophical, political, or religious factors, many people are once again recognizing the benefits of being close to the soil and producing their own food. Along with this movement has come public pressure for better labeling on food so the consumer understands what they're eating, a substantially increased demand for certified organic products, and a greater awareness of the dangers associated with much of the food manufacturing industry. These are positives steps in the right direction, and our involvement in gardening and food production will help this trend to become more popular and permanent.

The prophetic counsel to produce food does not suggest that a division of labor is inherently problematic or inadvisable; we're not being told to provide everything we need, and not exchange with others or purchase things we can't ourselves produce. Rather, the purpose of producing your own food is to build up the storage and skills necessary to preserve independence both in the short and long term. Trading and obtaining food from other locations is a wonderful thing, but must be complemented by also producing at home. It is important that we balance the benefits of a division of labor with the need to acquire and maintain skills of self-sufficiency and provident living that come as a result of producing one's own food. As one author writes:

> Although concentration of food production on large farms in certain geographic areas—such as California, Florida, or Mexico—may be a more efficient way to produce food from a narrow economic perspective, there are high costs involved that are not internalized in the price system. These include the loss of farms and farming communities in other regions of the United States, loss of knowledge about local farming conditions and effective ways

to cope with them, and loss of control or means of influencing important decisions about agricultural production. The advantages of "economic efficiency"—lower food costs and greater year-round availability of seasonal crops to consumers—must be balanced against these negative effects.[33]

This balance does not necessarily require that families tear out all their landscaping and create a large garden to provide for all of their own food. The balance can still be obtained through a division of labor—albeit a more local, informed one. Those unable to maintain their own garden, or maintain one large enough to provide for all their own food, can buy from local farmers who often grow their crops more naturally than the large agricultural plants. Community Supported Agriculture (CSA) is a growing movement whereby individuals can buy "shares" in a farm to fund the farmer's efforts and in later months reap what that farmer sowed. This dovetails with the First Presidency's counsel in 1942:

> Let every Latter-day Saint that has land produce some valuable, essential foodstuff thereon and then preserve it; or if he cannot produce an essential foodstuff, let him produce some other kind and exchange it for an essential foodstuff; let them who have no land of their own and who have knowledge of farming and gardening, try to rent some either by themselves or with others and produce foodstuff thereon and preserve it. Let those who have land produce enough extra to help their less fortunate brethren.[34]

Division of labor is a marvelous thing while it is feasible. However, during times of war, famine, or other prolonged emergency, the store shelves are quickly cleared out, distribution ceases, and individuals are left unable to obtain things they cannot themselves create, or which they do not already have in storage. To prepare for those times, and also to reap the benefits that come even while a diverse and enticing market is available, producing food is essential. The counsel from Church leaders has been clear on this matter, and a final summary can be found in the words of Orson Pratt in 1875:

> And the time will come, when we shall find ourselves restricted, and when it will be very important indeed for us to patronize home productions, and cease sending our millions abroad for

importations, for the gate will be shut down, and circumstances will be such that we cannot bring things from abroad; and hence the necessity of the exhortation that we have received from time to time, to engage with all our hearts in the various branches of industry necessary to make us self-sustaining, and to carry them out with all the tact and wisdom which God has given to us, that we may become free and independent in all these matters, free before the heavens, and free from all the nations of the earth and their productions, so as being dependent upon them is concerned.[35]

Producing food is as much about providing for one's daily needs as it is fostering independence from other people. The personal responsibility to produce food and its resulting benefit of independence, or individual liberty, is one that has largely been ignored by the Latter-day Saints, despite consistent counsel to the contrary. Our collective independence in the present as well as in times of emergency depends in large measure upon reversing this trend by acquiring and maintaining the skills and resources to produce one of the most basic and essential necessities: our food.

SUGGESTIONS

The following suggestions are offered on how to better fulfill the responsibility of producing your own food:

1. PLANT A VEGETABLE GARDEN.

Choosing a location on your property where the sun will shine at least six hours daily. If the natural soil is insufficient to maintain a garden, you can grow the garden in boxes above ground or replace the soil. Determining what you want to grow will depend on the climate and availability of sunlight in your location. Consult local garden shops or organizations to find the best practices in your area. Choosing how to grow your produce can be either simple or complicated. For those just getting started, even a tomato plant in a small pot is a good first step. Those wanting to increase their output beyond what the average, unskilled gardener can achieve might look into methods such as Square Foot Gardening (www.squarefootgardening.com) or Mittleider Gardening (www.growfood.com).

Another important thing to consider is storing your seeds. Whether you do this to save money, preserve genetic diversity, or better understand and be involved in every part of the process, saving seeds for future seasons is something all gardeners should consider doing. See www.howtosaveseeds.com or www.seedsave.org for more information.

2. PLANT FRUIT TREES, VINES, AND BUSHES.

Unlike vegetable plants, the trees, bushes, and vines that bear fruit do not need to be replanted on a yearly basis. However, they usually will not bear any fruit for several years once they are planted, so it is important to get them in the ground as soon as possible. Before planting, be sure to research how large the tree or plant will become once full grown so you can space them accordingly. Also keep in mind that some bear fruit yearly, while some only bear fruit every other year.

3. KEEP LIVESTOCK.

If you have enough land and local laws allow it, it's a good idea to raise animals as part of your food production process. Chickens, rabbits, ducks, sheep, and milk goats are generally easier to care for than some others, but regardless of what you choose, you'll want to research what food they will need, what shelter you'll have to provide, and how best to care for them to keep them healthy and productive. Keeping bees is also a great idea (they'll help to pollinate your plants) and the honey they produce can be stored indefinitely. Be sure to start small and simple before later including other animals, both for your own adjustment as well as that of the animals you'll be raising.

4. PRESERVE YOUR FOOD.

Seasonal produce can be stored and used later, providing a family the ability to extend their crop throughout the year. There are various types of food storage, each of which works better for different kinds of food. Drying food with a dehydrator or even the sun can extend the life of your produce. You can also bottle the food, a more complicated process that should be learned and followed closely to avoid any danger. Another option is to salt the food, which can especially work well for certain meats. Each of these and any other food preservation methods should be researched in detail to avoid health risks and any loss of your precious food.

NOTES

1. Foley, *Jefferson Cyclopedia*, 322.
2. John A. Widtsoe, *Discourses of Brigham Young*, vol. 3 (Salt Lake City: Deseret Book, 1925), 450.
3. Ezra Taft Benson, "Prepare for the Days of Tribulation," *Ensign*, October 1980.
4. "Three Arrested on Charges of Illegally Producing, Selling Unpasteurized Milk," Los Angeles County District Attorney's Office, August 3, 2011, accessed May 12, 2012, http://da.lacounty.gov/mr/archive/2011/080311a.htm.
5. "Raw Foods Raid—The Fight for the Right to Eat What You Want," Reason TV, November 27, 2010, accessed May 12, 2012, http://reason.com/blog/2010/11/17/raw-foods-raid-fight.
6. See the list at http://www.farmtoconsumer.org/farm-raids.html for examples.
7. "Rawesome foods raided: A sad day for America," *Washington Times*, August 6, 2011, accessed May 12, 2012, http://communities.washingtontimes.com/neighborhood/omkara/2011/aug/6/rawsome-foods-raided-sad-day-america/.
8. The Bledsoes' account of this event can be read at http://shanonbrooks.com/2011/10/people-live-dirt-roads-monte-laura-bledsoe-quail-hollow-farm-csa/.

9. "FDA's Response to FTCLDF Suit over Interstate Raw Milk Ban," Farm-to-Consumer Legal Defense Fund, April 26, 2010, accessed May 12, 2012, http://farmtoconsumer.org/litigation-FDA-status.htm.

10. "Restrictions on the Shipment of Florida Citrus to Out-of-State Locations," USDA, December 19, 2006, accessed May 12, 2012, http://www.aphis.usda.gov/newsroom/content/2006/12/holiday_citrus.shtml.

11. "Warning Letter," FDA letter to Diamond Food, Inc., February 22, 2010, accessed May 12, 2012, http://www.fda.gov/iceci/enforcementactions/warningletters/ucm202825.htm.

12. "FDA Says Walnuts Are Illegal Drugs," *Life Extension Magazine*, August 2011, accessed May 12, 2012, http://www.lef.org/magazine/mag2011/aug2011_FDA-Says-Walnuts-Are-Illegal-Drugs_01.htm.

13. The president of Asgrow Seed Company, a subsidiary of Monsanto, said in 1994 that "If you put a label on genetically engineered food you might as well put a skull and crossbones on it." See Harvey Blatt, *America's Food: What You Don't Know About What You Eat* (Cambridge: Massachusetts Institute of Technology, 2008), 97.

14. Leslie A. Duram, *Encyclopedia of Organic, Sustainable, and Local Food* (Santa Barbara: ABC-CLIO, 2010), 163.

15. "Noted Food Safety Expert Michael R. Taylor Named Advisor to FDA Commissioner," US Food and Drug Administration, July 7, 2009, accessed May 12, 2012, http://www.fda.gov/NewsEvents/Newsroom/PressAnnouncements/2009/ucm170842.htm.

16. "Monsanto Nation: Taking Down Goliath," Organic Consumers Association, July 27, 2011, accessed May 12, 2012, http://www.organicconsumers.org/articles/article_23693.cfm.

17. Michael Pollan, "A Flood of U.S. Corn Rips at Mexico," *Los Angeles Times*, April 23, 2004, accessed May 12, 2012, http://michaelpollan.com/articles-archive/a-flood-of-u-s-corn-rips-at-mexico/.

18. Few anti-illegal immigration advocates have connected the dots and realize that one of the largest reasons why an upsurge in illegal immigration has occurred over the past few years is because of the government's own flawed economic policies.

19. "First They Came for the Socialists . . . ," *Holocaust Encyclopedia*, United States Holocaust Memorial Museum, accessed May 12, 2012, http://www.ushmm.org/wlc/en/article.php?ModuleId=10007392.

20. For example, the Food Safety Modernization Act passed Congress in late 2010 under highly questionable circumstances and was signed into law by President Obama over the winter break. This law significantly expands the authority and scope of the FDA, empowering it with increased recall powers, oversight, regulation, and "preventative" tools to monitor the food supply and respond to outbreaks or other issues.

21. "Sugar on Maui," Alexander & Baldwin Sugar Museum, accessed

May 12, 2012, http://www.sugarmuseum.com/sugar.html/frameset
.exhibits.html.

22. Christopher Weber and H. Scott Matthews, "Food Miles and the
Relative Climate Impacts of Food Choices in the United States,"
Environmental Science and Technology, Nov. 28, 2007.

23. "Health Facts," National Resources Defense Council, November 2007,
accessed May 12, 2012, http://www.farmlandinfo.org/documents/37291/
foodmiles.pdf.

24. Ludwig von Mises, *Human Action* (Auburn: The Ludwig von Mises
Institute, 1998), 157.

25. Ezra Taft Benson, "Prepare for the Days of Tribulation," *Ensign*, Nov.
1980, 32.

26. Spencer W. Kimball, *Ensign*, Nov. 1974, 6.

27. Vaughn J. Featherstone, "Food Storage," *Ensign*, May 1976, 117.

28. Marion G. Romney, in Conference Report, Apr. 1975, 165.

29. Spencer W. Kimball, "Family Preparedness," *Ensign*, May 1976, 124.

30. "Farmer in Chief," *New York Times*, October 9, 2008, accessed May 12,
2012, http://www.nytimes.com/2008/10/12/magazine/12policy-t.html.

31. "Victory gardens sprout up again," *Los Angeles Times*, January 10,
2009, accessed May 12, 2012, http://www.latimes.com/features/la-hm-
victory10-2009jan10,0,2585914,full.story.

32. Ibid.

33. Jonathan M. Harris, ed., *Rethinking Sustainability: Power, Knowledge,
and Institutions* (The University of Michigan Press, 2000), 233.

34. In Conference Report, Apr. 1942, 88–97.

35. Orson Pratt, *Deseret Evening News*, vol. 8, Oct. 2, 1875, #265.

FAMILY

Between the omnipotent state and the naked individual looms the first line of resistance against totalitarianism: the economically and politically independent family, protecting the space within which free and independent individuals may receive the necessary years of nurture.[1]

—Michael Novak

From the beginning, The Church of Jesus Christ of Latter-day Saints has emphasized family life. We have always understood that the foundations of the family, as an eternal unit, were laid even before this earth was created! Society without basic family life is without foundation and will disintegrate into nothingness.[2]

—President Spencer W. Kimball

QUESTIONS TO PONDER

1. How can you encourage your children (or spouse, siblings, or parents) to become more responsible?

2. Why was the proclamation on the family created? What has happened in the world, as it relates to families, since it was delivered in 1995?

3. How do adultery, divorce, abuse, and other threats to families undermine the cause of liberty?

4. Why do you think President Harold B. Lee stated that "the most important work you and I will ever do will be within the walls of our own homes"?

*I*n his 1859 book *On Liberty*, the British political economist John Stuart Mill called for "experiments of living"[3] to compare and contrast different lifestyles in pursuit of finding out which is of the most worth. In many cases, such experimentation ranges between being beneficial and benign. Living in a large or small home, eating organic versus processed food, having elderly parents live in one's own home or in a care facility, giving children an allowance tied to the completion of chores or with no strings attached—these and many more family decisions do allow for the flexibility and variety to see what best works for each family. In other cases, however, the experiment goes horribly wrong. This is the case with the experiment—some might call it a revolution—regarding the nature of the family unit itself. While the results of experimentation with the family unit in the past several decades offer one alarming statistic after another, the concern is not only about the families themselves; the consequences of this social upheaval have significantly negative implications for the cause of liberty.

Every year, approximately one million children will see their parents separate due to divorce.[4] Forty-five percent of all American children can expect their families to break up before they reach the age of eighteen.[5] The data and conversation surrounding divorce has historically focused primarily on the main actors in the marriage: the husband and wife; rarely do the children, if there are any, receive significant attention. However, the increasingly negative trends surrounding marriage and family are developing to a large extent among those whose parents terminated their own marital vows. One example comes from a study, conducted over the course of nearly three decades, of children whose parents were divorcing in the 1970s.[6] The authors note that many of the children of divorced parents, now as adults, were not married or interested in becoming married. Many had no interest in having their own children. More than half of them had decided not to have children for fear of putting any potential posterity through the same difficult childhood that they had experienced. Forty percent of the adult children of divorced parents interviewed never married, and among those who did go on to marry, about 40 percent ended up divorced. Having experienced firsthand the familial destruction that divorce brings, it makes sense that the children would grow up to be wary of making, or have difficulty keeping, their own marital commitments. While sometimes certainly necessary, divorce today has become as common as marriage itself. The consequences of this circumstance have helped shape a society where liberty is on the decline—welfare dependence, violence, irresponsibility, ignorance, and a host of other social ills can be directly traced back to the overwhelming amount of unnecessarily "broken" families.

As prevalent as divorce is, many believe that the situation is improving. Commentators often point to studies that show the divorce rate peaking in the 1980s—after a surge during the 1960s and 1970s— and declining slightly since that time. One of the main influences in this decline is the fact that many couples today simply do not get married, and thus are not counted in the marriage and divorce statistics. Cohabitation—when a couple lives together without getting married— is, in the view of some marriage analysts, "the largest unrecognized threat to the quality and stability of children's family lives."[7] Whereas prior to 1970 only about 1 percent of all American couples cohabited, that number has skyrocketed fourteen-fold.[8] Sidestepping the obvious problems and impact surrounding the cohabiting relationship itself and again focusing on the children brings to the surface another wave of alarming data. Today, approximately 24 percent of American children are born to cohabiting couples (up from 14 percent in 2002[9]), and another 20 percent live at some point during their childhood with an unrelated adult cohabiting with their biological parent.[10] The effects of this circumstance are quite numerous, but perhaps the most prevalent is the substantially increased potential for child abuse. According to the Fourth National Incidence Study of Child Abuse and Neglect, a study conducted by the US Department of Health and Human Services, children living with their biological mother and her cohabiting boyfriend are around *eleven times more likely* to be physically, sexually, or emotionally abused than children living with their married biological parents.[11] Children living with both of their parents who are cohabiting still suffer abuse four times more often, on average, than those living with their married parents.[12] The number of couples opting for cohabitation and either delaying or refusing to marry has exploded in recent years. According to the US census, "the number of unmarried couples living together increased tenfold from 1960 to 2000,"[13] and today almost 8 million couples are living together outside of marriage.[14] By the time a child is two years old, 30 percent of cohabiting parents have gone their separate ways, while only 6 percent of couples who married will have divorced.[15] This steep rise in cohabitation, and its corresponding negative consequences, has contributed to the United States having the lowest rate of all Western countries of children being raised by both biological parents: 61 percent.[16] Seen today as a step in the courting process, living together has become the new norm. As a result, commitment has taken a backseat to convenience.

What does all of this have to do with liberty? How does the responsibility of creating strong families play a part? While the conventional battle for freedom pits the individual against the state, it is the family that gives both any relevance whatsoever. The family is not a mediating institution between the individual and the state, but an *originating* institution without which neither individuals nor states would even exist. How individuals interact with one another directly and indirectly via the state can be boiled down to the social, political, moral, and economic lessons (whether correct or incorrect) learned in their respective families. Consider what today's adults have learned in their own households growing up as youth. Were they taught the value of hard work, the virtue of love, or the importance of character and commitment? Were they taught to be kind to others, treat others' property with respect, or care for those in need? Do families damaged by divorce or corrupted by cohabitation produce, in the aggregate, the virtues and values needed to create a society of free people? Is the importance of responsibility taught by word and deed to children in households where commitments of fidelity and marriage are avoided or violated?

Persuading other adults to become responsible is an important task, albeit one met with relatively little success. Focusing instead on the rising generation—instilling these values and traits in people when they are impressionable, quick to adapt, and willing to learn—can yield much more success. As one anonymous quote says, "It is easier to build strong children than to repair broken men." What kinds of children are being "built" in experimental family situations?

The most basic benchmark of any society is the caliber of the families that comprise it. What, then, does this "experiment of living" have to show for itself? Reviewing these trends two decades ago, cultural historian James Lincoln Collier offered this commentary:

> We have abandoned our children. Between a soaring divorce rate
> and an equally soaring rate of children born to unwed mothers, it
> is now the case that the majority of our children will spend at least

a portion of their childhoods in single parent homes—in effect being raised without fathers. A large minority will spend their entire childhoods essentially without fathers, and a considerable number will not even know who their fathers are.

This is an extremely unusual circumstance—perhaps unique in human experience. *In no known human society, past or present, have children generally been raised outside of an intact nuclear family.* The nuclear family is one of the most basic of all human institutions, a system of doing things so fundamental that until this century it occurred to very few people that life could exist without it.[17]

An ever-increasing proportion of American families either cannot or do not fulfill some of the basic functions for which the family exists—to serve as the primary system for the provision of education, welfare, and health to the young, the sick, and the elderly. The gradual abandonment of the nuclear[18] family structure has brought with it a destabilization or outright dissolution of mediating institutions—churches, charities, fraternal organizations, and so on—which has encouraged the encroachments of the government into areas once taken care of by voluntary associations. At least $100 billion is spent per year in America on government programs, whether police, prisons, welfare, or court costs, to try and deal with the consequences of broken families.[19] Indeed, the colossal growth of the state, and the corresponding infringement of individual liberty, can be traced in part to the systemic dysfunction and destruction of many of the nation's families.

The police state has grown as a result of increased crime, due in part to the abandonment of fathers—the "most harmful demographic trend of this generation," as one author on the subject puts it.[20] Deprived of the love and support needed to develop into mature, responsible, and moral adults, children raised by a single parent are more likely than their peers to become criminals later in life.[21]

The welfare state has likewise grown due to the unwillingness or inability of families to take care of their own. Single mothers working two jobs, needy children, aging parents, and a long list of other cases have all resulted in government policies meant to help provide for those in need. Funding these programs has necessitated a double-faceted form of theft from the American taxpayer, both directly through taxation and indirectly through creating new money to fund such programs, causing inflation. Whether taking money directly from somebody who might need it or by devaluing the money a person has saved through inflation, this financial strain on American families often compels mothers to leave the home in pursuit of additional income, prompts fathers to seek a second job to make ends meet, and otherwise increases stress and strain on families who otherwise might not have had such a burden. Since divorce rates increase as couples experience financial tension,[22] the relationship between the welfare state and broken families is symbiotic. Broken families create additional dependence upon the programs that are part of the welfare state, and the funding of such programs then causes financial strain, which in turn creates more broken families.

The warfare state has expanded by sending spouses around the world to leave their families, causing the overall divorce rate among members of the military to rise from 2.6 percent in 2001 to 3.7 percent in 2011.[23] But the effects on the family are far greater than that: an America soldier dies every day and a half, on average, in Iraq and Afghanistan—often leaving behind a spouse and children who become dependent upon government welfare programs to survive.[24] Even worse, veterans kill themselves at a rate of one every eighty minutes.[25]

Unsurprisingly, the nanny state has also expanded, as the government believes that parents are not doing a sufficient job of being responsible themselves and encouraging their kids to do the same. Cell phone bans while driving, healthy eating regulations, zoning and landscaping laws, and even prohibitions on purchasing lightbulbs, toys in Happy Meals, and lemonade from kids on the side of the road have become hallmarks of the increasingly intrusive nanny state.

While many other factors play a part in the exponential expansion of the state's size and scope, the nuclear family is an important gatekeeper and arbiter of whether the state will increase or diminish in power. In a document called "The Divine Institution of Marriage," the LDS Church stated that family is a "vital instrument for rearing children and teaching them to become responsible adults."[26] When that instrument becomes dull or discarded, all of society suffers in the long run. Elder Neal A. Maxwell explained:

> Can we really afford a society in which the family, our most basic institution, is further diminished? Most of us revolt at the idea of having children raised by the state, but step by small step we are moving in that direction. If our society's success depends on having a critical mass of citizens with a sense of fair play and

justice, and with love and concern for others, where do citizens usually acquire those crucial virtues, if we acquire them at all? We usually acquire them first and best in the family. The family garden, as has been said, is still the best place to grow happy humans. Society already pays terrible costs for the products of tragically flawed families, but if our nation further undermines the average family, the costs will be catastrophic.

What we do with the family is going to determine what happens to our whole society. The wise Catholic writer, G. K. Chesterton, observed years ago that only men to whom the family is sacred will ever have a standard by which to criticize the State, because "they alone can appeal to something more holy than the gods of the city."[27]

Liberty is irrelevant without family. Indeed, the perpetuation of the human race through nuclear families is what first makes life, liberty, and the pursuit of happiness at all possible. The most important and effective place to learn the lessons of agency, liberty, and responsibility are in the home. Other mentors and influences can have a positive impact on a child and offer exposure to ideas and experiences that otherwise might not be provided, but a child who does not have access to parents who teach their children these things by word and example is at a significant disadvantage. Children who do not gradually learn to become independent of their parents will soon find themselves as adults depending on the government. Responsibility must be taught and learned within the family unit; otherwise society becomes full of adult infants unable to take care of themselves.

While in some cases a "broken" family is a necessity, whether due to death, abuse, or other unfortunate circumstances, the overwhelming majority of such families result from factors that could have been resolved by a couple committed to one another and their children. Further, simply being married does not assure that the union will be a healthy and successful one, or that the husband and wife will be good parents raising children to be intelligent, independent, and responsible. The nuclear family faces both internal and external threats, and the radical experimentation conducted over the past several decades has produced a series of negative consequences that puts the future of responsibility and liberty at risk.

Divorce and cohabitation are significant influences that are substantively altering society, but they are not the only ones. Another threat is the rise of homosexual couples seeking societal legitimacy and claiming to be an alternative form of family, equally capable of raising children. Today, more than 110,000 same-sex couples raise children in the United States, nearly double from a decade ago.[28] Through another tragic force, nuclear families around the world are decreased in size (and future ones denied existence altogether) through the institutionalized infanticide that sends roughly 115,000 unborn human beings to their death every single day.[29] From 1973 through 2008, nearly fifty million legal abortions have occurred in the United States.[30] Over forty million abortions are performed worldwide *each year*.[31] Less visible factors such as neglect, abuse, jealousy, pride, poor financial management and contention are no less significant, and likewise exist as real threats to families. Indeed, internal threats within nuclear families are equally if not more problematic than external experiments made at a societal level.

Marian Wright Edelman, president of the Children's Defense Fund, explains: "If the foundation of your house is crumbling, you don't say you can't afford to fix it while you're building astronomically expensive fences to protect it from outside enemies. The issue is not, 'are we going to pay,' it's are we going to pay now, up front, or are we going to pay a whole lot more later on."[32] The pressing matter for each family, then, is determining where and how it is most vulnerable and taking corrective and protective measures to counteract the attacks. This is not a topic meant only for religious or academic discussion. The family unit is legitimately under attack, and the government is rapidly growing in light of the increasing irresponsibility such attacks help cultivate. Families must be strengthened—life, liberty, and the pursuit of each person's happiness hang in the balance.

THE POWER OF THE PROCLAMATION

The Book of Mormon recounts the story of Amalickiah, a scheming and power-lusting individual who desired to be king and employed flattery and deceit to gain a significant following. He "led away the hearts of many people to do wickedly" and encouraged his group "to destroy the foundation of liberty which God had granted unto them" (Alma 46:10). In response to this uprising, Moroni grew angry, rent his coat, and on a piece of the fabric wrote: "In memory of our God, our religion, and freedom, and our peace, our wives, and our children" (Alma 46:12). Naming it the "title of liberty," Moroni used the phrase to rally the Nephites to their righteous cause, and close ranks against those wishing to attack their religion, their liberty, and their families.

Through his treachery, murder, and intrigue, Amalickiah became king of the Lamanites and used his new political position to breed animosity toward his former countrymen, the Nephites. As he prepared a military campaign "to overpower the Nephites and to bring them into bondage" (Alma 48:4), Moroni was preparing his people "to be faithful unto the Lord their God" (Alma 48:7). By strengthening the weakest fortifications and increasing their defensive barriers, Moroni "was preparing to support their liberty, their lands, their wives, and their children, and their peace" (Alma 48:10). Though these exhaustive efforts would later prove successful in repelling external attacks, Moroni had to also deal with internal dissensions that threatened to undermine the very cause for which the Nephites were fighting. A land dispute with the people of Morianton (see Alma 50:25–35), dissent by the king-men hoping to alter the form of government (see Alma 51:2–21), and other "wars and contentions among his own people" (Alma 51:22) weakened the Nephites' ability to repeal the Lamanite attacks. While Moroni was required to focus on cleansing the Nephites' inward vessel (see Alma 60:23), the Lamanites invaded a city that was not strong enough to survive the attack (Alma 51:22–23). Internal distractions and conflict had led to external weakness.

Who is raising the title of liberty today and defending the family against both external and internal attacks? What defensive measures are being employed to repel attacks, and what is being done to resolve the internal dissensions that undermine families? Consider the following report titled "Marriage in America: A Report to the Nation," issued in 1995 by the Council on Families in America. Stressing the importance of this foundational union in the family, the authors wrote:

> The divorce revolution—the steady displacement of a marriage culture by a culture of divorce and unwed parenthood—has failed. It has created terrible hardships for children, incurred unsupportable social costs, and failed to deliver on its promise of greater adult happiness. The time has come to shift the focus of national attention from divorce to marriage. . . . To reverse

the current deterioration of child and societal well-being in the United States, we must strengthen the institution of marriage . . . . Strengthening marriage . . . must become our most important goal. For unless we reverse the decline of marriage, no other achievements—no tax cut, no new government program, no new idea—will be powerful enough to reverse the trend of declining child well-being. . . . We call for the nation to commit itself to this overriding goal: To increase the proportion of children who grow up with their two married parents and decrease the proportion of children who do not. . . . Who, today, is still promoting marriage? Who is even talking about it? In place of a national debate about what has happened to marriage there has been silence—stonecold silence.[33]

During the same year that this challenge was issued, President Gordon B. Hinckley introduced a document with which Latter-day Saints are now very familiar: "The Family: A Proclamation to the World." After some remarks to the sisters in the October 1995 general Relief Society meeting, and prior to reading the proclamation in its entirety, he stated the following:

With so much of sophistry that is passed off as truth, with so much of deception concerning standards and values, with so much of allurement and enticement to take on the slow stain of the world, we have felt to warn and forewarn. In furtherance of this we of the First Presidency and the Council of the Twelve Apostles now issue a proclamation to the Church and to the world as a declaration and reaffirmation of standards, doctrines, and practices relative to the family which the prophets, seers, and revelators of this church have repeatedly stated throughout its history.[34]

The sophistry, deceit, and temptation described by President Hinckley stem in part from the experimentation on the family over the past several decades. These are not mere words he casually decided to include in his address, but rather a description of the world we live in—a world that surrounds us with lies, half-truths, immorality, and corruption at every turn. Rarely do Latter-day Saints find themselves having to actively thwart an external attack against their lives, liberties, or families. Rather, Satan's most effective bait is to use the "slow stain" method described by President Hinckley, whereby spiritual promptings to be anxiously engaged in a good cause are steadily ignored until the flaxen cords of bondage (2 Nephi 26:22) become nearly unbreakable. The world's ever-changing value systems are almost always at odds with the fixed standard required by God. Latter-day Saints are part of "a chosen generation, a royal priesthood, an holy nation, a peculiar people; that ye should shew forth the praises of him who hath called you out of darkness into his marvellous light" (1 Peter 2:9). But the sophistry and slow stains continue to assault the family, despite this noble calling. Clear back in his day, Brigham Young foresaw the temptation of Babylon's stains, and warned against them. Mosiah Hancock records that Brigham had seen, in a dream, the Latter-day Saints "drinking in the spirit of Babylon until one could hardly tell a Saint from a black-leg."[35] Brigham continued:

> Many of this people for the sake of riches and popularity, will sell themselves for that which will canker their souls and lead them down to misery and despair. It would be better for them to dwell in wigwams among the Indians than to dwell with the gentiles and miss the glories which God wishes them to obtain. I wish my families would see the point and come forth before it is too late. For oh, I can see a tendency in my families to hug the moth-eaten customs of Babylon to their bosoms. This is far more hurtful to them than the deadly viper; for the poisons of the viper can be healed by the power of God, but the customs of Babylon will be hard to get rid of.[36]

The changing customs of Babylon, including the change in attitudes regarding the nature and importance of marriage and family, have not let up since Brother Brigham expressed his concern about them. Indeed, they have significantly worsened. In his address, President Hinckley noted that he and the other General Authorities still to this day "have felt to warn and forewarn." It would seem, given the repetitive nature of the warnings, that the society in which we live still has not gotten the message.

This proclamation to the world on the subject of the family serves as a modern title of liberty—one which, if ignored or rejected, will "bring upon individuals, communities, and nations the calamities foretold by ancient and modern prophets."[37] It emphatically declares that "marriage between a man and a woman is ordained of God and that the family is central to the Creator's plan for the eternal destiny of His children." It affirms that all individuals are created in God's image and have "a divine nature and destiny." It rejects gender-bending societal trends by declaring that "Gender is an essential characteristic of individual premortal, mortal, and eternal identity and purpose." It takes on the staggering statistics surrounding unwed pregnancy and cohabitation, stating that "God has commanded that the sacred powers of procreation are to be employed only between man and woman, lawfully wedded as husband and wife." It addresses abortion, referring to the "the sanctity of life" and its "importance in God's eternal plan." It describes the "solemn responsibility" that both husband and wife have to care for one another and their children in an atmosphere of "love and righteousness." The proclamation declares that "The family is ordained of God," and thus should not be experimented with contrary to God's commandments. "Marriage between man and woman is essential," it states, and the children brought into this world "are entitled to birth within the bonds of matrimony, and to be reared by a father and a mother who honor marital vows with complete fidelity." In short, it offers clarity and light to a world filled with confusion and darkness.

It is important to remember that the external and internal attacks against the family are not merely cultural trends or happenstance developments as society progresses. Since they attempt to change what God has ordained, they are therefore either instigated or supported by Satan. A year following the release of the proclamation, Elder Robert D. Hales described Satan's role in these attacks:

> Because of the importance of the family to the eternal plan of happiness, Satan makes a major effort to destroy the sanctity of the family, demean the importance of the role of men and women, encourage moral uncleanliness and violations of the sacred law of chastity, and to discourage parents from placing the bearing and rearing of children as one of their highest priorities.[38]

In response to this effort on Satan's part, the proclamation declares that "individuals who violate covenants of chastity, who abuse spouse or offspring, or who fail to fulfill family responsibilities will one day stand accountable before God." Thus, while the "moth-eaten customs of Babylon" entice individuals to "call evil good and good evil" (Isaiah 5:20), the proclamation persuades God's children to understand and implement the commandments and characteristics of what marriage and family were ordained by God to be. The consequences of our actions relating to the family unit are eternal; salvation, as Elder Hugh B. Brown taught, "is essentially a family affair, and full participation in the plan of salvation can be had only in family units."[39] It is little wonder why Satan works tirelessly and cunningly to undermine this fundamental institution.

The power of this proclamation lies in the willingness and ability of those who believe its precepts to adopt and promote them. The French political economist Frédéric Bastiat once wrote that "the worst thing that can happen to a good cause is, not to be skillfully attacked, but to be ineptly defended."[40] If those who best understand how and why the family is ordained of God do not live worthy of that knowledge and defend the family unit from attack, then who will? Remember the question posed by the authors of the report mentioned earlier: "Who, today, is still promoting marriage? Who is even talking about it? In place of a national debate about what has happened to marriage there has been silence—stonecold silence." Whether with marriage specifically or the family more generally, there has been a profound imbalance in fighting back against society's slow but strong stain. The proclamation was given not as a declaration of new doctrine, but a summary of what God's prophets have for ages been communicating to his children. Have we been listening? More important, what are we doing about it?

"Why do we have this proclamation on the family now?" asked President Hinckley. "Because the family is under attack. All across the world families are falling apart. The place to begin to improve society is in the home. Children do, for the most part, what they are taught. We are trying to make the world better by making the family stronger." Loving, responsible, and strong families do not merely stand a greater chance at eternal salvation—the world becomes a better place, as President Hinckley noted, by their very existence. Responsibility is better taught to children and exemplified by their parents. Love is fostered between family members and cultivated toward neighbors. Committed parents seeking to raise their children to be self-reliant and productive members of society demonstrate hard work. Only in an environment where these and other related and important values can be consistently nurtured, tested, and strengthened will individual liberty have any chance of success. Strong families resist the encroachments of a nanny state; they alone, as Elder Maxwell noted, "can appeal to something more holy than the gods of the city."

Strengthening Marriage

Individual liberty is, perhaps paradoxically, best preserved through the *communal* family unit. Just as the Revolutionary War was not fought and won by General George Washington alone, so too are our rights reclaimed and defended today through a team effort. The joint effort between family members in cultivating a recognition and fulfillment of personal responsibility has historically proven to be the best way to help maturing individuals become independent. At the head of the family, of course, are the mother and father; no family would exist, let alone succeed, without these two founding members. While families must be strengthened in order to preserve liberty, marriages must likewise be strengthened to preserve families.

What is marriage? Marriage is a covenant, or promise, that a man and woman make to each other and to God. In Latter-day Saint families, however, this is no mere contract to be terminated upon death—marriage is meant to be eternal. Those covenanting to abide the law of celestial marriage promise to remain faithful to one another and to God throughout all eternity; to confine intimate affections and sexual relations to each other; to live in ways that contribute to happy and successful family life; and to "be fruitful, and multiply, and replenish the earth" (Genesis 1:28). God's promises for those who faithfully adhere to this covenant include eternal life in the world to come and the glory of the celestial kingdom (see D&C 88:4), and an inheritance of "thrones, kingdoms, principalities, and powers" (see D&C 132:19).

Marriage is, as President Joseph Fielding Smith said, "an eternal principle upon which the very existence of mankind depends."[41] These are not words used lightly. President Smith continued: "No ordinance connected with the gospel of Jesus Christ is of greater importance, of more solemn and sacred nature, and more necessary to the eternal joy of man than marriage in the house of the Lord." The Church of Jesus Christ of Latter-day Saints teaches that "Marriage is sacred, ordained of God from before the foundation of the world."[42] The proclamation on the family similarly states that "Marriage between man and woman is essential to [God's] eternal plan." In the scriptures, the Lord teaches that men should cleave unto their wives, and "be one flesh" (Moses 3:24).

The commandment to "cleave" is perhaps the single most rejected aspect of marital union today. Estimates on infidelity in marriage vary, ranging from 40 percent to 76 percent of all marriages having at least one member committing an affair and thus failing to cleave to one another.[43] And whether a divorce results from such infidelity or for any number of other reasons (some of which are certainly necessary), divorce itself is a refusal to cleave, or at least the end result of not cleaving during the term of the now-broken marriage. To "cleave" means to unite, or to be united with. Thus, the foundational marital relationship is (ideally) one of unity, cohesion, and fidelity. Having noted that "it is not good that man should be alone" (Abraham 5:14), God made "an help meet" for him. Indeed, as Benjamin Franklin once observed, "A single man has not nearly the value he would have in a state of union. He is an incomplete animal. He resembles the odd half of a pair of scissors."[44] Paul taught the Saints in Corinth: "Neither is the man without the woman, neither the woman without the man, in the Lord" (1 Corinthians 11:11). Elder David A. Bednar further explained the importance of this man/woman partnership:

> By divine design, men and women are intended to progress together toward perfection and a fulness of glory. Because of their distinctive temperaments and capacities, males and females each bring to a marriage relationship unique perspectives and experiences. The man and the woman contribute differently but equally to a oneness and a unity that can be achieved in no other way. The man completes and perfects the woman and the woman completes and perfects the man as they learn from and mutually strengthen and bless each other.[45]

Marriage is not just a commitment between two loving people, nor is it meant only for their own enjoyment and edification. Marriage is the divinely ordained institution by which God's children are brought into this mortal realm, "entitled," as the proclamation states, "to birth within the bonds of matrimony, and to be reared by a father and a mother who honor marital vows with complete fidelity." Marriages that bring children into this world are far more significant and influential than many myopically believe. What those marriages produce has long-lasting temporal, as well as eternal, consequences. As President Spencer W. Kimball said: "Marriage is perhaps the most vital of all the decisions and has the most far-reaching effects, for it has to do not only with immediate happiness, but also with eternal joys. It affects not only the two people involved, but their families and particularly their children and their children's children down through the many generations."[46]

With such a lasting impact, whether for good or for bad, marriages are a focal point for both God and Satan. God wishes success and happiness, and Satan wishes failure and misery. It's little wonder, then, that individual marriages, and the institution of marriage itself, are facing overwhelming internal and external threats. Satan, an eternal bachelor condemned to the misery his actions have produced, "seeketh that all men might be miserable like unto himself" (2 Nephi 2:27). If Satan can weaken or destroy the marital bond between husband and wife, as Elder Joseph B. Wirthlin noted, "he can cause more misery and more unhappiness for more people than he could in any other way."[47]

To understand how marriage should be strengthened, it's important to first recognize and understand how it is under attack. The scriptures are replete with references to a metaphorical marriage between the Savior and his people, in which Christ refers to himself as the "Bridegroom," and the Church as his bride. Elder James E. Talmage analyzed the breakdown of this marital relationship after Christ established his Church while on the earth in great detail in his book, *The Great Apostasy.* Throughout the book, Elder Talmage focuses on two main sources of the betrayal of Christ's covenant: internal and external. In the following paragraph, he notes the greater influence of one source over the other:

> Persecution [from external sources] at most was but an indirect cause of the decline of Christianity and the perversion of the saving principles of the gospel of Christ. The greater and more immediate dangers threatening the Church must be sought within the body itself. Indeed, the pressure of opposition from without served to restrain the bubbling springs of internal dissension, and actually delayed the more destructive eruptions of schism and heresy. A general review of the history of the Church down to the end of the third century shows that the periods of comparative peace were periods of weakness and decline in spiritual earnestness, and that

with the return of persecution came an awakening and a renewal in Christian devotion. Devout leaders of the people were not backward in declaring that each recurring period of persecution was a time of natural and necessary chastisement for the sin and corruption that had gained headway within the Church.[48]

Likewise, while many are prone to point a finger of blame towards external factors that threaten marriage, the most significant threats are internal ones. Increased premarital cohabitation, laws that attempt to alter marriage to include homosexual relationships, no-fault divorces—all these are but externalities that are secondary threats to each couple's marriage. As was the case with the early Church, the primary threats to today's marriages come from within. Indeed, the external threats just mentioned, and many more which exist, can in fact serve to strengthen one's marriage and increase fidelity between spouses and to God. The scriptures offer many examples of people being humbled through adversity and becoming stronger in their faith as a result. The Apostle Paul "[took] pleasure in infirmities, in reproaches, in necessities, in persecutions, in distresses for Christ's sake: for when I am weak," he said, "then am I strong" (2 Corinthians 12:10).

What, then, are the internal threats that undermine marriages? Consider the following passage by Joseph Milner, an eighteenth-century English reverend and church historian, quoted extensively in Elder Talmage's book. While Milner is referring to the internal threats that led to the early Church's demise, they are similarly applicable to marriages between husband and wife.

> During this whole century the work of God, in purity and power, had been tending to decay. . . . Outward peace and secular advantages completed the corruption. Ecclesiastical discipline, which had been too strict, was now relaxed exceedingly; bishops and people were in a state of malice. Endless quarrels were fomented among contending parties, and ambition and covetousness had in general gained the ascendency in the Christian Church. The faith of Christ itself appeared now an ordinary business; and here terminated, or nearly so, as far as appears, that first great effusion of the Spirit of God, which began at the day of Pentecost. Human depravity effected throughout a general decay of godliness; and one generation of men elapsed with very slender proofs of the spiritual presence of Christ with His Church.[49]

In other words, the Church was plagued with division, dissension, loose standards and morals, a lack of observance of covenant promises, anger, contention, selfishness, and a rejection of God's Holy Spirit. Similarly analyzing some of the problems besetting marriages, President James E. Faust cited "selfishness, immaturity, lack of commitment, inadequate communication, [and] unfaithfulness"[50] as examples. It should be noted that every item on that list as an *internal* threat. As with the fortifications needed to protect families from external threats, husband and wife should take proactive steps to counteract the carnal problems President Faust listed. To fight selfishness, spouses should serve one another, spend time thinking about and looking after the other's needs and desires, and place the concerns of others, where possible, before his or her own. To fight immaturity, spouses must seek after experiences that will mature their spiritual and emotional capacities, such as service, sacrifice, and education. To fight a lack of commitment, spouses must sacrifice to fulfill their obligations to the other spouse and their children, and prioritize them above other secondary demands on his or her time. To fight inadequate communication, spouses should hold family councils, conduct daily family prayer, and engage in conversation on enlightening and uplifting topics. To fight unfaithfulness, they must reserve their intimate actions, feelings, and thoughts only for their spouse, and none else.

Once these and other important steps are taken to ensure that their marriage is strengthened against internal threats, husband and wife can, in a united and more focused effort, turn their attention to the external ones. Each can do things to lessen the impact of ever-changing societal norms and influences, such as abstaining from media that sends less-than-virtuous messages right into the family room. They can reduce demands on their time that take them out of the home and away from opportunities for interaction with the other spouse and their children. They can manage their finances wisely and ignore enticing opportunities to take on debt in pursuit of entertainment or material acquisitions. They can become involved in the public arena, through education and persuasion, to defend the institution of marriage itself against those who seek to redefine its very meaning.

Each marriage is of course different, and the threats facing each one will vary depending on the individuals who comprise it—their backgrounds, their personalities, their interests, and their temptations.

Captain Moroni's strategy to strengthen the Nephites weakest fortifications (see Alma 48:9) is one that should be replicated in each marriage. Husband and wife together should, in a spirit of humility and unity, review their own weaknesses, their deficiencies, and their greatest areas of temptation, and then more proactively and thoroughly implement actions that will allow them to correct sinful or bad behavior.

Marriage is not a relationship, however, that should be relegated to the defensive position throughout life. Christians have been instructed to "be . . . an example of the believers" (1 Timothy 4:12), and to let their light shine before men (Matthew 5:16). In a world where marriage is quickly becoming loosely defined, deemed as irrelevant or unnecessary, and viewed as a temporary commitment more likely to end in divorce than not, positive examples of marriage are extremely important. Elder Neal A. Maxwell stated that "Latter-day Saints therefore have no choice but to stand up and to speak up whenever the institution of the family is concerned, even if we are misunderstood, resented, or brushed aside."[51] As President Hinckley once observed, "we are compelled by our doctrine to speak out."[52] In a society teeming with chaos, controversy, and contention, strong marriages can demonstrate through word and deed the power, peace, and protection that such a bond creates. As Elder Maxwell noted: "The ways of the world receive constant reinforcement—should not the ways of heaven?"[53]

STRONG FAMILIES WEAKEN THE STATE

Strong marriages result in responsible families, and responsible families help produce a healthy society in which people voluntarily and lovingly look after one another. The fight for individual liberty often takes place in the halls of government, but if the fight only occurs there, it will be lost. The heroes in the battle for liberty are not only the activist raising awareness about important issues, the legislator repealing unjust laws, and the hardworking individuals donating to help fund the cause of liberty. Indeed, the silent and often unnoticed heroes are arguably the most important actors in this fight—the men and women who unite together into families, raise responsible children, sacrifice and serve one another, and by their example awaken and inspire countless others to follow suit.

Unfortunately, some of the largest threats to a stable society and the fight for individual liberty come not from the state, but the individuals who comprise it: spouses who don't keep their commitments to one another and to their children; parents who govern their children with an authoritarian, impatient style; fathers who abandon their families to pursue selfish interests, leading the wife and children to depend on others for their basic needs; children who rebel against their parents and resist spending time with their family; and celebrities and other influential individuals who promote lifestyles and attitudes that undermine the family unit. King Benjamin told his people that "I cannot tell you all the things whereby ye may commit sin; for there are divers ways and means, even so many that I cannot number them" (Mosiah 4:29). So, too, with those who unconsciously undermine the fabric that keeps families intact and able to resist the internal and external influences which threaten them—with so many ways to destroy family unity and strength, we can at times become our own worst enemy.

Elder M. Russell Ballard noted that "Societies at large are strengthened as families grow stronger. . . . And when families work and play together, neighborhoods and communities flourish, economies improve, and less government and fewer costly safety nets are required."[54] Intact, functional families strengthen society because society is nothing more than a term used for the voluntary interactions between individuals, working in peaceful exchange one with another. As families create a microcosm of society within their own home, interacting with one another for each person's benefit and interest, this trend trickles upward to foster a society with more voluntary interactions, and fewer coercive ones. Society is weakened through the use of coercion when the state decides to intervene and compel or prevent an action it believes to be right. The state, as historian Murray Rothbard noted, "is an antisocial instrument, crippling voluntary interchange, individual creativity, and the division of labor."[55] A paternalistic state is anathema to a society of independent and responsible individuals voluntarily interacting with one another. Thus, as families and societies become more responsible and increase in independence relative to the state, the state consequentially diminishes in size and scope. In other words, as families become stronger, it becomes easier to reclaim and defend individual liberty.

Conservative author Robert Nisbet once wrote that "It is the nature of both family and state to struggle for the exclusive loyalty of their respective, and overlapping, members."[56] In this environment where "Caesar" requires that its subjects render unto it what they should instead be rendering unto God (see Matthew 22:21[57]), individuals must decide to which institution they will profess their allegiance and support.

SUGGESTIONS

The following suggestions are offered on how to better fulfill the responsibility of creating and maintaining strong families:

1. HOLD FAMILY HOME EVENING.

In September of 1970, a priesthood bulletin announced that "in a recent meeting the First Presidency and Council of the Twelve approved the setting aside of Monday night for holding family home evening throughout the entire Church. Encouragement is now given to stakes, missions, wards, and branches to reserve Monday evening for family home evening."[58] (Interestingly, *Monday Night Football* first aired on September 21, 1970.) While family home evening became formalized with this announcement, encouragement to hold a weekly home evening existed back to 1915 under President Joseph F. Smith's leadership.

During these evenings, families are encouraged to pray and sing together, read the scriptures, teach the gospel, and participate in unity-building activities such as games, outings, art projects, and so on. Echoing the similar counsel from Church leaders both before and after, President Ezra Taft Benson taught that "Family home evenings should be scheduled once a week as a time for discussions of gospel principles, recreation, work projects, skits, songs around the piano, games, special refreshments, and family prayers. Like iron links in a chain, this practice will bind a family together, in love, pride, tradition, strength, and loyalty."[59]

2. HOLD FAMILY SCRIPTURE STUDY.

While education is a personal responsibility, learning in a collaborative fashion with others provides an opportunity to discuss, consider alternative perspectives, and challenge your thoughts and beliefs. Individual scripture study is essential, but studying God's word in a family setting is also important. "Families are greatly blessed," taught President Howard W. Hunter, "when wise fathers and mothers bring their children about them, read from the pages of the scriptural library together, and then discuss freely the beautiful stories and thoughts according to the understanding of all."[60] The commitment to set this as a family goal, the consistency in doing it each day, adding variety to what is read and discussed, and looking for ways to help each family member individually apply scriptural lessons are all things that will help this practice produce spiritual rewards.

3. HOLD FAMILY COUNCIL.

Many church leaders have emphasized the importance of family councils as an opportunity to instruct, edify, and correct one another in an atmosphere of love and righteousness. Elder L. Tom Perry taught that "Each family organization should include a family council comprised of all members of the family unit. Here the basic responsibilities of the family organization can be taught to the children. They can learn how to make decisions and act upon those decisions. Too many are growing to marriageable age unprepared for this responsibility. Work ethics and self-preparedness can be taught in a most effective way in a family council."[61]

Councils should be a setting where the father (or, if absent, the mother) presides and counsels together with the other family members regarding circumstances or topics of relevant concern. They should be presented as an opportunity for honest and open communication, so problems may be resolved, questions may be answered, and conflict may be resolved. Consider setting goals for improvement both individually and together as a family, and then follow up in future councils to ensure accountability is taught and demonstrated.

4. HAVE DINNER TOGETHER.

In a recent general conference, Elder Dallin H. Oaks highlighted the importance of daily dinner together as a family. After noting that the number of families who usually eat dinner together has declined 33 percent, he stated: "This is most concerning because the time a family spends together eating meals at home [is] the strongest predictor of children's academic achievement and psychological adjustment. Family mealtimes have also been shown to be a strong bulwark against children's smoking, drinking, or using drugs. There is inspired wisdom in this advice to parents: what your children really want for dinner is you."[62]

Dinner is an excellent time to review how each person's day went at work, school, or home. With each family member often having busy and different schedules, a coordinated meal where all are present provides a calm setting to converse with one another, share stories, express frustrations, tell jokes, and otherwise enjoy one another's company. In large families, consider ways to ensure that each individual has a voice; taking turns sharing something can allow opportunities for shy children or indifferent teenagers to open up. Scripture reading can also be included at the end of the meal to take advantage of the moment and share a quick spiritual thought.

5. PRAY TOGETHER REGULARLY.

President Hinckley offered this suggestion: "I submit that a return to the old pattern of prayer, family prayer in the homes of the people, is one of the basic medications that would check the dread disease that is eroding the character of our society. We could not expect a miracle in a day, but in a generation we would have a miracle."[63] Stressing the importance of such prayers, President Kimball once observed that "In the past, having family prayer once a day may have been all right. But in the future it will not be enough if we are going to save our families."[64]

Simply offering thanks and requesting God's help is not enough, of course. Families united in prayer in hope of obtaining something have work to do. President Marion G. Romney stated that "The efficacy of our prayers depends on how we care for one another."[65] Use the family council as an opportunity to plan how family members can better meet each other's needs, and thus be instruments in God's hands to answer one another's prayers.

NOTES

1. Michael Novak, *The Spirit of Democratic Capitalism* (New York: Simon & Schuster, 1982).
2. Spencer W. Kimball, "Families Can Be Eternal," *Ensign*, Nov. 1980.
3. John Stuart Mill, *On Liberty* (Boston: Ticknor and Fields, 1863), 109.
4. Barbara Dafoe Whitehead, *The Divorce Culture* (New York: Vintage Books, 1998), 83.
5. Ibid.
6. See Judith S. Wallerstein, *The Unexpected Legacy of Divorce* (New York: Hyperion, 2000).
7. W. Bradford Wilcox, "Why Marriage Matters: Thirty Conclusions from the Social Sciences," National Marriage Project, accessed May 12, 2012, http://www.virginia.edu/marriageproject/pdfs/WMM_summary.pdf.
8. Ibid.
9. "Births to cohabiting couples dramatically increase," *Baptist Press*, April

20, 2012, accessed May 12, 2012, http://www.bpnews.net/bpnews
.asp?id=37654.

10. Wilcox, "Why Marriage Matters."

11. W. Bradford Wilcox, "Cohabitation and the abuse of America's children," *Deseret News*, May 15, 2011, accessed May 12, 2012, http://www. deseretnews.com/article/700135164/Cohabitation-and-the-abuse-of-Americas-children.html. It is important to note that these statistics show correlation and causation; cohabiting does not necessarily lead to child abuse. Other factors surrounding cohabitation, such as the type of people who are more likely to do it, certainly influence the outcome of how the children involved will be treated.

12. Ibid.

13. "Cohabitation is replacing dating," *USA Today*, July 17, 2005, accessed May 12, 2012, http://www.usatoday.com/life/lifestyle/2005-07-17-cohabitation_x.htm.

14. "The Downside of Cohabiting Before Marriage," *New York Times*, April 14, 2012, accessed May 12, 2012, http://www.nytimes.com/2012/04/15/opinion/sunday/the-downside-of-cohabiting-before-marriage.html.

15. Kalman M. Heller, Ph.D., "The Myth of the High Rate of Divorce," accessed May 12, 2012, http://www.drheller.com/divorcemyths.html.

16. "Majority of Children Live With Two Biological Parents," United States Census Bureau, February 20, 2008, accessed May 12, 2012, http://www.census.gov/newsroom/releases/archives/children/cb08-30.html.

17. James Lincoln Collier, *The Rise of Selfishness in America* (Lincoln, NE: iUniverse, Inc., 2005), 246.

18. "Nuclear family" is a sociological term used to describe a family consisting of two parents and one or more children.

19. "The Taxpayer Costs of Divorce and Unwed Childbearing," Institute for American Values, 2008, accessed May 12, 2012, http://www.americanvalues.org/pdfs/COFF.pdf.

20. David Blankenhorn, *Fatherless America: Confronting Our Most Urgent Problem* (New York: HarperCollins, 1995), 1.

21. Karen Heimer, "Gender, Interaction, and Delinquency: Testing a Theory of Differential Social Control," Social Psychology Quarterly 59 (1996), 39–61.

22. "Money Fights Predict Divorce Rates," *New York Times*, December 7, 2009, accessed May 12, 2012, http://economix.blogs.nytimes.com/2009/12/07/money-fights-predict-divorce-rates/.

23. "Military Divorce Rates Continue Steady Climb," Military.com, December 14, 2011, accessed May 12, 2012, http://www.military.com/news/article/military-divorce-rates-continue-steady-climb.html.

24. Nicholas D. Kristof, "A Veteran's Death, the Nation's Shame," *New York Times*, April 14, 2012, accessed May 12, 2012, http://www.nytimes

.com/2012/04/15/opinion/sunday/kristof-a-veterans-death-the-nations-shame.html.

25. Ibid.

26. "The Divine Institution of Marriage," Newsroom, The Church of Jesus Christ of Latter-day Saints, August 13, 2008, accessed May 12, 2012, http://www.mormonnewsroom.org/article/the-divine-institution-of-marriage.

27. Neal A. Maxwell, "The Prohibitive Costs of a Value-free Society," *Ensign*, Oct. 1978.

28. "Family Formation and Raising Children Among Same-sex Couples," The Williams Institute, January 2012, accessed May 12, 2012, http://williamsinstitute.law.ucla.edu/research/census-lgbt-demographics-studies/family-formation-and-raising-children-among-same-sex-couples/.

29. "U.S. Abortion Statistics," Abort73.com, April 18, 2012, accessed May 12, 2012, http://www.abort73.com/abortion_facts/us_abortion_statistics/.

30. Ibid.

31. "Worldwide Abortion Statistics," Abort73.com, May 26, 2011, accessed May 12, 2012, http://www.abort73.com/abortion_facts/worldwide_abortion_statistics/.

32. "The Child First Movement," Huffington Post, June 14, 2011, accessed May 12, 2012, http://www.huffingtonpost.com/daniel-heimpel/the-child-first-movement_b_875035.html.

33. Council on Families in America, *Marriage in America: A Report to the Nation* (New York: Institute for American Values, 1995), 1.

34. Gordon B. Hinckley, "Stand Strong against the Wiles of the World," *Ensign*, Nov. 1995.

35. The origin of the term "black-leg" appears to come from the ancient dislike of the rook (crow) because of its ravenousness and its feeding off of cornfields. "Rook" became used as a term of disapproval or abuse, and later was applied to those who took advantage of others. Since the rook is black and has black legs, the nickname "black-leg" later become common to describe a similar type of person.

36. Mosiah Lyman Hancock, *The Life Story of Mosiah Lyman Hancock*, typescript, Harold B. Lee Library, Brigham Young University, 73.

37. "The Family: A Proclamation to the World," http://www.lds.org/family/proclamation.

38. Robert D. Hales, "The Eternal Family," *Ensign*, Nov. 1996, 65.

39. Hugh B. Brown, in Conference Report, Oct. 1966, 103.

40. Frédéric Bastiat, *Economic Sophisms* (Irvington-on-Hudson, Foundation for Economic Education, 1996), 107.

41. Joseph Fielding Smith, in *Improvement Era*, vol. 73 (Salt Lake City: YMMIA, 1970), 2.

42. "The Divine Institution of Marriage," Newsroom.
43. D. M. Buss and T. K. Shackelford, "Susceptibility to infidelity in the first year of marriage," *Journal of Research in Personality*, 31, 1997, 193–221.
44. Sydney George Fisher, *The True Benjamin Franklin* (Philadelphia: J. B. Lippincott Company, 1899), 127.
45. David A. Bednar, "Marriage is Essential to His Eternal Plan," Worldwide Leadership Training Meeting: Supporting the Family, February 2006, http://www.lds.org/library/display/0,4945,6558-1-3363-3,00.html.
46. Spencer W. Kimball, *Marriage and Divorce* (Salt Lake City: Deseret Book, 1976), 2.
47. Joseph B. Wirthlin, "Spiritually Strong Homes and Families," *Ensign*, May 1993, 68.
48. James E. Talmage, *The Great Apostasy* (Salt Lake City: Deseret Book, 1994), 84–85.
49. Ibid., 87.
50. "The Enriching of Marriage," *Ensign*, Nov. 1977, 9.
51. Neal A. Maxwell, "Take Especial Care of Your Family," *Ensign*, April 1994.
52. Gordon B. Hinckley, "Why We Do Some of the Things We Do," *Ensign*, Nov. 1999.
53. Neal A. Maxwell, *Not My Will, But Thine* (Salt Lake City: Deseret Book, 1988), 133–34.
54. M. Russell Ballard, "That the Lost May Be Found," *Ensign*, May 2012.
55. Murray Rothbard, *The Ethics of Liberty* (New York: New York University Press, 1998), 187.
56. Robert Nisbet, *Prejudices: A Philosophical Dictionary* (Boston: Harvard University Press, 1982), 110.
57. For an interesting interpretation of this verse, see "Render Unto Caesar . . . ," LDS Liberty, accessed May 12, 2012, http://www.ldsliberty.org/render-unto-caesar/.
58. "I Have a Question," *Ensign*, Jan. 1987.
59. Ezra Taft Benson, "Salvation; A Family Affair," *Ensign*, July 1992, 4.
60. Howard W. Hunter, "Reading the Scriptures," *Ensign*, Nov. 1979, 64.
61. L. Tom Perry, "The Need to Teach Personal and Family Preparedness," *Ensign*, May 1981, 88.
62. Dallin H. Oaks, "Good, Better, Best," *Ensign*, Oct. 2007.
63. Gordon B. Hinckley, "The Blessings of Family Prayer," *Ensign*, Feb. 1991.
64. "The Greatest Challenge in the World—Good Parenting," *Ensign*, Nov. 1990, 33.
65. Marion G. Romney, "Welfare Services: The Savior's Program," *Ensign*, Oct. 1980.

FAITH AND
MORALITY

I am inclined to think that, if faith be wanting in him [the citizen], he must be subject; and if he be free, he must believe.[1]

—Alexis de Tocqueville

Religious faith is a store of light, knowledge, and wisdom and benefits society in a dramatic way when adherents engage in moral conduct because they feel accountable to God.[2]

—Elder Quentin L. Cook

QUESTIONS TO PONDER

1. Is there a connection between moral decay and the loss of liberty in society?

2. Do you see God's commandments as being burdensome or liberating?

3. If Satan "sought to destroy the agency of man" in the war in heaven, have his methods changed today?

4. As people decrease in righteousness, should the government intervene and enforce God's laws?

*T*he city later named Nauvoo, Illinois, was an uninhabited swamp before the Saints began to make it into their new home. Forced to flee Missouri in early 1839, they quickly turned the

235

land into a thriving city, which, at its peak in 1845, had a population of between twelve thousand and fifteen thousand.[3] The constant immigration of new converts created one logistical hurdle after another; renting a room or locating other temporary quarters was often difficult during the early 1840s. Even so, under Joseph Smith's direction and through the Saints' organization and cooperation, the city quickly overcame those hurdles, and Nauvoo expanded rapidly and successfully. The Illinois legislature had approved a very strong charter for the new city, giving Nauvoo powers that many other cities did not possess.[4] While relative peace existed, the city flourished. On one occasion, a member of the Illinois legislature visited Joseph Smith in Nauvoo and while there inquired of him regarding how he was able to preserve such perfect order while governing so many people—noting further that it was a circumstance the legislature had found impossible to replicate elsewhere. The Prophet Joseph replied that it was easy to do, and then elaborated: "I teach them correct principles, and they govern themselves."[5]

Think of it: a member of the state legislature impressed and intrigued at the sight of so many people taking care of themselves and living in peace. An entire city of people behaved in a way unlike any other city in that state, eager to be responsible, peaceful, and productive. Nauvoo was free. It was independent. Its citizens were fulfilling their responsibilities. "We do not go out of Nauvoo to disturb anybody," Joseph told a group of his followers. "Why, then, need they be troubled about us? Let them not meddle with our affairs, but let us alone."[6] Joseph was able to gather a people who were ready and willing to look after themselves and one another—people who actively sought out those "correct principles" he referenced, and then attempted to act accordingly. Thus, their ability to become independent and responsible was a direct result of living the principles of their faith.

The connection between faith in God and individual liberty has been dismissed or denigrated at times but nevertheless remains true. It was a connection frequently recognized and remarked upon by America's founders, who often stated that faith and morality were precursors to liberty. "Our Constitution was made only for a moral and religious people," observed John Adams. "It is wholly inadequate to the government of any other."[7] President George Washington wrote that "Of all the dispositions and habits which lead to political prosperity, religion and morality are indispensable supports. . . . Reason and experience both forbid us to expect, that national morality can prevail in exclusion of religious principles."[8] Benjamin Franklin agreed: "Only a virtuous people are capable of freedom. As nations become more corrupt and vicious, they have more need of masters."[9] Patrick Henry listed "virtue, morality, and religion" as the "great pillars of all government." He continued: "This is the armor . . . and this alone, that renders us invincible. These are the tactics we should study. If we lose these, we are conquered, fallen indeed . . . so long as our manners and principles remain sound, there is no danger."[10]

An atheist or agnostic may take issue with the above quotes (and hundreds of others which affirm the same idea), alleging that one does not need religion nor a Judeo-Christian moral framework to be free and defend liberty. They would actually be right; one need not be baptized or read the scriptures in order to live responsibly and morally. The principles of the gospel of Jesus Christ are found, in fragments, in a variety of religions and philosophies. Abiding by Christ's teachings does not require first being a member of his Church. Thus, a person can be living a clean, moral, Christian life without even being Christian. One need not even know whom Jesus Christ is to serve and love others, for example. As with many general rules, there is an exception to the claim that faith and morality are necessary responsibilities to live free and defend one's liberty against the encroachment of big government. But while such exceptions exist—in other words, while atheists and agnostics can indeed be strong allies in the cause of liberty—the principles of the gospel of Jesus Christ provide the surest way of becoming free. As the prolific German writer Johann Wolfgang von Goethe said, "What is the best government? That which teaches us to govern ourselves."[11] Joseph Smith, as we can see, was on to something.

Why were the citizens of Nauvoo a responsible people able to take care of themselves and become independent of outside assistance? What were the "correct principles" Joseph taught the followers of Christ to understand and implement? And more importantly, how can we become responsible and free by applying those same principles today? As with other important questions, these should be answered after first understanding the definition of what is being discussed. What, then, is a principle? Elder Richard G. Scott offered the following definition: "Principles are concentrated truth, packaged for application to a wide variety of circumstances. A true principle makes decisions clear even under the most confusing and compelling circumstances."[12] What principles in the gospel of Jesus Christ will lead to increased liberty and societal order?

Throughout his ministry, Jesus Christ taught many concentrated truths, intending them to be applied to a wide variety of circumstances. Perhaps foremost amongst his messages was the commandment to love one another. "A new commandment I give unto you," he taught his disciples, "that ye love one another; as I have loved you" (John 13:34). In his Sermon on the Mount, Jesus taught his disciples that simply loving their proverbial neighbors was insufficient. "Love your enemies," he said. "Bless them that curse you, do good to them that hate you, and pray for them which despitefully use you, and persecute you" (Matthew 5:44). The principle of loving others was so much a part of Christ's message that the Apostle John simply stated that "God *is* love" (1 John 4:8, emphasis added). The two greatest commandments given to men deal with love: "And thou shalt love the Lord thy God with all thy heart, and with all thy soul, and with all thy mind, and with all thy strength: this is the first commandment. And the second is like, namely this, Thou shalt love thy neighbour as thyself. There is none other commandment greater than these" (Mark 12:30–31). One of the main purposes of the restored gospel itself is to "convince" God's children to pursue peace (see 1 Nephi 14:7), a state accomplished through consistent, collective love.

Would today's geopolitical conflict endure if all of God's children loved their brothers in other nations? Would America's most dangerous cities be plagued by crime if parents raised their children in love and neighbors loved one another? Would torture, fraud, adultery, theft, vandalism, or neglect of those in need exist at all in a society where love prevailed? Like Nauvoo, the Nephite society after Christ's visit to the Western Hemisphere adhered to "correct principles" and thus governed themselves in peace and harmony for many years. Their universal adoption of the gospel of Jesus Christ led to "no contention in the land, because of the love of God which did dwell in the hearts of the people" (4 Nephi 1:15). As we seek to likewise become responsible and free by loving others, it is important to remember that love is best considered a verb, rather than just a noun. *Love* is an action word; rather than simply feeling love or helplessly falling into it, we actively choose to love others through our actions. As William Shakespeare said, "They do not love, that do not *show* their love."[13] The action of loving others—both friends and enemies—is service. The Apostle Paul taught the Saints, "ye have been called unto liberty; only use not liberty for an occasion to the flesh, but by love serve one another" (Galatians 5:13). A society whose members love one another will serve each other, resulting in a smoothly functioning community where individual liberty comes as a natural and welcome side effect.

A related "correct principle" taught by Jesus was what has become known today as the "Golden Rule." The scriptural source for this principle is Matthew 7:12, where the Master taught his disciples that "all things whatsoever ye would that men should do unto you, do ye even so to them." Referred to as "the formula for successful relationships with others" by President Ezra Taft Benson,[14] this principle is found in many other religions as well. Judaism teaches: "What is hateful to you, do not to your fellow man" (*Talmud*, Shabbat, 31a). Islam teaches: "No one of you is a believer until he desires for his brother that which he desires for himself" (*Sunnah*). Buddhism teaches: "Hurt not others in ways that you yourself would find hurtful" (*Udana-Varga* 5, 18). Confucianism teaches: "Is there one maxim which ought to be acted upon throughout one's life? Surely it is the maxim of loving-kindness: Do unto others what you would have them do unto you" (*Analects* 15, 23). "Wherever it is found and however it is expressed," taught Elder Russell M. Nelson, "the Golden Rule encompasses the moral code of the kingdom of God. It forbids interference by one with the rights of another. *It is equally binding upon nations, associations, and individuals.*"[15] In teaching this correct principle to his followers, Christ stated that "this is the law and the prophets," a phrase used to describe the Hebrew scriptures at that time. "The Law" refers to the first five books of the Old Testament, or what the Jews call the Torah. The subsequent words of the prophets, recorded in the rest of the Old Testament, were referred to as "The Prophets." Thus, to state that "this is the law and the prophets" effectively means that the "Golden Rule" was the underlying principle pervading existing scripture; dozens of books of scripture and all of God's law were distilled down into a single suggestion: do unto others as you would have them do unto you. As with the concept of loving others, consider how fully and sincerely implementing this principle would revolutionize relationships, from intimate to international. How would diplomacy change worldwide if countries sought to adhere to this important standard? How might residents in the same community become closer and more willing to help one another if they treated their neighbors the way that they would like to be treated?

Another principle conveyed in Christ's teachings is the eternal "law of the harvest." Teaching his disciples through parable, Christ referenced soils and seeds to demonstrate how planting seeds would yield different results depending on the nature of the soil. This was no mere gardening lesson—Jesus was helping others to understand the spiritual application of this pattern. The Apostle Paul later summarized the idea by simply saying that "whatsoever a man soweth, that shall he also reap" (Galatians 6:7; see also D&C 6:33). The Lord later emphasized this law by stating that "There is a law, irrevocably decreed in heaven before the foundations of this world, upon which all blessings are predicated— And when we obtain any blessing from God, it is by obedience to that law upon which it is predicated" (D&C 130:20–21). Our thoughts, words, and deeds become seeds sown that eventually must be reaped—whether to help or hinder us. Committing adultery, stealing another person's property, being dependent upon others—these and many more circumstances produce, in the aggregate, a society where liberty is lost and Christ's commandments are institutionally violated. Alternatively, a person who regularly does good works—one who is "anxiously engaged in a good cause" (D&C 58:27)—can create a ripple effect whereby those he serves are inspired to act likewise, creating a revolution of righteousness that trickles upward to change all of society. Whether for good or for evil, our actions determine the future; building a strong community, country, or world begins with each individual thinking and acting in a way such that they later reap peace and love. President David O. McKay taught:

> There is one responsibility which no man can evade and that responsibility is personal influence. Man's unconscious influence, the silent, subtle radiation of his personality. The effect of his words and acts. These are tremendous. Every moment of life he is changing to a degree the life of the whole world.
>
> Every man has an atmosphere which is affecting every other. Man cannot escape for one moment from this radiation of his character. This constantly weakening or strengthening of others. He cannot evade the responsibility by saying it is an unconscious influence. He can select the qualities he would permit to be

radiated. He can cultivate sweetness, calmness, trust, generosity, truth, justice, loyalty, nobility, and make them vitally active in his character. By these qualities he will constantly affect the world. This radiation to which I refer comes from what a person really is, not from what he pretends to be. Every man by his mere living is radiating sympathy, sorrow, or morbidness, cynicism, or happiness or hope, or any other hundred qualities. Life is a state of radiation and absorption. To exist is to radiate. To exist is to be the recipient of radiation.[16]

The experiences of Nauvoo, the Nephite society after Christ's visit, the early Saints after Christ's resurrection (see Acts 4:31–35) and other groups throughout history demonstrate what can happen when correct principles are lived by each individual. In the following remarks, President Howard W. Hunter offers an important analysis regarding what happens when these principles are *not* implemented—referencing the Law of the Harvest specifically, but generally describing what the rejection of the gospel of Jesus Christ will cause to happen.

There appears to me to be a trend to shift responsibility for life and its processes from the individual to the state. In this shift there is a basic violation of the Law of the Harvest, or the law of justice. The attitude of "something for nothing" is encouraged. The government is often looked to as the source of wealth. There is the feeling that the government should step in and take care of one's needs, one's emergencies, and one's future.

Just as my friend actually became a slave to his own ignorance and bad habits by refusing to accept the responsibility for his own education and moral growth, so, also, can an entire people be imperceptibly transferred from individuals, families, and communities to the federal government. . . .

What is the real cause of this trend toward the welfare state, toward more socialism? In the last analysis, in my judgment, *it is personal unrighteousness.* When people do not use their freedoms responsibly and righteously, *they will gradually lose these freedoms* . . .

If man will not recognize the inequalities around him and voluntarily, through the gospel plan, come to the aid of his brother, . . . he will find that through "a democratic process" he will be forced to come to the aid of his brother. The government will take from the "haves" and give to the "have nots." Both have lost their freedom. Those who "have," lost their freedom to give voluntarily of their own free will and in the way they desire. Those who "have not" lost their freedom because they did not earn what they received. They got "something for nothing," and they will neither appreciate the gift nor the giver of the gift.

Under this climate, people gradually become blind to what has happened and to the vital freedoms which they have lost.[17]

Faith in God and adherence to the moral standard he has established—a morality which includes not just sexual morality (such as chastity) but also justice, honesty, integrity, and other characteristics[18]—must be widely embraced if society is to enjoy any semblance of peace and prosperity. Liberty cannot long exist amongst a people who ignore their personal responsibilities and violate God's commandments. The founders were right to recognize the inherent bond between virtue and freedom. Samuel Adams once declared that the "truest friend to the liberty of his country" is one who "tries most to promote its virtue."[19] To become free, a person must have faith in God. Of course, a mere belief does not spark the change necessary to lead a person to become independent and free; like love, the word "faith" is better understood as a verb. To become free, one must not only have faith in God, but also be faith*ful* to him. Obeying God's commandments—implementing the "correct principles" he taught—is the seed that must be sown to later reap liberty. As Jesus said: "If ye continue in my word, then are ye my disciples indeed; and ye shall know the truth, and the truth shall make you free" (John 8:31–32). Faith and morality are inseparably connected to the principles Joseph referred to. These principles are readily discernible and well known, but individuals struggle to be faithful to them. Elder Scott noted that, "While easy to find, true principles are not easy to live until they become an established pattern of life." He continued:

> They will require you to dislodge false ideas. They can cause you wrenching battles within the secret chambers of your heart and decisive encounters to overcome temptation, peer pressure, and the false allure of the "easy way out." Yet, as you resolutely follow correct principles, you will forge strength of character available to you in times of urgent need. Your consistent adherence to principle overcomes the alluring yet false life-styles that surround you. Your faithful compliance to correct principles will generate

criticism and ridicule from others, yet the results are so eternally worthwhile that they warrant your every sacrifice.[20]

Though certainly worthwhile, the results that come from faith in God and obedience to his moral standard are often difficult to obtain. Held up as an ideal by many, they are consistently practiced by only a relative few. Even worse, they are sometimes so misinterpreted that people openly violate them while claiming to uphold them. For example, throughout the world's history many offensive wars have been waged in the very name of perpetuating Christian principles. But these deviations from principle (whether great or small) are not applications of those principles, but rather apostasy from them. Arriving at a point where an entire community of individuals can govern themselves can only happen through the correct principles found in the gospel of Jesus Christ. Thus, the proper course to combat the state's intervention into our lives and defend our liberty is to seek after and apply these principles—in short, to obey God's commandments and be responsible for ourselves and those within our stewardship.

While faith and morality are essential responsibilities that must be fulfilled if liberty is to be effectively defended, what happens when they are not widely adopted? When society becomes so wicked that people are routinely and openly shirking their responsibilities and completely abandoning God's moral standard, what recourse is available to prevent total moral decay?

A JUSTIFICATION FOR STATISM?

A common argument employed by Christian conservatives is that because people are unrighteous, the government must do for them what they will not do for themselves. Those who advance this argument often point to some common examples to support their claim. Because people do not give enough to charity, the welfare system is needed to take care of those unable to provide for themselves. Because children whose families are poor or who live in remote areas would otherwise not have access to a school, a public education system must be financed by taxpayers to provide education for all. Because drug use is harmful, regulations and prohibitions are needed to criminalize the production and consumption of these illicit substances. The list is lengthy, and each justification is based on the core idea behind this argument: widespread immorality and irresponsibility implicitly authorize the government's attempts to enforce a standard of morality that people would otherwise abandon.

The diagnosis made by these individuals is not inaccurate; morality and responsibility have been in decline over the past several decades, and now are either ignored or routinely denigrated in the public square. But is the proposed remedy worthy of support? Does the decline in morality and responsibility justify the government's intervention as a last-ditch effort to counteract society's moral decay? Writing on this subject recently, Elder D. Todd Christofferson is thought by some to have suggested exactly that. Like the proponents of the pro-state argument above, Elder Christofferson made a correct diagnosis:

> The societies in which many of us live have for more than a generation failed to foster moral discipline. They have taught that truth is relative and that everyone decides for himself or herself what is right. Concepts such as sin and wrong have been condemned as "value judgments." As the Lord describes it, "Every man walketh in his own way, and after the image of his own god" (D&C 1:16).[21]

From this determination of what is wrong, Elder Christofferson notes that, "As a consequence, self-discipline has eroded and societies are left to try to maintain order and civility by compulsion. The lack of internal control by individuals breeds external control by governments." On the surface, this observation appears to offer support for the scenario previously described. If understood this way, it would in fact seem to justify the state's use of compulsion and control to foster moral discipline. In other words, because so much of society has embraced immorality and irresponsibility, external influences are needed to shore up the moral deficiencies of the people.

Elder Christofferson continued his remarks by citing commentary from the prolific conservative columnist Walter Williams. "Policemen and laws can never replace customs, traditions and moral values as a means for regulating human behavior," Williams wrote. He continued: "At best, the police and criminal justice system are the last desperate line of defense for a civilized society. Our increased reliance on laws to regulate behavior is a measure of how uncivilized we've become."[22] Those attempting to justify statism because of moral decay may have found superficial wiggle room in the initial words from Elder Christofferson, but his inclusion of this commentary suggests that the opposite is in fact the better course. An institutionalized criminalization of social evils may be a defense against them, as Williams observed, but this obvious development of government control and compulsion does not become inherently right merely because it is "the last desperate line" for a civilized society. Necessity does not confer morality.

The wrong question in this discussion is whether the government is needed to promote and enforce morality. What should be addressed is whether the tools at the disposal of government will in fact promote and enforce morality. What can government do, other than coerce? It can fine, imprison, and physically assault those it alleges to have committed an offense against its laws. Are such tools an effective or moral means of promoting God's moral code? The obvious answer to this question is a negative one, for eternal laws are not fulfilled nor enforced through temporal coercion by one of God's children against another. "To deal with men by force," wrote Ayn Rand, "is as impractical as to deal with nature by persuasion."[23] God's moral ends do not justify mankind's immoral means. There is a better way.

Elder Christofferson's continuing remarks further explode the idea that immorality justifies statist interventions that otherwise would be wrongful and unjust. Noting that under a statist approach to enforcing moral discipline "there could never be enough rules so finely crafted as to anticipate and cover every situation," he argued that "*this approach leads to diminished freedom for everyone*" (emphasis added). In other words, this embrace of statism to uphold some arbitrary societal standard is not ideal. In fact, it breeds bondage.

Where the proponents of statist restraints on society ultimately fail is in conflating descriptions with prescriptions. Simply because something is observed to happen does not mean that that thing *should* happen, or that its happening is morally acceptable. The *description* in this case is the unsurprising development of increasing government intervention as society's standards decrease. But simply because that description generally holds true, it does not imply that it is itself the *prescription* for what should happen. In other words, because the power of the state tends to increase as people become immoral and irresponsible, it does not therefore follow that we should accept that increase as the right or best mechanism of counteracting that moral failure.

This idea was also included in Elder Christofferson's address. Citing the words of the Catholic Bishop Fulton J. Sheen, he said: "We would not accept the yoke of Christ; so now we must tremble at the yoke of Caesar." Caesar's reign was not morally justified by the people's rejection of Christ as their leader, but it is unsurprising that a depraved and wicked people would become overpowered by a centralized authoritarian state, in many ways openly welcoming and attempting to morally justify that state's "yoke."

The way to promote the responsibilities of faith in God and morality is not to empower the state as the enforcer of that divine standard, but rather to counteract evil through education and persuasion. When the Zoramites became wicked, Alma renounced his political power (and thereby rejected the use of statist coercion) and instead became a missionary. "And now, as the preaching of the word had a great tendency to lead the people to do that which was just—yea, it had had more powerful effect upon the minds of the people than the sword . . ." (Alma 31:5). Modern revelation likewise upholds the use of persuasion over coercion to promote righteousness. Noting that almost all men abuse whatever authority they get to "exercise unrighteous dominion," the revelation states that our influence on others must be "by persuasion, by long-suffering, by gentleness and meekness, and by love unfeigned" (D&C 121:29, 41).

The intervention of the state is not only immoral itself (not operating with any legitimately delegated authority) but also often breeds further immorality even as it attempts to suppress it. (Consider the results and side effects of the "war on drugs" as one of myriad examples.) A related quote by President J. Reuben Clark demonstrates the proper method of encouraging moral discipline:

> For America has a destiny—a destiny to conquer the world—not by force of arms, not by purchase and favor, for these conquests wash away, but by high purpose, by unselfish effort, by uplifting achievement, by a course of Christian living; a conquest that shall leave every nation free to move out to its own destiny; a conquest that shall bring, through the workings of our own example, the blessings of freedom and liberty to every people, without restraint or imposition or compulsion from us; a conquest that shall weld the whole earth together in one great brotherhood in a reign of mutual patience, forbearance, and charity, in a reign of peace to

which we shall lead all others by the persuasion of our own righteous example.[24]

The state's compulsion is antithetical to the persuasion by which the moral and virtuous principles of Christianity must be spread. When society begins to morally decay, those who turn to the state advocate an immoral act itself—the use of coercion against an individual who has sinned or shirked their responsibility, but who has not violated the rights of another person. They therefore perpetuate the very thing they claim to be trying to stop, and in so doing become hypocrites.

The state can only legitimately exist to secure to each individual his natural and unalienable rights. Encouraging and enforcing a moral standard is a topic that must therefore be left to families, churches, and other non-governmental institutions. Elder Christofferson observed that "In the end, it is only an internal moral compass in each individual that can effectively deal with the root causes as well as the symptoms of societal decay." Those who instead attempt to justify and advocate for statism as a backstop to that societal decay must recalibrate their own internal moral compass so as not to promote immorality in the name of fighting immorality.

Criminalizing immoral behavior will never compensate for an absence of morality. The lack of individual self-control does not justify external control on the part of government, but it certainly does explain it. Irish statesman Edmund Burke explained why:

> Men are qualified for civil liberty, in exact proportion to their disposition to put moral chains upon their appetites . . . . Society cannot exist unless a controlling power upon will and appetite be placed somewhere, and the less of it there is within, the more there must be without. It is ordained in the eternal constitution of things, that men of intemperate minds cannot be free. Their passions forge their fetters.[25]

Faith in God and obedience to his moral standard require a voluntary discipline that the state cannot replicate. The Saints in Joseph's day who lived the gospel's principles and governed themselves as a result are an example of the byproduct of such voluntary discipline. That independence is predicated on first following such principles; only after living righteously can we then claim the blessing of liberty that follows. Defending that liberty thus also requires promoting morality, for an immoral and irresponsible people will not only accept the illegitimate interventions of the state—they will openly beg for them. The necessary strategy to oppose that trend and counteract moral decay is to ensure each person's "internal moral compass" is correctly calibrated—and obeyed. When that occurs, men will finally put moral chains upon their own appetites and will thus be qualified to enjoy and defend liberty.

AGENCY: FAITH'S FOUNDATION

While volumes of books could be dedicated to compiling and discussing the correct principles of the gospel that must be implemented to have a free society, understanding their common thread can be achieved by instead focusing on a more foundational level. Faith and morality are important responsibilities, but they are extensions of a more fundamental element in the gospel of Jesus Christ: agency. Just as a compass must be tuned to true north in order to be accurate and usable, one's "internal moral compass" must be calibrated according to this guiding standard. By correctly understanding agency, one can then better exercise faith in the God who gave him that gift, and more fully follow his teachings.

Agency is not free. The phrase "free agency," while used by many Latter-day Saints, appears nowhere in scripture. While it is not necessarily incorrect to describe agency as free, danger arises when "free" is incorrectly defined. To many, freedom implies exemption from penalties or consequences. Such individuals "advocate absolute freedom without regard to consequences," as President James E. Faust taught.[26] This definition would imply that "free agency" means choice without cost or penalty—a result in direct opposition to what agency requires. Rather, agency is free in that we are free to make choices without compulsion. For this reason the scriptures state that "men are free according to the flesh . . . and they are free to choose liberty and eternal life, through the great Mediator of all men, or to choose captivity and death, according to the captivity and power of the devil" (2 Nephi 2:27; see also 2 Nephi 10:23). As part of our agency, we are held accountable for the choices we do make, along with their corresponding consequences.

While the scriptures do not refer to "free agency," they do reference "moral agency." The Lord notes that "every man may act in doctrine and principle pertaining to futurity, according to the moral agency which I have given unto him, that every man may be accountable for his own sins in the day of judgment" (D&C 101:78). The connection of these two words illustrates the importance of morality in correctly understanding and applying the eternal gift of agency. It is "by our *righteous* choices and actions," taught Elder Robert D. Hales, that "we liberate [others] from darkness by increasing their ability to walk in the light."[27] That liberation—independence from ignorance and bondage—is a natural byproduct of the correct use of agency. The purpose of faith in God and obedience to his commandments—indeed, the very reason we were given our agency (see Abraham 3:25)— is to one day return to his presence. Elder Dallin H. Oaks said that this goal "will result from a steady succession of covenants, ordinances, and actions, *an accumulation of right choices.*"[28] Faith and morality are clearly important in eternal matters, but their temporal implications are no less significant. Using our agency to obey God's commandments will liberate us from bondage, whether it be spiritual, temporal, financial, political, or otherwise. Life, liberty, and the pursuit of happiness gain greater meaning and potential as we bring our actions in line with God's divine standard. As President David O. McKay said, "Man's responsibility is correspondingly operative with his free agency. Actions in harmony with divine laws and the laws of nature will bring happiness, and those in opposition to divine truth, misery."[29]

Properly understanding agency is essential to recognizing how God operates, and by extension, how we should operate. In the *Lectures on Faith*, Joseph Smith taught that "three things are necessary, in order that any rational and intelligent being may exercise faith in God unto life and salvation. First, the idea that he actually exists. Second, a correct idea of his character, perfections, and attributes. Third, an actual knowledge that the course of life which he is pursuing, is according to his will."[30] Having a correct idea of God's character and attributes is therefore required in order to correctly have faith in (and thus obey) God. One such character or attribute is the unbending respect for the agency of each of his children. President Hunter explained:

> To fully understand this gift of agency and its inestimable worth, it is imperative that we understand that God's chief way of acting is by persuasion and patience and long-suffering, not by coercion and stark confrontation . . . He always acts with unfailing respect

for the freedom and independence that we possess. He wants to help us and pleads for the chance to assist us, but he will not do so in violation of our agency. He loves us too much to do that, and doing so would run counter to his divine character.[31]

In our congregations we sometimes sing a hymn that couches this idea in doctrinal and poetic prose:

> Know this, that ev'ry soul is free
> To choose his life and what he'll be;
> For this eternal truth is giv'n:
> That God will force no man to heav'n.
> He'll call, persuade, direct aright,
> And bless with wisdom, love, and light,
> In nameless ways be good and kind,
> But never force the human mind.
> Freedom and reason make us men;
> Take these away, what are we then?
> Mere animals, and just as well
> The beasts may think of heav'n or hell.[32]

If the responsibilities of having faith in God and abiding by his moral standard are required to successfully enjoy and defend individual liberty, then the more fundamental element of agency must first be understood and adhered to. By coercing others to act a certain way, even if that end goal is virtuous and praiseworthy, we employ tactics that God himself rejects. Statism is not a solution for immorality and irresponsibility.

While many might profess faith in God, not everybody follows his counsel to operate only through persuasion. When God the Father and Jesus Christ appeared to Joseph Smith and informed him that the fullness of the gospel would soon be restored, Joseph was told that the existing religions were all wrong. Referring to the followers of those other faiths, Joseph was further told by God that "they draw near to me with their lips, but their hearts are far from me, they teach for doctrines the commandments of men, having a form of godliness, but they deny the power thereof" (Joseph Smith—History 1:19). Many people verbally affirm that they love and follow Christ, but a review of their actions often reveals an irreconcilable inconsistency, demonstrating that they either do not have a correct idea of God—his "character, perfections and attributes"—or that they are, as Jesus so often said of the most pious in his day, hypocrites.

It is important to recall that a mighty war was waged over the question of agency. Satan sought to destroy the agency of man (see Moses 4:3), and his proposal was ultimately rejected. Still, he influenced a significant number of God's children—ironically employing agency in an effort to destroy it. Understanding Satan's methods to destroy agency helps to more clearly define it and allows us to more effectively reject and actively oppose policies, practices, and arguments that employ the same methods.

One of Satan's illegitimate proposals was to "redeem all mankind, that one soul shall not be lost" (Moses 4:1), a method which clearly would not allow God's children to choose whether they would obey his law and merit returning to his presence. One who "cannot look upon sin with the least degree of allowance" (D&C 1:31) clearly could not accept a system whereby all mankind, regardless of their sins, would be ushered back into his celestial environment. As Joseph Smith said, "The contention in heaven was, Jesus said there would be certain souls that would not be saved, and the devil said he could save them all . . ."[33] Despite this righteous roadblock, Lucifer was able to persuade many of his spiritual siblings to support him in his quest for power. How could such a campaign become so successful? Why would so many of God's children, who lived in his presence, be deceived into supporting Lucifer's goal to save all of mankind?

The answer to that question illuminates the strategies employed by those seeking to destroy agency today. One of the enemy's main methods of recruiting followers was to flatter those looking for an easy way out. In the Book of Mormon, Samuel the Lamanite noted that the Gadianton Robbers had used this method with the Nephites: "If a man shall come among you and shall say . . . do whatsoever your heart desireth . . . ye will receive him, and say that he is a prophet" (Helaman 13:27). The sinful segment of society looking to justify iniquity supported those who told them that they were not committing any wrong. Similarly, Satan proposed to his followers that all of mankind would be saved, regardless of their action—an enticing option for many who feared the damning possibilities of misused agency. It was an argument used by Nehor who taught, "that all mankind should be saved at the last day, . . . for the Lord had created all men, and had also redeemed all men; and, in the end, all men should have eternal life" (Alma 1:4). The Book of Mormon also describes countless others who believe that a loving God looks past sin after a simple confession, and that if any form of punishment does exist for sin, "God will beat us with a few stripes, and at last we shall be saved in the kingdom of God" (2 Nephi 28:8). The accountability aspect of agency rigidly requires that all of God's children face the consequences of their thoughts, their words, and their deeds. As such, Satan's campaign to remove that accountability and act however they pleased, even in clear contradiction to God's commandments, would always be an enticing argument to make. Nephi noted that this argument would be extremely popular in the last days:

> Yea, and there shall be many which shall teach after this manner, false and vain and foolish doctrines, and shall be puffed up in their hearts, and shall seek deep to hide their counsels from the Lord; and their works shall be in the dark. (2 Nephi 28:9)

Numerous other scriptural examples exist which demonstrate the false and vain and foolish doctrine of somehow being exempt from the accountability that agency requires. The Zoramites were a people that "would not observe to keep the commandments of God," yet who believed that they would be saved (see Alma 31:9,16). The people of Ammonihah, among the most wicked of groups recorded in the Book of Mormon, "did not believe in the repentance of their sins" (Alma 15:15). The story of the Gadianton Robbers, however, offers a much clearer understanding of how Satan's followers perpetuate this false doctrine. This group began when its founder, Gadianton, united a group of assassins with a secret oath for the purpose of helping and defending one another (Helaman 2:4–5). Whereas the Lamanites had been trying for around five centuries to defeat the Nephites militarily and bring them into bondage through direct attacks, the Gadiantons "did obtain the sole management of the government" (Helaman 6:39) in only twenty-six years. The key to their success is the driving force of every form of tyranny in our own day. It is therefore important to understand how they operated in order to recognize and combat the same strategies being used today.

Rather than attacking from the outside like the Lamanites, the Gadiantons primarily worked from the inside. This group made oaths "to help such as sought power to gain power" and to "murder, and to plunder, and to lie, and to commit all manner of wickedness and whoredoms" (Ether 8:16). Their goal was to gain power and to sin without consequence (see Helaman 6:22–24). Like with Satan's premortal plan, the Gadiantons "had *seduced* the more part of the righteous until they had come down to believe in their works and partake of their spoils, and to join with them in their secret murders and combinations" (Helaman 6:38; emphasis added). In other words, they pacified those who might have otherwise opposed their wicked deeds by offering them the opportunity to partake in their spoils and be protected while pursuing the same evil ends. Thus, the Gadianton goal "to keep [the people] in darkness" (Ether 8:16) was accomplished, in part, by undermining the morals of the people—enticing them to sin without any concern for the consequence.

The Gadiantons did not only work through persuasion among the people, however; a group of people seeking to become exempt from the consequences of their evil actions may conveniently alter the law so as to codify that exemption. Whereas Nephite law was once "correct, and . . . given them by the hand of the Lord" (Mosiah 29:25), in just two decades "their laws had become corrupted" because "they had altered . . . the laws" (Helaman 4:22). The implementation of illegitimate laws, which enabled evil and exempted it from any legal remedy, led to the corresponding corruption of the entire civilization:

> For as their laws and their governments were established by the voice of the people, and they who chose evil were more numerous than they who chose good, therefore they were ripening for destruction, for the laws had become corrupted.
>
> Yea, and this was not all; they were a stiffnecked people, insomuch that they could not be governed by the law nor justice, save it were to their destruction. (Helaman 5:2–3)

In the end, the Nephite civilization was destroyed not through an external enemy, but by moral decay and a corrupt legal system that ruled by "the laws of their wickedness" (Helaman 6:24). The prophet at the time, Helaman, records that the Gadiantons were "letting the guilty and the wicked go unpunished because of their money; and moreover to be held in office at the head of government, to rule and do according to their wills, that they might get gain and glory of the world, and, moreover, that they might the more easily commit adultery, and steal, and kill, and do according to their own wills" (Helaman 7:5). Satan's plan to redeem all of mankind finds its mortal application in such societies and legal systems, whereby agency is undermined by detaching consequences from choices. When men feel they are able to be governed not by the laws of justice and of God, but by "the laws of their wickedness," then they will feel emboldened to engage in evil acts that otherwise might not occur. In short, when consequence is removed from the choices that individuals make, they will increasingly make bad choices.

Dark works usually inhibit individual liberty as much as they attack agency and encourage evasion of God's commandments. Jesus noted that those who did not have faith in God were condemned, explaining that "this is the condemnation, that light is come into the world, and men loved darkness rather than light" (John 3:19). Why did the Jews at the time of Christ love darkness over the light? Why did they reject their Savior, the Light who had come into the world? Jesus stated it was "because their deeds were evil." Wicked men embraced the cover of darkness over the exposing, sanitizing light of day. It is a trend that has existed as long as good and evil themselves have existed. Jesus taught that "every one that doeth evil hateth the light, neither cometh to the light, lest his deeds should be reproved" (John 3:20). By promoting a moral code and legal standard which "call[ed] evil good, and good evil; that put darkness for light, and light for darkness" (Isaiah 5:20), the Gadiantons sought, like Satan, to destroy the agency of man. By attacking agency, they thus discouraged faith in God and a moral code of conduct. By enticing people to apostatize from the gospel, the Gadiantons destroyed individual liberty, gained control of the government (see Helaman 6:39), persecuted the few who clung to their faith (see Helaman 7:5), and ultimately caused the implosion of the entire civilization (see Ether 8:21). President Hinckley made clear the connection between the Gadiantons' activity as related in the Book of Mormon and our own day:

> [The Book of Mormon] is a chronicle of nations long since gone. But in its descriptions of the problems of today's society, it is as current as the morning newspaper and much more defini-tive, inspired, and inspiring concerning the solutions to those problems.

I know of no other writing that sets forth with such clarity the tragic consequences to societies that follow courses contrary to the commandments of God. Its pages trace the stories of two distinct civilizations that flourished on the Western Hemisphere. Each began as a small nation, its people walking in the fear of the Lord. Each prospered, but with prosperity came growing evils. The people succumbed to the wiles of ambitious and scheming leaders who oppressed them with burdensome taxes, who lulled them with hollow promises, who countenanced and even encouraged loose and lascivious living, who led them into terrible wars that resulted in the death of millions and the final extinction of two great civilizations in two different eras.

No other written testament so clearly illustrates the fact that when men and nations walk in the fear of God and in obedience to his commandments, they prosper and grow, but when they disregard him and his word, there comes a decay which, unless arrested by righteousness, leads to impotence and death.[34]

Written for our day, the Book of Mormon and its doctrinal teachings, scriptural stories, and related principles—such as those mentioned by President Hinckley—are meant to be applied to our lives. A concluding chapter written by Moroni shortly before his death conveys an even more explicit need to apply what was recorded. After describing the "secret combinations"—groups like the Gadianton robbers—Moroni writes the following:

Wherefore, O ye Gentiles, it is wisdom in God that these things should be shown unto you, that thereby ye may repent of your sins, and suffer not that these murderous combinations shall get above you, which are built up to get power and gain—and the work, yea, even the work of destruction come upon you, yea, even the sword of the justice of the Eternal God shall fall upon you, to your overthrow and destruction if ye shall suffer these things to be.

Wherefore, the Lord commandeth you, *when* ye shall see these things come among you that ye shall awake to a sense of your awful situation, because of this secret combination which shall be among you; or wo be unto it, because of the blood of them who have been slain; for they cry from the dust for vengeance upon it, and also upon those who built it up.

> For it cometh to pass that whoso buildeth it up *seeketh to overthrow the freedom of all lands, nations, and countries*; and it bringeth to pass *the destruction of all people*, for it is built up by the devil, who is the father of all lies . . . (Ether 8:23–25; emphasis added)

The attack on agency has consisted of the same method, whether by Satan in the war in heaven or by his followers here on Earth. Those who "teach after this manner, false and vain and foolish doctrines" seek to gain power, be free from the consequences of their bad decisions and evil actions, corrupt the population to make their deeds popularly acceptable, and alter the legal system to avoid any accountability. Their successes can be seen in the size and scope of the modern welfare state, the forced taxpayer bailout of banks and other companies, the legalization of torture and the denial of due process for alleged criminals, the promotion of immorality in multiple forms of media, so-called "stimulus" programs to offer money to individuals, corporations, and states, and a host of other political, social, and financial activities. The war in heaven wages on today, and the individuals employing Satan's methods—whether they know it or not—still seek to destroy the agency of man.

Framed in this context, the observations made by the founders regarding liberty's dependence upon faith and morality gain significant strength. Faith in God means more than merely attending church, praying regularly, or paying a tithe. Adhering to God's moral laws means more than merely abstaining from adultery, not telling any lies, and obeying the Word of Wisdom. Faith and morality are necessary for liberty because they are inseparably connected to agency—as Elder David A. Bednar explained, "faith in Christ inspires us to exercise our moral agency in compliance with gospel truth, invites the redeeming and strengthening powers of the Savior's Atonement into our lives, and enlarges the power within us whereby we are agents unto ourselves."[35] The personal responsibility of faith in God and moral living require the correct and righteous use of moral agency, resulting in independence, wisdom, and true liberty. As President Benson said, "righteousness is an indispensable ingredient to liberty."[36] While society can in the aggregate accommodate those who disbelieve in God and defy his laws, a system and culture of faith and morality must exist in order to protect liberty. Without it, those employing Satan's methods will more easily "overthrow the freedom of all lands, nations, and countries" because Americans, like the Nephites of old, will willingly barter away[37] their liberty by embracing a system that rejects God, undermines agency, and promotes both immorality and irresponsibility. The choice is ours, and "the voice of the people" (see Mosiah 29:26) will ultimately carry the day. Nephi noted that all of God's children "are free to choose liberty and eternal life through the great Mediator of all men, or to choose captivity and death, according to the captivity and power of the devil; for he seeketh that all men might be miserable like unto himself" (2 Nephi 2:26–27). "Liberty and eternal life"—the ultimate reward—cannot be obtained without the choice (the exercise of moral agency) to have faith in God and adhere to his moral standard.

SUGGESTIONS

The following suggestions are offered on how to better fulfill the responsibility of faith in God and adherence to his moral standard:

1. GAIN AN UNDERSTANDING OF MORAL AGENCY.

Those charged with preaching the gospel of Jesus Christ are told by God to "first seek to obtain my word" (D&C 11:21). The pattern of education before action applies equally to members and missionaries alike. As Satan is still seeking to undermine our agency, and if we are to fight back just as was necessary in the war in heaven, then it's crucial to first obtain God's "word" regarding what agency is; we cannot defend that which we do not understand. Review the scriptures looking for references to agency, as well as stories such as the Gadianton robbers' exploits, which demonstrate how agency is attacked. For those looking for compiled information to more easily understand the issue, consider reading *Satan's War on Free Agency* by Greg Wright.

2. STRENGTHEN YOUR FAITH IN GOD.

As the Prophet Joseph taught, to have faith in God it is necessary to first understand his character, perfections, and attributes. Engage yourself in serious scripture study, focusing on the nature of God, and how he operates in relation to his children. As you ponder these things, pray to God to receive a spiritual witness of what you're reading. Actively work to obey his commandments so you can more fully enjoy the gift of the Holy Ghost, and strengthen your testimony about the truthfulness of the restored gospel of Jesus Christ. Your righteous actions will lead you to not only have greater faith in God, but also to be more faithful to him.

3. AVOID CORRUPT MEDIA.

Joseph Smith noted that the "correct principles" of the gospel enabled the Saints in Nauvoo to become independent and enjoy (albeit for a limited time) peace and prosperity. Those principles are openly mocked and routinely ignored from secular sources, which consider them antiquated and restrictive. When he had the vision of the tree of life, Lehi observed that the individuals in the great and spacious building (which represented the "world and wisdom thereof") were "in the attitude of mocking" and "did point the finger of scorn" at those following Christ. The open attacks on faith and morality were popularly supported and widely practiced; "as many as heeded them," records Lehi, "had fallen away" (See 1 Nephi 8:33–34). In our day, the media is replete with similar mocking and scorn. Such sources of information and entertainment should be avoided. For a helpful guide about regarding what to avoid, see the "Entertainment and the Media" chapter of the Church's *For the Strength of Youth* pamphlet.

4. ARREST MORAL DECAY BY RIGHTEOUSNESS.

President Hinckley's quote referenced in this chapter noted that "unless arrested by righteousness," moral decay would lead "to impotence and death." God's same methods of promoting righteousness should be patterned after in our own lives so as to be most effective and correct. Recall President Hunter's words: "God's chief way of acting is by persuasion and patience and long-suffering, not by coercion and stark confrontation." Through education, persuasion, and creative activism, the cause of righteousness (and thus the cause of liberty) can gain ground in the war that has been occurring since the council in heaven. There are, of course, as many methods of arresting moral decay by righteousness as there are people who are willing to do it. Consider your own talents and resources, and determine how you might more "anxiously [be] engaged in a good cause" in order to "bring to pass much righteousness" (D&C 58:27).

NOTES

1. de Tocqueville, *Democracy*, 24.
2. Quentin L. Cook, "Let There Be Light!" *Ensign*, Oct. 2010.
3. At its peak in 1845, Nauvoo was the second largest city in Illinois. Chicago, the largest, had a population at the time of about fifteen thousand.
4. Nauvoo's charter afforded it powers such as an extremely independent militia; authority for the city council to pass any laws not in conflict with the US or Illinois Constitution, effectively allowing the council to circumvent statutory law; and court authority to review all writs made against Nauvoo citizens, allowing the local (and friendly) court to protect Joseph Smith and other targeted citizens from trumped up charges.
5. As quoted in "The Organization of the Church," *Millennial Star*, Nov. 15, 1851, 339.

6. Roberts, *History of the Church,* vol. 4, 470–71.

7. Charles Francis Adams, ed., *The Works of John Adams*, vol. 9 (Boston: Little, Brown, 1854), 229.

8. Edward Charles M'Guire, *The Religious Opinions and Character of Washington* (New York: Harper & Brothers, 1836), 74.

9. Benjamin Franklin, *The Memoirs of Benjamin Franklin*, vol. 1 (New York: Derby & Jackson, 1859), 604.

10. As quoted in Jared Sparks, ed., *The Writings of George Washington*, vol. 11 (Boston: Russell, Shattuck, and Williams, 1836), 558.

11. Johann Wolfgang von Goethe, *The Maxims and Reflections of Goethe* (New York: The MacMillan Company, 1906), 107.

12. Richard G. Scott, "Acquiring Spiritual Knowledge," *Ensign*, Nov. 1993, 86.

13. *The Plays of William Shakespeare*, vol. 3 (London: C. Bathurst, 1778), 76; emphasis added.

14. Ezra Taft Benson, *Teachings of Ezra Taft Benson* (Salt Lake City: Deseret Book, 1988), 447.

15. Russell M. Nelson, "Blessed Are the Peacemakers," *Ensign*, Nov 2002, 39; emphasis added.

16. David O. McKay, "The Mission of Brigham Young University," April 27, 1948, accessed May 12, 2012, http://education.byu.edu/mckay/48apr27 .html.

17. Howard W. Hunter, "The Law of the Harvest," BYU Devotional, Mar. 8, 1966; emphasis added.

18. Morality is often too narrowly defined, reduced only to sexually oriented behavior. It is instructive to note the various items included in the Topical Guide as being related to morality: charity, chastity, cleanliness, courage, grace, honesty, integrity, justice, life (sanctity of), modesty, prudence, purity, righteousness, self-mastery, steadfastness.

19. William V. Wells, ed., *The Life and Public Services of Samuel Adams*, vol. 1 (Boston: Little, Brown: 1866), 22.

20. Scott, "The Power of Correct Principles."

21. D. Todd Christofferson, "Moral Discipline," *Ensign*, Oct. 2009.

22. Walter Williams, "Laws Are a Poor Substitute for Common Decency, Moral Values," *Deseret News*, Apr. 29, 2009, A15.

23. Ayn Rand, "The Metaphysical Versus the Man-Made," *Philosophy: Who Needs It* (New York: Signet Books, 1984), 32.

24. J. Reuben Clark, quoted in Jerreld L. Newquist, ed., *Prophets, Principles, and National Survival* (Salt Lake City: Publishers Press, 1964), 60.

25. Edmund Burke, *The Works of Edmund Burke*, vol. 3 (Boston: Little, Brown, 1839), 326.

26. James E. Faust, "Obedience: The Path to Freedom," *Ensign*, May 1999.

27. Robert D. Hales, "Agency: Essential to the Plan of Life," *Ensign*, Nov. 2010; emphasis added.

28. Dallin H. Oaks, "The Challenge to Become," *Ensign*, Nov. 2000; emphasis added.
29. David O. McKay, "Free Agency . . . the Gift Divine," *Improvement Era*, Feb. 1962, 86.
30. Joseph Smith, *The Book of Doctrine and Covenants of The Church of Jesus Christ of Latter-day Saints* (Liverpool: S. W. Richards, 1852), 29.
31. Howard W. Hunter, "The Golden Thread of Choice," *Ensign*, Nov. 1989, 18.
32. "Know This, That Every Soul is Free," Hymns, no. 240.
33. Thomas Ward, ed., *The Latter-day Saints' Millennial Star*, vol. 5 (Liverpool: Thomas Ward, 1845), 91.
34. Gordon B. Hinckley, "The Power of the Book of Mormon," *Ensign*, June 1988, 2.
35. "Elder Bednar Fulfills Assignment in Europe," *Church News and Events*, September 27, 2011, accessed May 12, 2012, http://www.lds.org/church/news/elder-bednar-completes-tour-through-europe.
36. Ezra Taft Benson, "The Constitution—A Glorious Standard," *Ensign*, May 1976.
37. John Taylor recorded: "These secret combinations were spoken of by Joseph Smith, years and years ago. I have heard him time and time again tell about them, and he stated that when these things began to take place the liberties of this nation would begin to be bartered away." See George F. Gibbs, ed., *Journal of Discourses*, vol. 22 (Liverpool: Albert Carrington, 1882), 143.

CONCLUSION

Neither the wisest constitution nor the wisest laws will secure the liberty and happiness of a people whose manners are universally corrupt. He therefore is the truest friend of the liberty of his country who tries most to promote its virtue, and who, so far as his power and influence extend, will not suffer a man to be chosen onto any office of power and trust who is not a wise and virtuous man.[1]

—Samuel Adams

In these days of uncertainty and unrest, liberty-loving people's greatest responsibility and paramount duty is to preserve and proclaim the freedom of the individual, his relationship to Deity, and . . . the necessity of obedience to the principles of the gospel of Jesus Christ—only thus will mankind find peace and happiness.[2]

—President David O. McKay

Hans Monderman is a traffic engineer in Holland. Somewhat unique in his profession, he is not a fan of most road signs, considering them to be not only annoying but also dangerous. Such signs, to Monderman, convey failure on the part of the road designer to create a system that functions well. "The trouble with traffic engineers is that when there's a problem with a road, they always try to add something," he says. "To my mind, it's much better to remove things."

And that's what he did. For example, in northern Holland he designed a busy intersection that doesn't have a single traffic signal, road sign, or directional marker. This radical abandonment of nearly a century of traffic engineering might seem alarming to those who have been accustomed to looking for road signs as indicators for how to drive. Monderman's intersection is a junction between two busy two-lane roads that handles twenty thousand cars a day, as well as thousands of bicyclists and pedestrians. Where traffic lights, road markings, and pedestrian crossings once existed, Monderman put a roundabout void of any signs or signals telling drivers who has the right-of-way, how fast they may go, when to turn, and so on.

Imagine being a tourist in this country, approaching the intersection with a handful of other cars around you. As you reduce your speed and notice a complete absence of any signs, how would you react? What would you do? This initial hesitation—the pause to consider your actions—is precisely the point of Monderman's design. A journalist who witnessed the results of this design recorded his impressions as follows:

> Monderman and I stand in silence by the side of the road a few minutes, watching the stream of motorists, cyclists, and pedestrians make their way through the circle, a giant concrete mixing bowl of transport. Somehow it all works. The drivers slow to gauge the intentions of crossing bicyclists and walkers. Negotiations over right-of-way are made through fleeting eye contact. Remarkably, traffic moves smoothly around the circle with hardly a brake screeching, horn honking, or obscene gesture. "I love it!" Monderman says at last. "Pedestrians and cyclists used to avoid this place, but now, as you see, the cars look out for the cyclists, the cyclists look out for the pedestrians, and everyone looks out for each other. You can't expect traffic signs and street markings to encourage that sort of behavior. You have to build it into the design of the road."[3]

Just as traffic signs and street markings do not necessarily encourage or produce proper driving behavior, laws do not encourage responsibility. If anything, they makes us less responsible because we assume that everybody else is following the rules and that the government has everything under control. These laws create a false sense of security in which we look to the rules and regulations, and not to one another, to determine how to act and what to do. But this striking example— one which the journalist notes is "spreading around the globe, showing up in Austria, Denmark, France, Germany, Spain, Sweden, the UK, and the US"—epitomizes the symbiotic relationship between liberty and responsibility discussed in this book. As liberty is restored, people assume their responsibilities; as people become more responsible, they can claim, maintain, and defend more of their liberty.

Without a revolutionary return to personal responsibility, the American republic will be lost. Individuals have collectively surrendered their responsibility to the government, placing themselves in a subservient status to the state. Always looking to expand its power, the state has willingly and eagerly taken on the additional responsibilities, adding layers of new "road signs" along the way to regulate and control those for whom it now has responsibility. The state's attempt to discharge the duties that are actually ours does not work, however. Government systematically makes things worse, creates new problems, and overwhelmingly wastes and misdirects resources.

The state has historically been the greatest violator of individual liberty, for its collective, concentrated power suppresses the freedom of millions, whereas the common criminal or even the mastermind terrorist can only harm a limited few. States that have emphasized collective responsibility over personal responsibility have, without fail, become the hotbeds of tyranny that give rise to mass-murdering dictators and freedom-suppressing central planners. With America steadily moving in a similar direction, we are able to observe similar abuses of authority and violations of individual liberty at the hands of our own government.

James Madison once stated: "If men were angels, no government would be necessary."[4] This ignores the obvious fact that even with "necessary" government ruling its un-angelic subjects, those placed in positions of power are not angels, either. Similarly, Jesus Christ once called the Pharisees the "blind leaders of the blind," noting that "if the blind lead the blind, both shall fall into the ditch" (Matthew 15:14). America is likewise teetering at the ledge of a large ditch, being led ever more closely by irresponsible leaders encouraging the irresponsible masses to follow their every step.

When the state attempts to assume responsibility for those who will not take care of themselves and others, the very problems it attempts to resolve are only exacerbated. In truth, the state is a disease masquerading as its own cure; *by assuming responsibility, it encourages irresponsibility*. As the nineteenth-century English philosopher Herbert Spencer observed, "Indeed the more numerous public instrumentalities become, the more is there generated in citizens the notion that everything is to be done for them, and nothing by them. Each generation is made less familiar with the attainment of desired ends by individual actions or private combinations, and more familiar with the attainment of them by governmental agencies; until, eventually, governmental agencies come to be thought of as the only available agencies."[5] This something-for-nothing mentality has become pervasive in recent decades, and is predicated upon the complete abandonment of personal responsibility. Society is weakened as more and more people seek aid and comfort from the state—"that great fiction," said the French economist Frédéric Bastiat, "through which everybody endeavors to live at the expense of everybody else."[6]

In his endorsement of *Latter-day Liberty*, Representative Ron Paul wrote: "Those who advocate limited government necessarily must advocate strong religious, civic, and social institutions. These institutions, rather than the state, should act as the central organizing mechanisms in American society." These institutions require independent, responsible people to lead them, to volunteer in them, and to help promote and perpetuate their influence within society. Alexis de Tocqueville, in his detailed review of the budding American nation, marveled at the "immense assemblage of associations" formed for a variety of purposes. "If it is proposed to inculcate some truth, or to foster some feeling, by the encouragement of a great example," he wrote, "they form a society . . . . I have often admired the extreme skill with which the inhabitants of the United States succeed in proposing a common object to the exertions of a great many men, and in inducing them voluntarily to pursue it."[7] The state of individual liberty in American society during de Tocqueville's time is markedly different from what it is today—a day when rather than forming an association to pursue a desired goal, people first look to government.

A "mediating institution," like the word "society," is simply a term used to describe the voluntary interactions of peaceful people working toward desired goals for their own benefit, and that of others. Such associations fulfill a vital role in helping people interact with others, identify and fulfill others' needs, and learn more about the world around them. In recent decades, they have taken a backseat to government; whether by design or by consequence, the nanny state has taken over the house. American citizens have turned "we, the people" into "us, the citizenry" and "them, the agents of the state." The remedy to such a separation of power and influence—the remedy to reducing the state's role in our lives—is to increase personal responsibility, thereby minimizing the financial, social, and moral costs the state inevitably incurs.

During a visit in the United States in 2008, Pope Benedict XVI stated that "Freedom is not only a gift, but also a summons to personal responsibility." He continued:

> Americans know this from experience—almost every town in this country has its monuments honoring those who sacrificed their lives in defense of freedom, both at home and abroad. The preservation of freedom calls for the cultivation of virtue, self-discipline, sacrifice for the common good and a sense of responsibility towards the less fortunate. It also demands the courage to engage in civic life and to bring one's deepest beliefs and values to reasoned public debate. In a word, freedom is ever new. It is a challenge held out to each generation, and it must constantly be won over for the cause of good.[8]

This is our challenge. This is the curse and blessing of personal responsibility—"the agency of man, and . . . the condemnation of man" (D&C 93:31) depending on which way we choose. It is the only path toward reclaiming, maintaining, and defending individual liberty. All of the efforts to increase freedom by decreasing the influence and reach of government will be of little avail if we are not simultaneously working to become more responsible and encouraging others to do the same.

In their tragedies, ancient Greek dramatists often employed a literary device called a *deus ex machina*, whereby a difficult problem, often of the characters' own making, was suddenly and miraculously solved with an unexpected intervention. Actors portraying gods would be lowered by a crane onto the stage to save the mortals from the consequences of their own actions. A desire to be rescued from the consequences of their own irresponsibility is similarly found in the lives of far too many people today. While divine intervention is certainly important and welcome when given, the masses have instead come to deify their respective Caesars (see Matthew 22:20–21). The state has become their *deus ex machina*, supposedly saving them from themselves—a tragedy indeed, for all of us.

Thomas Jefferson once famously wrote that "The tree of liberty must be refreshed from time to time with the blood of patriots and tyrants. It is its natural manure."[9] He was wrong. The tree of liberty does not require the infrequent sacrifice of the lives of patriots to nurture its soil and encourage its continual growth. Rather, the tree of liberty must be continually nurtured with the consistent actions of personal responsibility—continual exertions during our lives, not a sacrifice of them. Only then can the tree grow large and bear fruit.

In the end, liberty is a choice—one that we cannot act upon without being accountable for our various personal responsibilities. God has given moral agency to each of his children, and allows us the opportunity to determine our own destiny and reap the consequences, for better or for worse. Lehi taught that all people "are free to choose liberty and eternal life, through the great Mediator of all men, or to choose captivity and death, according to the captivity and power of the devil." (2 Nephi 2:27). Liberty and eternal life are, of course, the consequences of good choices made over the course of a lifetime—a consistent fulfilling of personal responsibilities. God will not impose individual liberty upon us here on earth, nor will he force us back to heaven. The amazingly simple yet eternally profound aspect of our probationary state here on earth is that we can have whatever we want and are willing to work for. What will you choose? Society or the state? Freedom or tyranny? Independence or dependence? Responsibility or irresponsibility? Liberty and eternal life, or captivity and death? In five simple words, the Lord summed up the entire subject: *"thou mayest choose for thyself"* (Moses 3:17; emphasis added).

Whatever you choose, the choice is yours.

Notes

1. William Vincent Wells, ed., *The Life and Public Services of Samuel Adams* (Boston: Little, Brown, 1865), 22.
2. David O. McKay, in Conference Report, Apr. 1950, 37.
3. "Roads Gone Wild," Wired, December 2004, accessed May 12, 2012, http://www.wired.com/wired/archive/12.12/traffic.html.
4. Rossiter, *The Federalist Papers*, 290.
5. Herbert Spencer, *The Man versus the State* (Edinburgh: Williams & Norgate, 1894), 30.
6. Frédéric Bastiat, The Bastiat Collection (Auburn, AL: Ludwig von Mises Institute, 2007), 99.
7. de Tocqueville, *Democracy*, 129–30.
8. "Address of His Holiness Benedict XVI," White House, April 16, 2008.
9. Foley, *The Jefferson Cyclopedia*, 499.

APPENDIX

AMERICANS DEMAND INCREASED GOVERNMENTAL PROTECTION FROM SELVES

The following article, reprinted with permission from TheOnion.com, is satire.

NEW YORK—Alarmed by the unhealthy choices they make every day, more and more Americans are calling on the government to enact legislation that will protect them from their own behavior.

"The government is finally starting to take some responsibility for the effect my behavior has on others," said New York City resident Alec Haverchuk, 44, who is prohibited by law from smoking in restaurants and bars. "But we have a long way to go. I can still light up on city streets and in the privacy of my own home. I mean, legislators acknowledge that my cigarette smoke could give others cancer, but don't they care about me, too?"

"It's not just about Americans eating too many fries or cracking their skulls open when they fall off their bicycles," said Los Angeles resident Rebecca Burnie, 26. "It's a financial issue, too. I spend all my money on trendy clothes and a nightlife that I can't afford. I'm $23,000 in debt, but the credit-card companies keep letting me spend. It's obscene that the government allows those companies to allow me to do this to myself. Why do I pay my taxes?"

Beginning with seat belt legislation in the 1970s, concern over dangerous behavior has resulted in increased governmental oversight of private activities. Burnie and Haverchuk are only two of a growing number of citizens who argue that legislation should be enacted to protect them from their own bad habits and poor decisions.

Anita Andelman of the American Citizen Protection Group is at the forefront of the fight for "greater guardianship for all Americans."

"Legislation targeting harmful substances like drugs and alcohol is a good start, but that's all it is—a start," Andelman said. "My car automatically puts my seat belt on me whenever I get into it. There's no chance that I'll make the risky decision to leave it off. So why am I still legally allowed to drink too much caffeine, watch television for seven hours a day, and, in some states, even ride in the back of a pick-up truck? It just isn't right."

The ACPG has also come out in favor of California's proposed "soda tax," which addresses unhealthy eating habits.

"The legislation, if approved, would establish a tax on sodas and other beverages with minimal nutritional value, and the money would be used to fund programs that address the growing epidemic of child-hood obesity," Andelman said. "If our own government doesn't do something to make us get in better shape—or, for that matter, dress a little nicer—who will?"

Rev. Ted Hinson, founder of the Christian activist group Please God Stop Me, said he believes that the government will listen.

"For years, legislators have done an admirable job of listening to constituents who want the dangerous, undesirable behavior of their neighbors regulated," Hinson said. "That is a good sign for those of us who wish for greater protection from ourselves. But you should see the filth I still have access to, just by walking into a store or flipping on my computer. There is still much work to be done if we are going to achieve the ideal nanny-state."

Bernard Nathansen, an attorney for the Personal Rights Deferred Center in Oakes, VA, is one of many individuals working to promote "governmental accountability." His organization arranges class-action lawsuits on behalf of Americans who have been hurt by the govern-ment's negligence, including individuals who suffer health problems related to overexposure to sunlight.

"We can all agree that many choices are too important to be left up to a highly flawed individual," Nathansen said. "Decisions that directly affect our health, or allow us to expose ourselves to potential risks, should be left to the wiser, cooler heads of the government."

"But things like food and drug labels are half-measures," Nathansen said. "The regulations, however well-intentioned, often allow citizens the choice of ignoring the instructions. Many current laws were written primarily to protect others from our dangerous actions, with no concern for the deleterious effect our actions can have on ourselves. The government must do more."

To this end, Personal Rights Deferred has compiled an action list of more than 700 behaviors it wants regulated by state or federal authorities. The list includes such risky behaviors as swimming in cold weather and staying up all night playing video games.

"The fact is, personal responsibility doesn't work," Nathansen said. "Take a good look at the way others around you are living, and I'm sure you'll agree. It's time for the American people to demand that someone force them to do something about it."

PERSONAL RESPONSIBILITY IS THE PRICE OF LIBERTY

The following speech was given by Center for Small Government president Michael Cloud at the 2000 Libertarian Party national convention. It is included here with the author's permission.

number of years ago, Erich Fromm, a psychoanalyst, wrote a book entitled *Escape From Freedom*. He argued that people are born free, and yet they beg to be enslaved—they beg to be put in chains. He said they fear freedom. He said they seek out people who will lock them up and tell them what to do. They surrender their freedom piecemeal to the lowest bidder, step by step by step. They lick the boot that kicks them, and they love the people who take their freedom.

Erich Fromm was so close to the truth, and yet he missed the mark. People are not fleeing freedom. They are trying to escape personal responsibility. It is not freedom and choice and individual options and alternatives they're running from—it's from the heavy burden of the responsibilities that come with human life. They are seeking to surrender their responsibility—not throw away their liberty.

Have you read *Atlas Shrugged* by Ayn Rand? She brilliantly challenges our thinking. Whether you agree or disagree, whether you think she's right or think she's wrong, Ayn Rand makes you think.

If you asked Ayn Rand what *Atlas Shrugged* was about, she would tell you it's about the role of man's mind in human existence, the role of human ability and human thought in making our way through the world, and the indispensability of human intelligence in that equation.

True, but her book is also an anthem to personal responsibility. If you look at the heroes and the villains throughout the book, they're divided along the lines of responsibility and irresponsibility.

One of the sad failures in the book was a man named James Taggart. His opening lines—now, here's the head of a railroad. His opening lines when one of his employees comes to him saying, "We have a serious, serious problem with the railroad," is, "Don't bother me. Don't bother me. Don't bother me." Why should the head of the railroad be bothered with, well, running the railroad? Because he was seeking to escape personal responsibility. But whether you look at James Taggart or Wesley Mouch or any of the other scoundrels and villains throughout *Atlas Shrugged*, you'll realize they were characterized by a distinct desire to evade personal responsibility. The heroes, on the other hand, wore responsibility as a king wears a robe. As the master of his fate takes his life into his own hands, these people take responsibility into theirs. Whether you're looking at Hank Rearden or Dagny Taggart, whether you're looking at John Galt or Ragnar Danneskjöld or Francisco d'Anconia, all of the heroes in Atlas Shrugged are people who embrace responsibility as a birthright—not a burden.

Let's move on to one of my favorite writers, Robert Heinlein. I don't know if you've read the man. He's absolutely extraordinary. He writes wonderful juvenile novels as well as very interesting adult novels, everything from *The Green Hills of Earth* to *Stranger in a Strange Land* to *The Moon is a Harsh Mistress*. In every one of these books, you find a common theme. The theme is, Earth is going to hell in a hand basket, sometimes caused by extraterrestrials and sometimes caused by normal terrans. The problem is that it takes the responsibility of one person to change the world. And the hero in the Heinlein novels is the person who takes his life into his own hands, takes his fate into his own hands, and changes the world. Those are books about personal responsibility and their role in making the world a dramatically better place.

Let's move to a nonfiction book, *How I Found Freedom in an Unfree World*, by Harry Browne. This book was written in 1973. This book had a theme that you can run your life the way you want to run it, that you can live your life the way you want to live it, if you'll take your life back into your own hands. Several years ago, I met Harry Browne for the first time, and I had a conversation with him about the book. I said, "You know, Mr. Browne, I really like your book, but you know what?

You could have as easily called that book *How I Found Responsibility in an Irresponsible World.*" And he says, "Yeah, I could have, but then the book wouldn't have sold many copies, then, would it?" The man did have a point. You see, people love to be free, but they don't always love to be responsible, because freedom is easy and light and everybody wants it, and responsibility is dark and heavy and sounds like grown-ups. Responsibility seems like the burden; freedom seems like the blessing. What we have here is a failure of personal responsibility.

In America today, we're awash in a sea of irresponsibility. We're awash in a sea of recklessness, personal endangerment, self-indulgence, self-destructiveness, and behavior that could best be characterized as human demolition derby. You see, in America, we look at big government and we say, "My gosh, look at the American people. We have surrendered our freedoms to the federal government. We have given them up. We have given up our birthright for a bowl of pottage. We have given up our liberty." Well, I believe that's wrong. I don't believe the American people have given up their liberty. I believe that they have given up their personal responsibility, because government doesn't grow by seizing freedom, but by *assuming responsibility.* And that's the dirty little secret.

Let's take a look at government involving itself in responsibility. Let's look at where and how government shoulders responsibilities that we, as free men and free women, ought to shoulder ourselves. Government comes to us and says, "Oh, look at the burden of educating your children. How could you ever possibly choose schools that will turn your children into functional literates? Let us do it. We can do a far better job than you can as a private citizen. How could you determine what good and bad teachers would be, what good and bad programs would be?"

They've said, "Deciding on what a school is, deciding what a good education is, is too big a burden, too great a calling for you as an individual. Surrender the responsibility to government. Let government decide how and when and where your children will be educated and what they'll learn and not learn, what values they will be taught and what values they won't be taught. You let us assume the burden of educating your children, and you can just rely upon us."

And we did. We did turn our children over to government—their minds, their souls, their futures, their values, their decisions, their thought processes. But it didn't stop with educating children. Government looked to us and said, "Look at of caring for the poor. Look at all the people in society who have less than you do. Look at the disadvantaged. Look at the firm and the frail. Look at the people who don't have the kinds of goods you do. Look at those who are barely squeaking by. Let us assume the burden of caring for the poor. Let us assume the burden of making certain that they and their children will have enough food and shelter around them. Let us make certain that they are cared for in a way that really matters." And we surrendered our personal compassion. We surrendered the tie that holds communities together about caring for our own poor, about acting on behalf of those less fortunate than ourselves. We surrendered the responsibility of caring for the poor to the government, and the freedom to help the poor went with it.

But it didn't stop there. Government said, "Wait a minute. There's a huge burden with health care. Look at the expense of a hospital stay. You can work your whole life, you can diligently save money, you can have good health insurance (or as good as you can afford after huge taxes), and yet, if you have a catastrophic illness, three days or three weeks in the hospital can bankrupt you, can take everything you've earned your whole life. Give us the responsibility of caring for your health. Give us the responsibility for the hospitals and the hospices. Give us the responsibility for taking care of your health." And we thought, "Government can do that better than we can. Government can handle huge amounts of money better than we can." And so the American people, piecemeal, year by year, step by step, have surrendered more and more of the responsibility of caring for our own health and providing for our own health care. And who did we surrender it to? The government. We let government shoulder the responsibility.

But they didn't stop there. What about the burden of looking out for us in our golden years? What about the elderly, the aged? What about people who work their whole life? They're 65, they're 70, and they haven't saved enough to support themselves. The government said, "Let us help them. Let us reach out. Let us give a hand up. Let us give a hand out, and we will assist them. We will make certain that those people are not doing without." And so what did we do? We allowed them to run a bottomless pit, a fraudulent Ponzi scheme called Social Security, under the promise that they would take responsibility for our golden years. Well, they have the gold, and we have years and years and years. When we surrendered the responsibility, we surrendered the liberty to care for ourselves, to plan for ourselves, to save for ourselves—and government grew by assuming that responsibility as well.

Let's look at the burden of disaster relief. You can't watch television for any period of time without seeing some new disaster occurring, some new crisis emerging. How in the world can the people living on the coast of Florida possibly foresee that there might be a hurricane? How could they possibly anticipate the idea that great winds and great waters might wash their homes away? Let the government pay the cost of handling that disaster. Or people whose homes get flooded, how could they possibly anticipate or foresee or think through the idea that because they're building their home on a floodplain that they might actually be placing themselves in harm's path? And what about people in California? How could anyone there ever possibly foresee that they might be in an earthquake? And if you want to know how insane that behavior is, I want you to visualize a subway being built in Los Angeles near the San Andreas fault. This is what happens when the burden of disaster relief, when the responsibility for disaster relief, is given to government. The government says to people, "Build your homes on the side of Vesuvius, and we will protect you from the lava."

We surrendered responsibility for educating our children, for caring for the poor, for health care, for looking out for our golden years, for disaster relief, and many, many other things—and the freedom went with it. Because, you see, individual liberty and personal responsibility are two sides of the same gold coin. You cannot throw away one side of the coin without also throwing away the other. You see, government doesn't grow by seizing liberty; it grows by assuming responsibility.

Because when we we surrender responsibility, we surrender authority over that area of our life. When we surrender authority over that area of our life, we surrender control over that area of our life. And when we surrender control, we surrender choice over that area of our life, which means we surrender individual liberty. I agree with Libertarian State Chair Mark Hinkle. He says, "Liberty is the prize; responsibility is the price." When we give up the price, we give up the prize, because we cannot have the prize if we will not pay the price. There's an old libertarian quote that I love very much, which says, "There ain't no such thing as a free lunch." There's a Spanish proverb where God says, "Take what you like and pay for it."

What is responsibility? Responsibility is the simplest concept in the world. It's so simple it gets overlooked, because obvious means overlooked. Responsibility means cause and effect. There's a phrase called karma. It's a Sanskrit phrase, and what it means is action and reaction or cause and effect. "As ye sow, so shall ye reap." That's karma. "Every action has an equal and opposite reaction." That, too, is karma. "By their fruit shall ye know them." That also is karma. And what they all acknowledge is the fact that cause and effect are undeniably linked, that we cannot separate them, that when we initiate the cause, we initiate the effect. When we will the cause, we will the effect.

When we say, "What is responsibility?," here's fundamentally what it means. When I say, "The match was responsible for the fire," I mean the match *caused* the fire. When I say that Jones was responsible for the project's success, I mean that Jones *caused* the project's success. In simple terms, responsible means caused.

What this brings us to is the idea of choice, because we, as human beings, have the choice to act or not act, to engage in a behavior or refrain from the behavior; but when we choose the action, we have chosen the consequence. We are responsible for the consequence. We made it happen. When we choose the path, we have chosen the destination, because responsibility means consequences.

Who is responsible in a given set of affairs? The person is responsible for his own actions. The person is responsible for the consequences of his own actions. You're responsible for your actions and I'm responsible for mine, and so is everybody else in the world. The funny thing about this is everybody knows this. This is a blinding flash of the obvious. I'm not telling you anything you don't already know. What I'm telling you is what people are trying to ignore in the area of politics. Responsibility affects that just as much as it affects us in every area of our life.

Elbert Hubbard said, "We are not punished for our sins, but by them." So, too, we're not rewarded for our virtues, but by them. It is contained in the action. That is where rewards and punishments come from. And what is the reward or punishment? It's a very simple concept. It's called consequences, the reaction to the action, the reaping to the sowing. Consequences. Good consequences reward us; bad consequences punish us. Good consequences are enjoyed; bad consequences are suffered. You see, consequences is the master teacher. It teaches us to act wisely, to save our money, to care for our health, to keep learning, because it pays off. But there are some people in the world who want to try to cheat cause and effect. Well, it can't be done. The only way you can even try to cheat cause and effect is to make someone else reap what you have sowed. When they try to cheat cause and effect, what they do is they say, "You reap what other people sow," or, "You sow what other people reap. You make the consequences, and other people take the consequences." And you know what this does? This discourages virtue and encourages vice. This penalizes wisdom and rewards folly.

To try to reverse cause and effect, to try to sever cause and effect, to try to cheat cause and effect, is the source of most of the problems we face. If you could get drunk on Friday night and your neighbor got the hangover on Saturday morning, you'd drink until you died! If you could eat as much as you want and your neighbor got fat, you'd eat until you exploded, because that's the way that people try to cheat consequences: through government. The government system puts other people between you and the consequences of your behavior. It lets other people reap the bad consequences when you act foolishly or stupidly or recklessly or without forethought, and it lets you lose the good consequences when you act prudently and well.

Let's look in two areas. For example, when an individual goes out and works very, very hard, earns a good living, and the government stands between them and the consequences of their behavior and says, "I want half of the crop that you sowed, I want half of your income," it's called an income tax. And what that does is it tries to sever cause and effect, it tries to break responsibility. And that's what happens when government assumes responsibility. When government stands between you and the consequences of your bad behavior, it acts as an airbag to protect you against things that you shouldn't be doing, things that you would learn soon enough you oughtn't be doing, and things you would stop doing if someone wasn't protecting you from the consequences.

Personal responsibility says that you own the consequences of your behavior. You own the results of your actions. When you initiate the cause, you own the effect. When you marry the cause, you marry the effect. When you engage in good behavior, it pays off and your life is better. When you engage in bad behavior, things don't go the way you want. And reality gives you an opportunity to grow by making it painful, by making it less convenient, and by making it harder for you. That is how we learn in life. And that is what government taking responsibility tries to cheat us out of—cheat us out of the learning to become more responsible and better, and cheat us out of the positive consequences and cheat us into believing that we can act recklessly and thoughtlessly and someone else will pick up the pieces. It allows government to put other people between you and the consequences of your behavior.

If a young lady wanting to engage in promiscuous sex knew full well that she would pay the cost of raising that child, that she would raise the child and the government would not give her a stipend, would not give her an apartment, would not give her a reason to engage in that behavior, she might learn two words: "birth control," or maybe just one: "no!" It is because she has been taught that there are no consequences to her, that someone else will pick up the pieces, that she broke it and someone else bought it. It's because people teach her that, that she engages in thoughtless, reckless, self-indulgent behavior. It's because of that that she cannot learn from the consequences of her behavior.

One of the problems in life is that people keep asking the wrong questions. In *Gravity's Rainbow*, Thomas Pynchon wrote, "If they can get you asking the wrong questions, they don't have to worry about the answers." And, you know, he was right. If we're always looking in the wrong direction, if we're always seeking the answer in the wrong area, we'll never find it. I don't know whether you've tried the World's Smallest Political Quiz. It's offered by Advocates For Self-Government. Several years ago, I went out and took the Advocates for Self-Government diamond chart, the World's Smallest Political Quiz, to a number of high school classes, and I got some rather interesting results. You might get similar ones if you go to your church, your charity, your local rotary club, your local Lions. You might get very interesting results—maybe a little different from mine.

I went to a high school class one day, and I said, "Here's how the World's Smallest Political Quiz works. You can't get it wrong. It's a map—it just lets you know where you are on the political chart. It helps you find where you fit, whether you're conservative or a liberal, whether you're libertarian, whether you're authoritarian, which of the quadrants you belong to." Well, we handed out the quiz, and we started seeing the results. About 60 or 70 percent of the class was falling into the libertarian quadrant. And my reaction was, "All right. Now we're going to win! Boy, ten years from now, the whole world will be libertarian! These people want to be free. High school students are demanding their freedom." And then it sunk in, and so I asked the question. I said, "I realize that each of you here wants to be free. I'd like around the class and ask yourself if you trust the other people in your class to be free?

Whereas 60 percent of the people said, "I want to be free!," when they looked around the numbers reversed. "Are you nuts? These people are crazy! You should lock them in rooms, feed them raw meat under the door. You shouldn't let these people be free! Me? I know I can trust me . . . but those people are totally nuts!"

Sometimes when we're asking people if they want to be free, we get the right answer. And yet, I think we're asking the wrong question. What is the right question? It's the responsibility question. Instead of asking people, "Do you want to be responsible for your own life?," try asking it this way: "Do you want your neighbors to be more responsible? Would you like to live in a world where everybody up and down your street, everybody you know, is responsible for the consequences of his or her behavior? Would you like to live in a world where people are prudent and thoughtful, where they act with foresight? Would you like to live in a world where people are 100 percent accountable for behavior? Would you like to live in a world where all of your neighbors are more responsible?" You see, that's the right question. You have to be intelligently altruistic here. You've got to ask yourself, "What kind of a world do I want to live in? Do I want to live in a world where people are responsible or irresponsible? Do I want to live in a world where people act with forethought or a world where they're reckless? Do I want to live in a world where people act with an eye toward the future, act in such ways as to enhance their health and make sure that their livelihood is well cared for and raised in good families? Do I want to live in that kind of a world or do I want to live in a world where people live their lives like it's a demolition derby?"

That is the right question. Do we want to live in a world where responsibility gets rewarded or where it gets penalized? Do we want to live in a world where people are more responsible, more often, in more situations? Or do we want to live in a world where people are reckless, thoughtless, brutish, boorish, and stupid? This is the right question. This is the libertarian question: "Do I want to live in a world where people are more responsible?" If they can get you asking the wrong questions, they don't have to worry about the answers because you'll get the right answer to the wrong question, not the right answer to the right question.

A lot of people are asked the wrong question when they're dealing with government: Would you like the government to protect you when you make mistakes? "Sure, that sounds great!" Would you like government to care for grandma and grandpa? "Yeah, that's wonderful!" Would you like government to pick up the tab on your health bill, even when you don't care for your health, even when you act foolishly, even when you ride around without wearing a seat belt or ride a motorcycle without wearing a helmet? Would you like government to pick up the bill when you engage in harmful, destructive, accidental behavior? "Wow that sounds like a great deal!," you might think. But it's the wrong question. The wrong question is the kind of question that we get answers to every day. Would you like government sure your life is safer? "Sure." Would you like government to you're never at risk of losing your job? "Sure." Would you like government to make sure you earn a good living? "Sure." Would you like government to guarantee that nothing ever goes wrong in your life? "Yeah, that would be great," you think. And it's with that dirty little lie that we surrender our liberty, because that's the wrong question.

You see, the question isn't, "Do you want government to do these things?" The question is, "What happens when it does? What happens to you and what happens to your neighbors?" Let's ask ourselves a few questions that might help us clarify this. Let's do something called a structural analysis. Take a look at three questions: what gets rewarded and penalized by a certain course of action, a certain policy; what gets taught by the policy; and third, what kind of people does that policy or that system nurture, encourage, or produce? Let's take Karl Marx's principle. "From each according to his ability, to each according to his need." Now, let's do a motivational analysis here. What gets rewarded in that kind of a system? Need. What gets penalized? Ability. What are you going to get lots of? Need. What are you going to get none of? Ability. As evidence, I offer you Washington, DC, or the old Soviet Union, which was sort of a Washington, DC with a real bad attitude. You see, under this sort of a system, what gets rewarded is the very worst in human behavior, and what gets penalized is the very best.

We need to ask ourselves what gets rewarded in a system of government dependency? What gets rewarded when government picks up the pieces for human behavior? What happens when they cover your losses and pick up your winnings? What kind of behavior gets rewarded? What kind of behavior gets penalized? What gets rewarded in a system where the government is responsible?

Well, let's take a look at what the government system provides us with. The government system provides us with dependency, because when government is responsible for certain things, we are dependent upon government to provide it. What does that do to us? It makes us dependent. What does that make us? It makes us passive. We wait for government to take care of the problem. We don't prevent it ourselves and we don't fix it ourselves. What does that do to us? It makes us weak. When government does for us what we should do for ourselves, our abilities atrophy, our abilities shrivel and shrink and ultimately disappear.

We've got a choice. We can either have a weak people and a strong and powerful government, or a strong and free people and a small, limited government. There aren't any other alternatives. So the government responsibility system causes us to be dependent, then passive, then weak. And then what does it do? *It makes us irresponsible.* It makes us reckless because there is no penalty for it.

"Engage in promiscuous sex. Don't worry about babies. Don't worry about sexually transmitted diseases. Don't worry about the consequences to your own image, to your own time. Don't worry about the consequences. Government will take care of it."

"You want to use hard drugs? You want to engage in behavior that damages your body and makes you less able to be healthy? Don't worry about it. Government will put together a methadone program."

"You want to engage in behavior that would not be accepted on the job? You want to flip off your boss, and treat people with rudeness? You want to be inconsiderate? You want to be a bad employee?" Government will guarantee your job so no one could fire you. Of course, in that kind of a system where you can't be fired, you'll never get hired either now, will you?

You see, it encourages us to be the most irresponsible and reckless people you can imagine when government always sweeps up the mess we create. After it makes us dependent and passive and weak and irresponsible, you know what's left? *Obedience.* Because we will do as we're told by the institution that holds our future, our retirement, our children's education, our health care, and every other facet of our life in its hands. When government is responsible for our life, government has authority over our life. When government has authority over our life, it has control of our life. When government has control over our life, it owns us.

That's the government responsibility system. What gets rewarded in that system and what gets penalized? What gets taught in that system? What gets taught by that system is that it's good to be weak, it's good to be dependent, it's good to be passive, it's good to be irresponsible, and it's good to be obedient. And what kind of people does this system nurture, encourage, and produce, and what kind does it keep from emerging? The kind of people who get nurtured and encouraged are dependent, irresponsible, thoughtless, and reckless people.

If you look around today and you say, "Why is the world in such a mess? Why aren't things far better than they are today?," you need to look no further than the fact that government has assumed responsibility for people's choices and actions. Government has agreed to pick up the pieces. But here's the dirty little secret: the dirty little secret is that it's your tax dollar that's picking up other people's pieces; your prudence is funding their recklessness; your wisdom is subsidizing their folly; your forethought is being drained and taken from you to subsidize the kind of spiritual weakness, inadequacy, and destructiveness that you see with those who choose the path of least resistance, because the path of least resistance leads to crooked rivers and crooked men.

That's the real problem with government being responsible. The problem isn't that somehow or other life is easier and better. The problem is that in a government dependency system, in a government responsibility system, life is nasty, brutish, short, and doggone miserable. I agree with Harry Browne who said, "In a marketplace, liberty rewards virtue and punishes vice. In a government system, government rewards vice and punishes virtue." Do you want your kids to grow up having their vices rewarded and their virtues hurt? Do you want your children to grow up to learn to be thoughtless and reckless and irresponsible and imprudent? Do you want your children to grow up to be obedient, dependent, and passive, relying upon the kindness of strangers? Because that's what a government dependency system creates.

Do you want a simple cure for this problem that's ailing America? Would you want the easiest, fastest way of making Americans more responsible, more often, under more circumstances? There's a very simple way to do it: free them! When people are free to embrace the consequences of their behavior, we learn very quick that it's *our* hangover on Saturday morning, that it is *our* broken things when we don't act with forethought. We learn very quickly and begin engaging in thoughtful, intelligent behavior.

A number of years ago, I went home and visited my mother and father for a weekend. I was grown up, at least I thought so. I was enlightened, mature. You know, any time you think that you're really mature and you think you're enlightened, go spend a weekend with your mom and dad. They'll push every button you got. You know why? They installed them! So I got up at 9:00 in the morning, a perfectly normal time for any decent person to get up. I wander out into the kitchen to go get a cup of coffee. My mom looked at me and my mom said, "Half your morning is gone. I've been up since 6:00!"

"Grumble, grumble, grumble," I thought. In the back of my mind, I had this vision that at midnight I'd be banging on her door, saying, "Half your night is gone, too, Mom!" But I was a house guest, so I didn't do it.

I said, "Where's the coffee?" And she said, "Oh, it's over by the sink." I walked over to the sink and I looked out the window, and there was a bird feeder. My mom and dad had one of those plastic bird feeders, which are very, very entertaining if you have cats and are certainly entertaining for people that like to see birds. And I saw this bird sitting on the edge of this empty bird feeder with this look like, "You owe me money!"

This bird says, "Where's the birdseed?" So I turned to my mom and said, "Where's the birdseed?" My mother said, "It's under the sink, but be sure and read the instructions." Instructions? How complicated could birdseed be? This is not rocket science! But sometimes mom does know best, and this is one of those times. I reached under the sink and I took out the package, which had the following instructions: "Bird feeders can provide hours of fun. We can see many, many different kinds of birds. But when the bird feeder becomes empty, leave it empty for a few days. Otherwise," it said, "the birds will come to depend upon you and not learn to fend for themselves." That is a sad testimony to America's progress, America's development, today, is that the makers of a bird feeder care more about self-reliance and personal responsibility of birds than we do with our children, our aged, and ourselves. We need to retake responsibility.

On my coat whenever I travel, I wear the Statue of Liberty pin. It symbolizes our libertarian dream. I can't think of anything that, to me, is just more American than seeing that wonderful Statue of Liberty giving a beacon through the dark night of big government, leading us in the correct direction. But, you know, when I look at that Statue of Liberty, I feel like something is missing. And I finally figured out what it was a number of years ago. We've got a Statue of Liberty on the East Coast. I'd really like it if America would put a Statue of Responsibility on the West Coast, because if you don't have freedom on one side and responsibility on the other, what's in between ain't worth much.

America needs to take back its freedom, and there's only one way to do it—and that is by taking back responsibility for our lives. We need to take back responsibility for educating our children according to our values, not the government's. We must take back responsibility for our health care and not leave it in the hands of a government. We need to take responsibility for our retirement, to plan for our own futures, to save our own pensions, rather than to throw it into that bottomless pit of a Ponzi scheme they call Social Security. We need to take back our retirement.

We need to take back responsibility for helping our neighbors and not let them sever the ties of compassion that bind us together to assist those less fortunate. We need to take responsibility in our own neighborhoods for helping those people get a hand up, not a handout. We need to reach into ourselves and take responsibility for everything from keeping ourselves out of the path of hurricanes and earthquakes and landslides and mudslides and lava flow. We need to build our homes where it's prudent and thoughtful.

We need to act with responsibility. *As we take back our responsibility, we take back our liberty.* The American dream is a dream of responsibility, of taking our lives back into our own hands, of embracing our destiny happily, in reaching out and grasping our possibilities, in standing on our own two feet and being willing, for better or worse, for richer or poorer, to take our own future seriously by acting with prudence, by acting responsibly.

We need to take back responsibility from government, and we'll find that freedom is on the other side of that gold coin. Personal responsibility is the price of liberty. But there's one secret we need to remember: personal responsibility is the prize as well.

INDEX

A

Abortion 214, 218
Acton, Lord 9
Adams, John 2–3, 6–8, 28, 58,
    141–42, 152, 236
Adams, Samuel 37, 242, 263
Agency 3–4, 15–17, 63, 72, 124,
    151, 248–50, 268
Alma 246
Amalickiah 214–15
Amulek 84
Andersen, H. Verlan 136, 166
Ashton, Marvin J. 100

B

Ballard, M. Russell 169, 226
Bastiat, Frédéric 180, 219, 266
Bednar, David A. 149, 221
Benjamin, King 69, 84, 176, 226
Benson, Ezra Taft 60, 64, 114, 118,
    123, 149, 164–68, 185, 197,
    228, 239, 256
bin Laden, Osama 23
Bloom, Allan 146
Book of Mormon 166, 172–73,
    214, 251–52, 254–55
Brown, Hugh B. 219
Brown, Victor L. 121
Burke, Edmund 247
Bush, George 22, 177

C

Charity 14, 84–85, 90, 94, 97, 101,
    117, 243
Christ, Jesus 97, 110, 112, 113, 119,
    138, 153, 155, 237–40, 242,
    250–51, 254, 265
Christofferson, D. Todd 244–47
Civic Duty
    has eternal consequences 174
    required of Latter-day Saints
        162, 170–74
    requires an education 165–66
    to promote liberty 178–79
    to support good, honest, and
        wise leaders 162–63, 166
    using the internet 169
    voting analysis 175
Clark, J. Reuben 59, 112, 246
Cleveland, Grover 117
Coercion 4–5, 72, 88, 93, 97, 226,
    245, 246–47, 249–50
Colton, Charles Caleb viii
Congress 22, 82, 117, 173, 174,
    177–78
Conspiracy, see Secret combinations
Constitution 8, 26, 39–40, 82, 117,
    140, 154, 164–67, 170–71, 174,
    191, 236, 263
Cook, Quentin L. 161, 235

D

De Tocqueville, Alexis viii, 82–83, 235, 266
Debt 59–66, 101
Declaration of Independence 27, 28, 58, 71, 150
DeMille, Oliver 145
Democide 33–36
Division of labor 6, 178, 196–201, 226
Divorce, see Family
Douglass, Frederick 137–40

E

Education
  a component of agency 151
  an individual responsibility 148
  importance for liberty 136, 151–52, 165
  in a conveyor belt system 145
  mediocre standard in America 141–43, 147
  to become like God 149
  trend toward conformity 145
  what Latter-day Saints should learn 138, 150
Eisenhower, Dwight D. 139
Eyring, Henry B. 115, 150

F

Faith
  in God over government 95
  must be voluntary 148, 247
  necessary for liberty 236–37, 256
  relationship to education 151, 155
  required for a healthy society 15, 242

strengthened through adversity 223
  to avoid debt 62
  to prepare for the future 111, 118
Family
  an originating institution 210
  effects of divorce 208–9, 215–16, 221
  experimentation regarding the family unit 208, 210–11, 216–17
  importance for liberty 210, 225–26
  increase in cohabitation 209
  internal threats 214, 223–24
  strengthened by strong marriages 220–25
  under attack 214–19
The Family: A Proclamation to the World 29, 83, 98, 216–18
Faust, James E. 7, 224, 248
FDA 6, 189–92
Featherstone, Vaughn J. 198
Financial freedom
  burden of debt 59–61
  comes through defense against temptation 66
  results in greater independence 67–69
  through entrepreneurialism 70–73
  to better preserve liberty 59, 73
First Presidency 108, 124, 130, 170–71, 179, 200, 216, 228
Food
  dangers of outsourcing 195
  examples of illegitimate raids 186–90
  excessive regulation 190–93, 195
  family gardens 198
  industrialization 196–98

storing extra for future needs
113, 114, 128–30, 198–200
For the Strength of Youth 126, 259
Frankl, Victor 1
Franklin, Benjamin 6, 17, 57, 71,
221, 237
Fyans, J. Thomas 61

G

Gatto, John Taylor 135, 142, 146
Gerry, Elbridge 39
Golden Rule 239
Good Samaritan 124
Grant, Heber J. 69, 84, 127
Gun control 24, 26, 34, 40–41, 43

H

Hafen, Bruce C. 98
Hales, Robert D. 62, 96, 107, 121,
218, 249
Hamilton, Alexander 80, 142
Hancock, John 58
Henry, Patrick 1, 21, 37–38, 237
Heston, Charlton 26
Hinckley, Gordon B. 18, 57, 60, 61,
64, 107, 109, 121, 141, 163, 164,
167, 168–69, 172, 173, 181,
216–17, 219, 225, 230, 254
Hitler, Adolf 34, 39
Holland, Jeffrey R. 102
Holocaust 35
Homosexuality 214, 223
Hunter, Howard W. 117, 228, 241,
249

I

Independence
a subset of interdependence
98–99
of entrepreneurs 72
of the Church 7, 60–61
through education 151–52
through financial freedom
67–69, 73, 80
through food production 199,
201
through preparedness 122, 124,
127
Isaiah 176, 254

J

Jackson, Andrew 136
Jacob 84, 176
Jefferson, Thomas 13, 21, 58, 71, 79,
136, 141, 152, 161, 166, 185,
267
Joseph 108–9, 112

K

Kimball, Heber C. 62, 109
Kimball, Spencer W. 75, 79, 96,
111, 121, 175, 178, 197–98,
207, 222, 230

L

Law of Consecration, see Charity
Law of Moses 32
Law of the Harvest 16, 90, 117, 240
Lee, Harold B. 169, 170
Lehi 165, 176, 258, 259, 268
Liberty
complementary to responsibility
8, 265
definition 13–14
importance of civic duty 162–63,
174, 178–79

importance of education 136, 152, 165, 179
importance of faith 236–37
importance of family 210, 213, 220, 225–26
importance of financial freedom 58–59, 67–69
importance of food production 187, 195 197–98
importance of morality 164–65, 242, 249, 256
importance of preparedness 119, 122, 127
importance of self-defense 26–27, 47
importance of welfare and charity 96–99
our duty to defend, see Civic Duty
threatened by broken families 209, 211
tied to action 9, 15, 60, 63, 98, 119, 124, 127, 151
Love 29, 84, 92, 94, 102, 123, 211, 218, 219, 238–39, 250

M

Madison, James 28, 39, 82, 117, 135, 142, 165, 265
Marriage 98, 113, 208–9, 215–25
Mather, Cotton 82
Maxwell, Neal A. 112, 212, 220, 225
McConkie, Bruce R. 13, 16, 114, 126, 162
McKay, David O. 4, 13, 72, 170, 240, 263
Media 45–46, 169, 179, 224, 256, 258–59
Mencken, H.L. 14, 145

Militia 26–27, 38–39, 40
Mill, John Stuart 208
Mises, Ludwig von 197
Monson, Thomas S. 60, 99, 107, 123–24, 167
Moral hazard 116
Morality
    as part of our civic duty 164
    enforcement by government 244–45
    necessary for liberty 7, 165, 236–37, 256
    spread by persuasion 246–47
    tied to agency 248–49
Moroni 140, 172, 174, 176, 255
Moroni, Captain 31, 66, 215, 225
Morris, Robert 58
Moses 167

N

Nanny state 5, 8, 212, 243
Nazi 34–36, 194
Nelson, Russell M. 148, 150, 239
Nephi 252, 257
Niemöller, Martin 194
Nisbet, Robert 227
Noah 111–12

O

Oaks, Dallin H. 113, 229, 249
Obama, Barack 87, 177, 178

P

Paine, Thomas 2–3, 73, 152
Paul 32, 84, 97–98, 165, 176, 221, 223, 239
Paul, Ron 266
Perry, L. Tom 69, 101, 123, 127,

168, 229

Persuasion 5, 14, 66, 149, 181, 224, 245, 246–47, 249–50, 253, 259

Pharaoh, see Joseph

Phelps, William W. 162

Pierce, Franklin 82

Police

 inability to protect individuals 41

 no obligation to protection people 42–44

 response time to accidents 42

Police state 5, 8, 22, 211

Pratt, Orson 200–201

Prayer 155, 224, 230

Preparedness

 a biblical pattern 108

 a function of the gospel 124

 a personal responsibility 117, 125

 both temporal and spiritual 111, 113

 failure of Latter-day Saints 114

 for the Second Coming 110, 115

 possible prophetic warning 109–10

 reasons why few prepare 120

 through provident living 119–22

 to become independent 122, 124, 127

Priesthood 14, 174, 176–77, 217

R

Rand, Ayn 245

Reagan, Ronald 41, 138

Responsibility

 an individual, voluntary effort 85

 complementary to liberty 8, 265

 lack of as justification for statism 8

 learned in the family unit 213, 219

 relationship to agency 4, 18

 relationship to liberty 3, 8–9, 15

 reduces the influence of the state 9

Revolution 27, 37–38, 47, 59, 152, 220

Robbins, Lynn G. 114

Roberts, B.H. 4

Romney, Marion G. 96, 198, 230

Roosevelt, Franklin D. 89

Rothbard, Murray 226

S

Samuel the Lamanite 151, 251

Satan 3, 7, 15, 18, 174, 217, 218–19, 222, 251–54, 256

Scott, Richard G. 237, 242

Second Amendment 26, 28, 39, 40

Secret combinations 172–74, 176, 178, 251–55

Sedwick, Theodore 47

Self-defense

 a common occurrence 25

 a responsibility which cannot be delegated 43, 44

 an individual right 26–27, 47

 importance of fulfilling the responsibility 29, 47

 tied to the right of property 26

 to prevent democide 36

 to protect one's family 29–30, 32

Self-reliance, see Preparedness

Sin 4, 17, 172, 176, 244, 251–53, 279

Slavery 137–38

Smith, Joseph 13, 30, 47, 60, 84, 96, 110, 150, 153, 167, 169, 236–37, 249–51

Smith, Joseph F. 32, 61, 228
Smith, Joseph Fielding 155, 220
Snow, Lorenzo 60
Social safety net, see Welfare
Standing army 38–39, 47
Steward 7, 9, 16–17, 18, 29, 60, 68, 83, 85, 97, 98, 100, 120–21, 122, 124, 126–27
Story, Joseph 39
Supreme Court of New York 44
Symmes, William 46

T

Talmage, James E. 113, 222, 223
Tanner, N. Eldon 57
Taylor, John 5, 7, 162
Tithing 60–61, 74, 100

U

Uchtdorf, Dieter F. 149, 151

V

Virgins, Parable of the 113–15, 121
Virtue, see Morality
von Goethe, Johann Wolfgang 237

W

Washington, George 7, 49, 135, 220, 236

War 27, 110, 139, 177
Warfare state 212
Webster, Noah 15, 36, 142, 152
Welfare 6
    early American history 81
    individual responsibility 83
    not the church's responsibility 123
    not the federal government's role 82, 85
    social safety nets 95–97, 99
    through charity 97
Welfare state 5, 8, 83, 84, 86–90, 116, 138, 211, 243
Widtsoe, John A. 150
Williams, Walter 5, 244
Winthrop, John 80
Wirthlin, Joseph B. 59, 85–86, 222
Woodruff, Wilford L. 122, 177
Work 124
Wythe, George 58

Y

Young, Brigham 31, 32, 47, 108–9, 123, 185, 217

Z

Zion 96–97, 99, 166

ABOUT THE AUTHOR

Photo by Scott Jarvie

*C*onnor Boyack is president of Libertas Institute, a public policy organization focused on advancing the cause of liberty in Utah. He is the author of *Latter-day Liberty: A Gospel Approach to Government and Politics*. Connor is a frequent guest on radio shows and regularly publishes opinion pieces in a variety of newspapers and websites. A California native and Brigham Young University graduate, he currently resides in Lehi, Utah, with his wife and two children.

For more information about this book or Connor, please visit
LATTERDAYRESPONSIBILITY.COM
You may also contact Connor directly at
CBOYACK@GMAIL.COM